THE POWER OF SOFT SKILLS
EMPOWERING YOUNG PROFESSIONALS

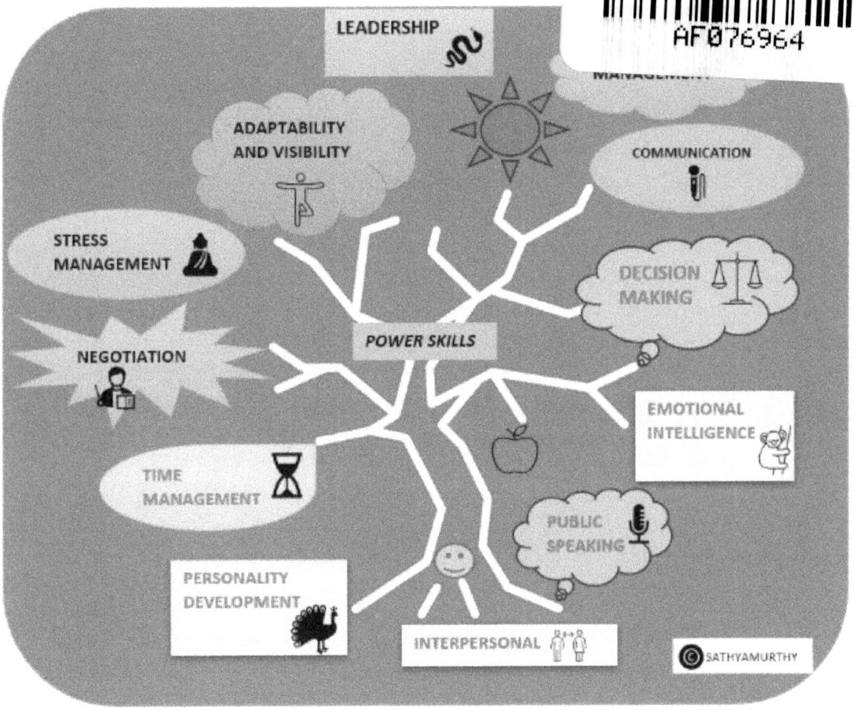

SATHYAMURTHY VAMAN

CLEVER FOX PUBLISHING
Chennai, India

Published by CLEVER FOX PUBLISHING 2024
Copyright © Sathyamurthy Vaman 2024

All Rights Reserved.
ISBN: 978-93-67072-73-8

This book has been published with all reasonable efforts taken to make the material error-free after the consent of the author. No part of this book shall be used, reproduced in any manner whatsoever without written permission from the author, except in the case of brief quotations embodied in critical articles and reviews.

The Author of this book is solely responsible and liable for its content including but not limited to the views, representations, descriptions, statements, information, opinions and references ["Content"]. The Content of this book shall not constitute or be construed or deemed to reflect the opinion or expression of the Publisher or Editor. Neither the Publisher nor Editor endorse or approve the Content of this book or guarantee the reliability, accuracy or completeness of the Content published herein and do not make any representations or warranties of any kind, express or implied, including but not limited to the implied warranties of merchantability, fitness for a particular purpose. The Publisher and Editor shall not be liable whatsoever for any errors, omissions, whether such errors or omissions result from negligence, accident, or any other cause or claims for loss or damages of any kind, including without limitation, indirect or consequential loss or damage arising out of use, inability to use, or about the reliability, accuracy or sufficiency of the information contained in this book.

Dedicated to

All those who bought my first book **"EPC made Ezee"**, *made it a success, and motivated me to write my second book.*

CONTENTS

Foreword .... *vii*
Foreword .... *ix*
Preface .... *xi*
Introduction .... *xv*
Acknowledgements .... *xvii*

Chapter 1: Emotional Intelligence 1
Chapter 2: Communication Skills 15
Chapter 3: Interpersonal Skills 43
Chapter 4: Conflict Management 67
Chapter 5: Stress Management 93
Chapter 6: Time Management 105
Chapter 7: Decision Making 124
Chapter 8: Leadership 142
Chapter 9: Adaptability and Visibility 160
- *Learning skill*
- *Observation skill*
- *Innovation skill*
- *Flexibility skill*
- *Collaboration skill*
- *Determination skill*
- *Open-mindedness*
- *Empathy*
- *Resilience skill*
- *Teamwork*

v

CONTENTS

- *Coaching and mentoring*
- *Motivation*

Chapter 10: Negotiation Skills 188
Chapter 11: Public Speaking 209
Chapter 12: Personality Development 225

- *Dressing and personal grooming*
- *Table manners*
- *Body language*
- *Email etiquette*
- *Command over the language*

Additional topics: 270
- I. 'Work From Home' (WFH), 'Remote work' or 'Telework.' ... 270
- II. Work-Life Balance 274
- III. Continuing Education 277
- IV. Rational use of social media 278
- V. Corporate ethics and business code of conduct 280
- VI. Diversity Equality and Inclusion – DEI 285
- VII. Performance Appraisal 286
- VIII. Upskilling 289
- IX. Personal branding 300
- X. Personality Check card 323
- XI. MBTI – Personality development assessment tool 333

"The man who graduates today and stops learning tomorrow is uneducated the day after" – **Newton D. Baker**

FOREWORD

Sathya and I go a decade back when we were working together in Chennai for an American MNC. I was the Director of the Engineering office and Sathya was managing the quality assurance division in it.

What stuck to me about him was his easy-going persona, his absolute comfort in public speaking and a being a beehive of crazy and out of box ideas to passionately improve engineering quality at work.

He eventually was one of the key members in turning the office around from a low-cost engineering center to the engineering center of choice for the Company that it is today, with some brilliant initiatives that made project delivery both challenging and enjoyable.

His outgoing and gregarious nature in addition to his passion and eagerness to mentor colleagues at work made me hand over the running of the company's Graduate Engineer Training Program in 2015 to him. And man, what a transformation he brought about…this book, the second from him, is all about what he learnt, understood and he thought, and I do agree, needed done to soft land young Engineers where they want to get in their careers.

Having spent 30++ years in the corporate world, one sure thing I can vouch for, is the power of 'Soft skills.' It is not enough to have good domain experience and knowledge; you also need to have effective vehicles to deliver them. This book will take the reader through all of it and some more.

When I started reading it, I was pleasantly surprised at the treasure trove of very useful information that is there in the book for young corporate

FOREWORD

professionals. In fact, anyone working in the corporate world will find this self-help book really useful and informative.

Over time, in my career, I have seen many aspiring and ambitious individuals getting waylaid for not able to communicate their ideas effectively within their teams and above. What possibly could have been fixed easily with mentoring from within the organization and some self-help, ends up into disillusionment and loss of confidence.

For any new or experienced corporate professionals, the sure shot way to land on your ambitions is to develop your soft skills in addition to of course perseverance. I strongly recommend that you read this book to get you where you aspire to be.

Happy reading!!

Kannan Iyer
Director of Engineering
Lamprell

FOREWORD

This book was introduced to me by Siva Ramalingam, (CEO, Fiori Asia) my friend, from school days. This is the second book of Sathyamurthy Vamanan.

Sathyamurthy comes with 35 years of illustrious experience and is a voracious reader.

Reading this book gave me an insight into how well Sathyamurthy Vamanan has worked towards bringing a concise reference manual for young graduates and entrepreneurs.

In this book, he has articulated the importance of the soft skills in a simple but highly effective way that would help an individual in their personal and professional journey. He has handpicked key ideas and theories by various specialists and has clubbed his own experience with it and has presented it well.

The chapters like Motivation, Time Management and How to make a Brand of Yourself by adopting few tips in the work environment will interest the readers. The idea of Personality Check Card will help everyone in understanding oneself and making life changes.

This book is to be read, re-read, and used as a regular reference by all aspiring young minds.

My best wishes to Sathyamurthy Vamanan.

V Sridhar
Chief Operating officer,
MK Agrotech, India.

PREFACE

The philosophy of Hinduism elucidates three fundamental qualities, (or Gunas), inherent in a human being: Sattva, Rajas, and Tamas.

> **'Sattva'** represents goodness, calmness, and harmony.

> **'Rajas'** embodies passion, activity, and movement.

> **'Tamas'** signifies ignorance, inertia, and laziness.

It is important to note that an individual is a composite of these three Gunas, known as Trigunas, (Three qualities) with varying degrees of dominance. These proportions are not static and fluctuate based on time, location, subject, and necessity.

In a similar vein, an individual's power skills (Soft skills) are contingent upon the identification and further refinement of the dominant trait. This explains why not everyone ascends to the position of a CEO, and not all CEOs are born leaders.

The ascent up the professional ladder *is not* solely determined by hard work or hard skills (hard skills are basically the technical skills and Credentials). This is exactly where 'power skills' (soft skills) are important. Without honing these skills, reaching the pinnacle of success remains an elusive goal.

Power skills are cultivated through consistent and conscious efforts and cannot be acquired merely by reading a book, attending a training session, or watching YouTube videos. These resources can only provide a broad guideline and techniques for an individual to develop further.

Then why this book?

PREFACE

Numerous esteemed authors, such as Edward de Bono, Stephen Covey, and Dale Carnegie, have extensively written on various soft skills.

However, for those seeking a comprehensive and easily understandable book that encompasses *all types of soft skills*, this volume stands out as an excellent choice.

"This book explores contemporary technological advancements and the evolving attitudes of new generations."

This book, in addition, offers practical tips and ideas. It is crucial to understand that learning is a continuous process, and perfection is achieved through practice. Miraculous transformations should not be expected in a short span of time.

Who needs this book?

Anyone with the right aptitude to learn and acquire new skills or hone up the existing skills.

"Although the primary focus of this book is on those who are employed, its insights and principles are applicable across various domains, including business, politics, and professional fields."

"This book is not intended as an academic text or a manual. Rather, it serves as a valuable reference, designed to guide individuals in exploring and developing essential power skills for their professional growth."

No matter what job you have in life. Your success will be determined 5% by Your academic credentials, 15% by Your professional experiences, and 80% by your Power of Soft skills.

The structure of the book

"This book is designed to be gender and language-neutral, utilizing simple language for clarity. The rhetoric used in this book is simple and clear, to keep the reader engaged.

PREFACE

The Chapters in this book are sequenced based on 'logic.' The order prioritizes 'foundational skills' like 'emotional intelligence' and 'communication,' which are crucial for *personal and professional interactions*. It then moves on to 'managing stress and time,' 'making decisions,' and 'leading effectively.' Finally, it includes skills that enhance 'visibility and personal growth.'

"The author has incorporated *'For Your Information'* sections at strategic points throughout the book to provide readers with enlightening and interesting information."

It is advisable not to rush through the book. Instead, read it chapter by chapter (as many chapters are interrelated), practice and rehearse, and then proceed to the next.

"It is not the strongest or the most intelligent of the species that survives, but the one that is most adaptable to change." – **Charles Darwin**

"75 percent of long-term job success depends on people skills, while only 25 percent on technical knowledge."

INTRODUCTION

*E*very year millions of students pass out of the educational institutions, but not all are getting employment, of their choice.

The reason could be many, but one glaring aspect is the lack of "soft skills." Not many possess these skills and a person who possesses these skills has an edge over the other.

According to research, the "power of soft skills" can be attributed to 75% of job success.

The term "power skills" has emerged as an alternative to "soft skills." While both terms refer to non-technical abilities, there is a subtle difference:

When one looks at the dictionary the meaning of 'soft,' is something like agreeable, somewhat subdued. Hence replacing soft with power would be apt.

Power skills encompass decision-making, addressing challenges, good judgment, effective communication, self-management, collaboration, and clarifying values.

Individuals must recognize their areas of strength and focus on enhancing those traits.

As the world rapidly evolves, we must keep pace with these changes to avoid being left behind.

Do not Just Focus on Your Technical Skills. Focus On Your Power Skills.

Let us embark on a journey into the realm of powerful soft skills.

> "I'm convinced that about half of what separates the successful, from the non-successful is pure perseverance." – **Steve Jobs**

ACKNOWLEDGEMENTS

I would like to express my profound gratitude to the esteemed corporate leaders and distinguished authors of the self-help genre who have inspired me to write this book.

My sincere thanks go to Mr. Kannan Iyer and Mr. Sridhar V, for graciously agreeing to write such a wonderful foreword.

I am also grateful for the latest technologies and tools that facilitated the processes of proofreading, grammar checking, and formatting.

Gratitude to my first employer, 'Larsen & Toubro Limited', India, for introducing me to the importance of soft skills in both personal and professional growth, way back in 1987.

A special thanks to 'Clever Fox', the publisher, for their unwavering support in bringing this book to fruition with remarkable speed and quality.

I am deeply thankful to my wife, 'Udaya', for her patience and meticulous proofreading of all the drafts and the final manuscript.

Lastly, I am profoundly grateful to 'Lord Shiva', for granting me the strength and wisdom to complete this endeavor.

CHAPTER 1

EMOTIONAL INTELLIGENCE

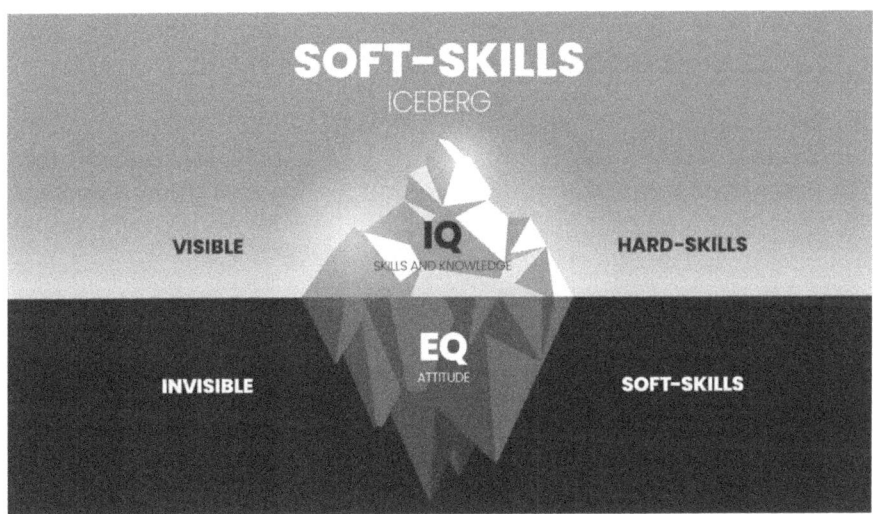

From my childhood, I have heard about Intelligence Quotient (IQ) and people say Albert Einstein had the best IQ in the world, (160) and so on. I never took the risk of undertaking any test to check my IQ.

IQ is a numerical measure of a person's cognitive abilities, particularly their reasoning, problem-solving, and analytical skills. It is often assessed through standardized tests.

The concept of IQ originated in the early 20th century and has been widely used to evaluate intellectual capacity. However, it is essential to recognize that intelligence is multifaceted, and IQ alone does not capture all aspects of a person's abilities or potential.

But today's buzz word is Emotional Quotient or Emotional Intelligence.

(Now the world is moving into Artificial Intelligence, which is entirely a different subject altogether).

Daniel Goleman's book "Emotional Intelligence: Why It Can Matter More Than IQ" comprehensively reviews the research, insights, and implications of emotional intelligence.

Here are the key points:

Emotions and the Human Brain

Emotions are strong impulses that guide our actions, helping us survive.

We have two minds: the emotional mind (intuitive and impulsive) and the rational mind (thoughtful and analytical).

Emotional hijacking occurs when emotions override rational thinking.

Our biological evolution has not caught up with modern lifestyles, leading to emotional mismatches.

What Is Emotional Intelligence?

Emotional intelligence involves self-control, regulating moods, empathy, and resilience.

Research suggests that IQ accounts for only 20% of success; the remaining 80% comes from factors like emotional intelligence.

Developing Emotional Intelligence

The book provides actionable ways to handle emotional distress and become more rational in our feelings.

In summary, emotional intelligence plays a crucial role in shaping our lives, relationships, and achievements, and it can be nurtured and developed.

A few excerpts from the book Emotional intelligence by Daniel Goleman

"A belligerent samurai, an old Japanese tale goes, once challenged a Zen master to explain the concept of heaven and hell. The monk replied with scorn, "You're nothing but a lout - I cannot waste my time with the likes of you!"

His very honor attacked, the samurai flew into a rage and, pulling his sword from its scabbard, yelled "I could kill you for your impertinence."

"That," the monk calmly replied, "is hell."

Startled at seeing the truth in what the master pointed out about the fury that had him in its grip, the samurai calmed down, sheathed his sword, and bowed, thanking the monk for the insight.

"And that," said the monk "is heaven."

The sudden awakening of the samurai to his own agitated state illustrates the crucial difference between being caught up in a feeling and becoming aware that you are being swept away by it. Socrates's injunction "Know thyself" speaks to the keystone of emotional intelligence: awareness of one's own feelings as they occur."

****

"People's emotions are rarely put into words, far more often they are expressed through other cues.

The key to intuiting another's feelings is in the ability to read nonverbal channels, tone of voice, gesture, facial expression, and the like."

****

"Anyone can become angry—that is easy. But to be angry with the right person, to the right degree, at the right time, for the right purpose, and in the right way—this is not easy. ARISTOTLE, The Nicomachean Ethics"

****

"Emotional self-awareness is the building block of the next fundamental emotional intelligence: being able to shake off a bad mood."

****

"Helping people better manage their upsetting feelings—anger, anxiety, depression, pessimism, and loneliness—is a form of disease prevention. Since the data show that the toxicity of these emotions, when chronic, is on a par with smoking cigarettes, helping people handle them better could potentially have a medical payoff as great as getting heavy smokers to quit."

****

Emotional Intelligence (EI), *also known as* **emotional quotient (EQ)**, refers to a person's ability to understand and manage their own emotions effectively, as well as their capacity to empathize with others and manage interpersonal relationships judiciously. Here are the key components of EQ:

Self-awareness: Being aware of your own emotional patterns, motives, and impact on others.

Self-regulation: Reacting proportionately to circumstances, pausing when needed, and controlling impulses.

Motivation: Intrinsic drive for personal development and success, not solely for external rewards.

Empathy: Understanding others' perspectives, being slow to judge, and showing compassion.

Social skills: Adeptness at working in teams and managing relationships.

Research suggests that EQ plays a significant role in various aspects of life, including mental health, relationships, job satisfaction, and academic performance.

Basic human emotions

Basic emotions are innate, universal, and automatic responses that play a crucial role in human behavior. Here are the fundamental ones:

Happiness: Characterized by contentment, joy, and well-being. It is expressed through smiling, relaxed body language, and an upbeat tone of voice.

Sadness: Associated with loss, disappointment, and grief. It often leads to tears, withdrawal, and a subdued demeanor.

Disgust: Evoked by unpleasant or repulsive stimuli. It triggers avoidance behaviors and facial expressions of distaste.

Fear: A survival response to threats. Fear activates the fight-or-flight system, causing heightened alertness and physical tension.

Surprise: Occurs when something unexpected happens. It is expressed through widened eyes, raised eyebrows, and a sudden intake of breath.

Anger: Linked to frustration, injustice, and conflict. Anger motivates action and can lead to aggressive behavior.

Remember, these basic emotions are deeply ingrained and influence our daily interactions and decisions.

A word of caution: Never ever try to suppress or control your emotions. Learn to manage or regulate them well.

Regulating the emotions

Effective emotional regulation is essential for well-being. Here are **practical strategies** to help you regulate your emotions:

Allow Your Emotions to Exist Without Judgment:

Acknowledge and accept your feelings without labeling them as good or bad. Create space for exploration.

Explore How You Feel:

Understand the factors influencing your emotions. Reflect on situations, thoughts, and triggers.

Name Your Emotions:

Label your feelings. This simple act enhances self-awareness and helps you manage them better.

Accept Your Emotions:

Avoid suppressing or denying emotions. Allow yourself to experience them fully.

Practice Mindfulness:

Techniques like meditation and deep breathing create mental space between emotions and reactions.

Identify Your Triggers:

Recognize situations or people that evoke strong emotional responses. Prepare to manage them.

Practice Self-Compassion:

Be kind to yourself during emotional difficulties. Treat yourself as you would a friend.

Challenge Negative Self-Talk:

Replace harsh inner dialogue with supportive, constructive thoughts.

Mindfulness

Mindfulness is a state of active, open attention to the present moment. It involves observing thoughts and feelings without judgment, allowing us to fully experience our inner processes. Here are the key aspects:

Understanding Mindfulness

To live mindfully means being fully present, reawakening to the present instead of dwelling on the past or anticipating the future.

We observe and label thoughts, feelings, and bodily sensations objectively, avoiding self-criticism and judgment.

Roots and History

Mindfulness has roots in Buddhist and Hindu teachings. In Buddhism, "sati" (attention, awareness, presence) is considered the first step toward enlightenment.

Jon Kabat-Zinn, a pioneer, developed **Mindfulness-Based Stress Reduction (MBSR)** in the late 1970s. It treats chronic pain by encouraging mindfulness.

Components of Mindfulness:

Awareness: Focusing on inner experiences, including the present moment.

Acceptance: Observing thoughts without judgment or avoidance.

Mindfulness integrates into therapies like **Mindfulness-Based Cognitive Therapy** and **Dialectical Behavior Therapy**.

Practicing Mindfulness

Pay attention to the present, whether through meditation or small moments during the day.

Overcome fears and insecurities about the past or future by learning to be present.

In summary, mindfulness cultivates peace, mental clarity, and better relationships.

Zazen meditation

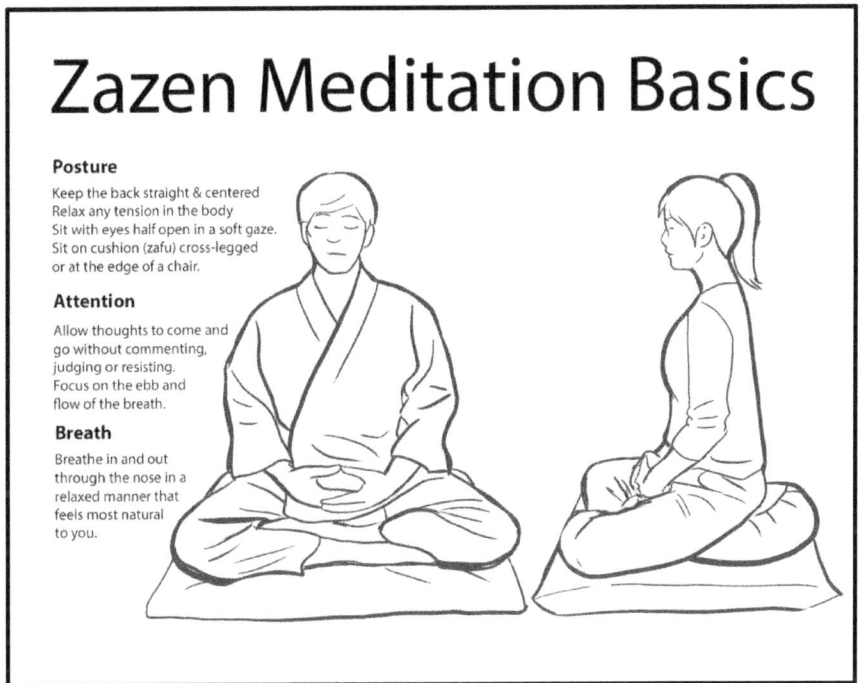

Let me narrate my own experience in Japan.

As a resolute practitioner of Yoga and meditation, I have spent over eight years faithfully following Sadguru's "Inner Engineering" meditation practice including the "Sambhavi Maha Mudra." This daily practice has granted me a measure of control over my body and mind, although enlightenment remains elusive.

Recently, my curiosity led me to explore Zazen—a venerable meditation technique with roots in ancient Japan. Living in Yokohama, I discovered that the **SOJIJI (Zen) Temple** offered Zazen classes in English on weekends.

One crisp Saturday morning, my journey unfolded. The sprawling Sojiji Temple, dating back to the 12th and 13th centuries, sprawled across acres—an architectural marvel. A monk greeted us and ushered us into a vast hall, the scheduled class time approaching.

At 9:45 AM, we sat alone, wondering if we were the sole participants. But then, like a harmonious chorus, more than twenty seekers arrived promptly at 9:55 AM.

Mostly, foreigners registered for the class; their eyes reflecting anticipation.

The monk guided us to the meditation hall, where we embarked on an hour of Zazen. Words fail to capture the experience: a silent communion with existence, a dance of stillness. It was, quite simply, **awe-inspiring**.

Post-Zazen, the monk graciously shared the temple's history. Curious, I asked about his daily routine. His laughter echoed through the hallowed halls as he explained that Zen Buddhism allowed its priests to lead normal family lives. They could eat, drink, and even marry. Assigned to manage specific temples, they balanced sacred duty with earthly bonds.

In the past, monasteries teemed with young acolytes. Now, double-digit attendance was rare. Times change, traditions evolve.

And so, I returned home, dedicating 20 to 40 minutes each evening to Zazen—a quiet voyage within.

There are many YouTube videos available to learn Zazen, and if you are interested, please have a look at them.

I can tell you one thing; *Zazen* is a powerful meditation and effective too.

Why am I bringing in Zazen suddenly? The reason is simple: Zazen or for that matter any type of *meditation*, will help oneself to practice '*mindfulness*.'

Relationship between Mindfulness and Emotional Intelligence

Mindfulness and **EI** are closely related, and practicing mindfulness can enhance your EI. Here is how they intersect:

Foundation for EI

Mindfulness is a key tool for understanding ourselves, our thoughts, and feelings. It fosters **self-awareness**, which is the **first component of EI**.

Self-awareness is the basis for developing other EI skills, such as empathy, self-regulation, and social awareness.

Sensitivity to Emotions

Mindfulness practices, like meditation, help us observe thoughts and feelings without judgment or reactivity.

This heightened awareness extends to emotions, allowing us to recognize and understand them better.

Emotional Intelligence Competencies

Open awareness in mindfulness facilitates sensitivity to emotions and their components (thoughts, physical sensations).

EI competencies, such as accurately perceiving and managing emotions, align with mindfulness principles.

In summary, practicing mindfulness can deepen your self-awareness and contribute to a more emotionally intelligent approach to life.

Buddhist doctrine distinguishes five aggregates.

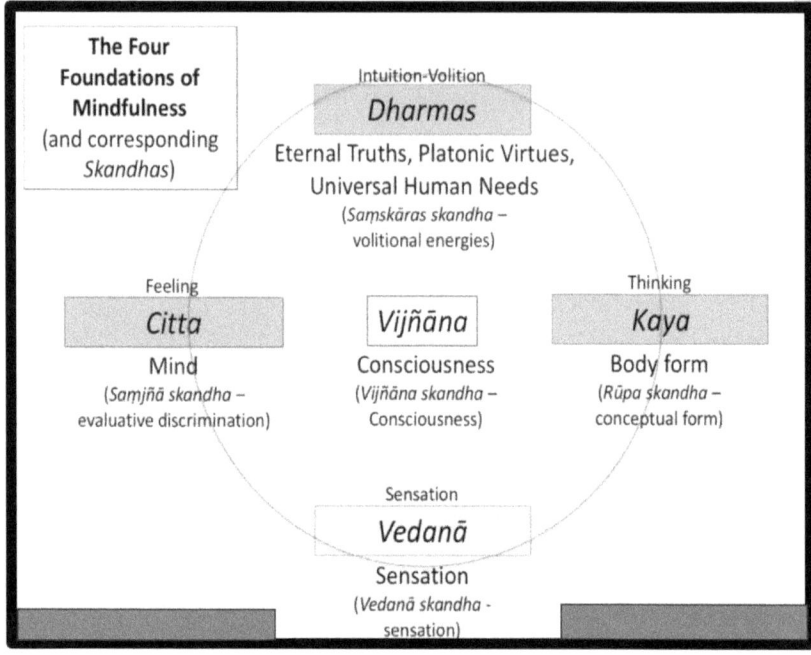

How to incorporate mindfulness into daily life?

Incorporating mindfulness into your daily routine does not require extra time or unique skills. Here are **simple ways** to be mindful throughout your day:

Morning Mindfulness

Start your day with intention. Take a few minutes to focus on your breath, set positive intentions, and appreciate the present moment.

Mindful Eating

Pay attention to your meals. Savor each bite, notice flavors, textures, and how food nourishes you. Avoid distractions while eating.

Mindful Movement

During exercise or daily activities, be present. Feel your body's movements, notice sensations, and appreciate the physical experience.

Mindful Technology Use

When using devices, pause and check in with yourself. Are you mindlessly scrolling? Take breaks, breathe, and refocus.

Mindful Moments Throughout the Day

Pause periodically. Observe your surroundings, senses, and emotions. Even a few seconds of mindfulness can be effective.

Evening Reflection and Relaxation

Before bed, reflect on your day without judgment. Practice deep breathing or gentle stretches to unwind.

Remember, little moments of mindfulness add up!

Role of Emotional Intelligence at workplace

Emotional intelligence (EI) plays a crucial role in the corporate workplace.

Improved Communication: Emotionally intelligent employees tend to be better communicators. They recognize and manage their emotions, allowing them to convey ideas clearly and confidently. For instance, during a nerve-wracking presentation, an emotionally intelligent employee stays in control, ensuring effective communication.

Conflict Resolution: EI helps manage conflict and negative emotions. Instead of reacting impulsively, emotionally intelligent individuals assess their feelings. They address issues from a stable, clear-headed perspective, leading to positive outcomes and maintaining harmonious relationships with colleagues.

Stronger Relationships: High EI fosters better connections with colleagues. Emotionally intelligent employees respect others' ideas and feelings, collaborate openly, and provide support. This contributes to a positive work environment and effective teamwork.

Remember, emotional intelligence influences interactions, stress management, and overall job performance. It is an asset in any professional setting!

For your information

"All-time best books – My pick

The 7 Habits of Highly Effective People – Stephen Covey

Think and Grow Rich – Napoleon Hill

The art of public speaking – Dale Carnegie

The Alchemist – Paulo Coelho

The Power of Positive Thinking – Normal Vincent Peale

Man's Search for Meaning – Victor Franki

How to win Friends and Influence people – Dale Carnegie

Don't say YES when you want to say NO – Herbert Fensterheim and Jean Baer

How to STOP worrying and START living – Dale Carnegie

Emotional Intelligence – Daniel Goleman

Lateral Thinking – Edward De Bono

Bhagvad Gita – (Original in Sanskrit, also available in 82 world language)

Tirukkural – (Original in Tamil, also translated into 102 world languages)

CHAPTER 2

COMMUNICATION SKILLS

One of my favorite and essential traits for anyone to succeed in life is communication skills.

Effective Communication

The dictionary defines communication as, "the imparting or interchange of thoughts, opinions, or information by speech, writing, or signs."

Communication is broadly divided into three categories:

Verbal Communication (as well as non-verbal)

Written Communication

Listening

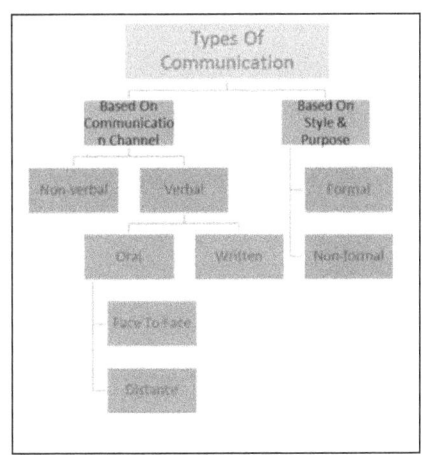

Communication process

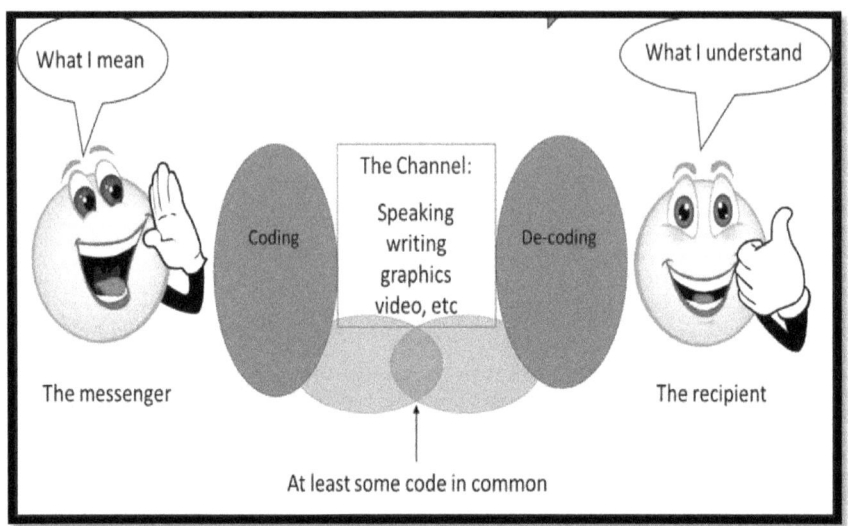

Active Listening: During a team meeting, an effective communicator listens attentively to colleagues, acknowledges their points, and responds thoughtfully. This fosters a collaborative environment and ensures everyone feels heard.

Clear and Concise Emails: When sending an email, an effective communicator ensures the message is clear, concise, and free of jargon. They use bullet points for easy readability and include a clear subject line and call to action.

Nonverbal Communication: In a presentation, an effective communicator uses appropriate body language, such as maintaining eye contact, using hand gestures to emphasize points, and adopting an open posture to engage the audience.

Constructive Feedback: Providing feedback in a way that is specific, actionable, and focused on behaviors rather than personal attributes. For example, saying, "I noticed that the MIS report was submitted late. In the future, please ensure it is submitted by the deadline," is more effective than a vague criticism, like "You are becoming lazy."

Empathy in Conversations: When a colleague is facing a personal issue, an effective communicator shows empathy by listening without interrupting, offering support, and respecting their feelings.

Conflict Resolution: During a disagreement, an effective communicator remains calm, listens to the other person's perspective, and works towards a mutually beneficial solution. They avoid blame and focus on resolving the issue.

Storytelling: Using storytelling to convey complex ideas in a relatable and engaging manner. For instance, a manager might share a success story to illustrate the benefits of a new strategy.

Negotiation: In a negotiation, an effective communicator clearly articulates their needs and interests while also understanding and addressing the concerns of the other party. This approach helps in reaching a win-win agreement.

Virtual Communication: During virtual meetings, an effective communicator ensures their technology is working, speaks clearly, and uses visual aids to enhance understanding. They also encourage participation from all attendees.

Public Speaking: Delivering a speech with confidence, clarity, and enthusiasm. An effective public speaker prepares thoroughly, knows their audience, and uses rhetorical devices to engage and persuade.

5C's of Communication

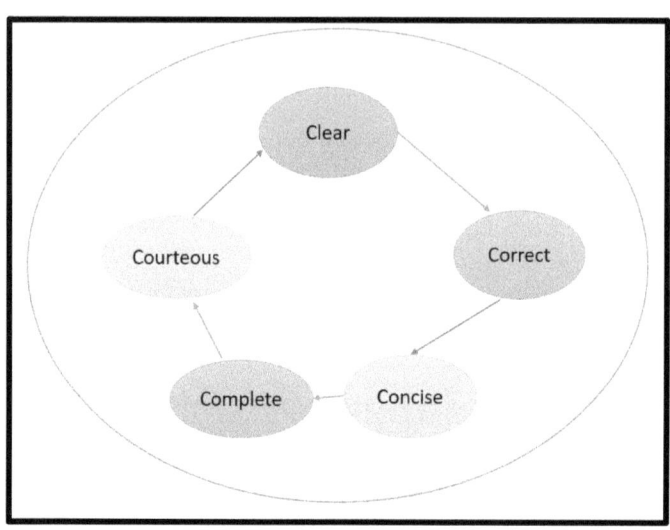

Have you ever noticed that during a typical communication process one uses only 7% words. That clearly depicts the importance of non-verbal communication techniques.

Communication barriers

Effective communication is essential in both personal and professional settings.

Let us explore some common communication barriers and strategies to overcome them:

Differences in Language and Culture:

Barrier: Language and cultural differences can lead to misunderstandings. Words may have different meanings across cultures, and regional dialects or jargon can cause confusion.

Overcoming Strategy: Foster cultural awareness, use simple language, and clarify meanings. Active listening helps bridge gaps.

Physical Barriers:

Barrier: Noise, distance, or outdated technology can hinder communication.

Overcoming Strategy: Choose quiet spaces, use effective communication tools, and ensure technology is up to date.

Emotional and Psychological Barriers:

Barrier: Our emotions (stress, anxiety) affect how we interpret messages.

Overcoming Strategy: Practice emotional intelligence, manage stress, and be aware of emotional biases.

Attitudinal Barriers:

Barrier: Personality conflicts, poor management, or lack of motivation hinder communication.

Overcoming Strategy: Foster open communication, encourage feedback, and address hierarchical issues.

Perceptual Barriers:

Barrier: Different viewpoints and biases impact communication.

Overcoming Strategy: Seek common ground, actively listen, and be open-minded.

Information Overload:

Barrier: Too much information overwhelms recipients.

Overcoming Strategy: Prioritize key points, use concise language, and avoid unnecessary details.

Cultural and Language Barriers:

Barrier: Cultural norms and language differences create misunderstandings.

Overcoming Strategy: Learn about other cultures, use plain language, and adapt communication styles.

Hierarchy and Power Dynamics:

Barrier: Unequal power levels affect communication flow.

Overcoming Strategy: Encourage open dialogue, create a supportive environment, and listen actively.

Poor Communication Channels:

Barrier: Inefficient channels hinder message delivery.

Overcoming Strategy: Choose appropriate channels (e.g., face-to-face, email, video calls) based on context.

Noise and Distractions:

Barrier: External noise or distractions disrupt communication.

Overcoming Strategy: Minimize distractions, choose quiet environments, and focus on the conversation.

Lack of Clarity and Context:

Barrier: Vague messages lead to confusion.

Overcoming Strategy: Be specific, provide context, and ask clarifying questions.

Emotional Barriers:

Barrier: Negative emotions (anger, fear) hinder effective communication.

Overcoming Strategy: Manage emotions, practice active listening, and choose words carefully.

Remember, adapting communication strategies based on the context and audience is crucial for overcoming these barriers.

Communication mix

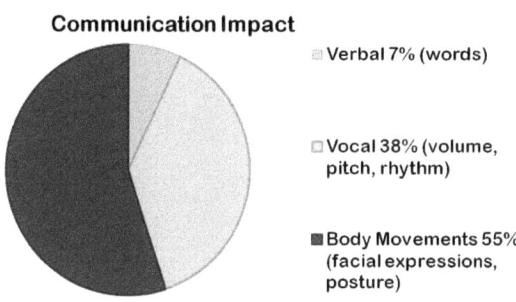

Written Communication

Essentials of Technical Writing

Technical writing is a specialized form of writing that focuses on conveying complex technical information clearly and understandably. Here are the essentials of technical writing:

1. **Audience Analysis**:
   Understand the target audience and their knowledge level, expertise, and familiarity with technical concepts.
   Consider their needs, goals, and potential challenges in comprehending the subject matter.
   Adapt the writing style, vocabulary, and level of detail to best suit the intended audience.
2. **Clarity and Simplicity**:
   Use clear and concise language to communicate technical information effectively.

Avoid jargon, acronyms, or technical terms that may confuse or alienate the audience.

Break down complex concepts into bite-sized information using plain language.

Structure the content logically, using headings, subheadings, and bullet points for clarity and easy navigation.

3. **Visual Communication**:

   Utilize visuals like diagrams, charts, graphs, or illustrations to enhance understanding.

   Ensure visuals are accurate, labeled appropriately, and support the written content.

   Use consistent formatting and layout to create visually appealing documents.

   Provide clear captions or explanations for visuals to aid comprehension.

4. **Organization and Structure**:

   Follow a logical and consistent structure in organizing information.

   Start with an introduction to provide context and purpose.

   Use headings and subheadings to break down the content into sections for easy navigation.

   Present information in a sequential and orderly manner.

   Summarize key points and provide a conclusion or summary at the end.

5. **Plain Language and Active Voice**:

   Use simple language that is easy to understand.

   Write in an active voice, which makes the writing more engaging and direct.

   Keep sentences short and to the point.

   Define technical terms or provide explanations when necessary.

6. **Accuracy and Precision**:

   Ensure the accuracy and validity of the technical information presented.

Verify facts, figures, and data using reliable sources.

Use precise language to avoid ambiguity or misinterpretation.

Provide citations or references for external sources used.

7. **User-Centric Approach**:

    Focus on the user's perspective and address their needs and concerns.

    Anticipate potential questions or areas of confusion.

    Provide clear and detailed instructions or procedures for using products or systems.

    Include troubleshooting tips or FAQs to help users overcome common issues.

8. **Revision and Editing**:

    Revise and edit the content for clarity, coherence, and grammatical correctness.

    Proofread for spelling, punctuation, and grammar errors.

    Eliminate unnecessary or redundant information.

    Ensure consistency in terminology and formatting.

9. **Documentation Maintenance and Updates**:

    Keep technical documents up to date with the latest information and changes.

    Regularly review and revise documents as needed.

    Establish version control and change management processes.

    Archive outdated or obsolete documentation.

10. **Collaboration and Feedback**:

    Collaborate with subject matter experts (SMEs) to ensure accuracy and completeness.

    Seek feedback from users or stakeholders to improve the documentation.

    Incorporate user feedback and suggestions to enhance usability.

    By following these essentials of technical writing, you can create clear, concise, and user-friendly technical documents that effectively communicate complex information to your target audience.

Report writing

Make it clear, crisp, simple and interesting,

Formula is WR³
- **Write it**
- **Review it**
- **Revise it**
- **Re-read it**

Some more tips.
- Language should be simple, yet professional.
- Use 'conducted' or 'performed' or 'carried out' instead of 'done.'
- Use 'informed' or 'advised' instead of 'told.'
- Reports should be written in third person.
- Break-up long sentences for clarity.
- Pay attention to the consistency of tone.

Contents of a report (Technical report)

- Cover sheet
- Executive Summary (where needed)
- Revision history
- Table of Contents
- HOLDS List (if applicable)
- Introduction, Background, and Purpose
- Abbreviations (this is necessary) and Glossary
- Body of the report
- Key Results
- Analysis
- Conclusions
- References
- Appendices

Depending on the nature of the report, the above list can be modified.

Importance of "Executive Summary"

The summary should:

- Briefly state the purpose and specific background – if any
- Outline the approach to the task, if applicable
- Indicate key aspects and salient results
- State the main outcomes and/ or conclusions

The summary should NOT:

- Provide general information or background
- Explain why you are conducting the activity
- Provide references to other sections
- Be slick, limit it to a page or two… Remember, this is for busy executives!!

Formatting

Why formatting is important?

- Look at it from the reader's point of view.
- A correctly formatted document gives the impression that care has been exercised.
- An ill-formatted document may make a reader doubt not just the formatting skills but more importantly, the technical content of the report as well.
- Paragraph spacing, line spacing, font size consistency, etc., are of paramount importance for the overall impact of your report!

Checks and balances: (checking the quality)

- Pay attention to fonts and font sizes.
- On tables across pages, use the 'Header Rows Repeat' feature.
- Appropriately superscript and subscript.
    - Example m^3/h instead of m3/h
- C_v instead of Cv

- Clarify units unambiguously
- 'Cut and Paste' without regard to content, tone, and blending with the overall report is an absolute NO.
- Number all the pages, it should be evident to the reader if something is missing/not printed.
- Each page within an appendix should also be numbered.
- Pay attention to logos, use only company and project-approved ones.
- Do NOT pull straight from a printer and submit.
- Use grammar check and spell check (MS Word features), but with caution.
- There are many tools like 'Grammarly,' which does a decent job.
- Check the physical copy contents manually before submission.
- When creating PDFs, derive as much as possible from native files (signed sheets may be an exception).
- Avoid repetition and/or contradictions between sections, and use consistent language.
- Maintain consistency of bullet styles.
- Avoid headings at the bottom of a page.
- Check the appropriateness of bold/italics, if used.
- Align both the right and left sides of a paragraph to achieve a clean look.
- Place File name, location, and revision in the footer.
- Do not use "&" in the middle of a sentence unless it is part of an abbreviation.

Nonverbal communication

Improving your non-verbal communication can greatly enhance how you convey messages and connect with others. Following the below strategies could help you to improve this skill:

1. **Maintain Eye Contact**
   Make appropriate eye contact to show engagement and interest. Avoid staring, but ensure you meet the other person's gaze regularly.
2. **Be Aware of Your Body Language**
   Adopt an open posture. Try to avoid crossing your arms or legs, as this can appear defensive. Stand straight or sit up straight to convey confidence.
3. **Use Facial Expressions**
   Express your emotions through your facial expressions. Smile when appropriate, and ensure your expressions match the tone of the conversation.
4. **Pay Attention to the Tone of Voice**
   Modulate your tone of voice to match the message you are conveying. A warm, friendly tone can make your communication more effective.
5. **Observe and Mirror**
   Observe others' non-verbal cues and mirror them subtly. This will .definitely help build rapport and make the other person feel more comfortable.
6. **Use Gestures**
   Incorporate natural gestures to emphasize your points. Avoid overdoing it but use your hands to help illustrate your message.
7. **Be Mindful of Personal Space**
   Respect personal space. Do not stand too close which can make others uncomfortable, while standing too far can seem disengaged.
8. **Practice Active Listening**
   Show that you are listening by nodding, maintaining eye contact, and responding appropriately. This reinforces that you are engaged in the conversation.
9. **Pay Attention to Incongruences**
   Ensure your non-verbal signals match your words. If there is a mismatch, it can create confusion and mistrust.

10. **Seek Feedback**

    Ask for feedback from trusted colleagues or friends about your non-verbal communication. They can provide insights into areas you might need to improve.

    By incorporating these strategies into your daily interactions, you can enhance your non-verbal communication skills and make your interactions more effective and meaningful.

Evaluating nonverbal signals	
Eye Contact	Is eye contact being made? If so, Is it overly intense or just, right?
Facial expression	What is their face showing? Is it mask like and unexpressive, or emotionally present and filled with interest?
Posture and gesture	Are their bodies are relaxed or stiff and immobile? Are shoulders tense and raised, or slightly sloped?
Touch	Is there any physical contact? Is it appropriate to the situation? Does it make you feel uncomfortable?
Intensity	Do they seem flat, cool, and disinterested?
Timing and pace	Is there an easy flow of information back and forth? Do nonverbal responses come too quickly or too slowly?
Sounds	Do you hear sounds that indicate caring or concern?

As you continue to pay attention to the nonverbal cues and signals you send and receive, your ability to communicate will improve.

Seven signals of success

1. **Upright steady posture** – Walk slowly, deliberately, and tall upon entering the room. While in conversation, leaning slightly forward is inviting.
2. **Maintain good eye contact** – a friendly 'eyebrow flash' when accompanied by a natural smile sends a strong positive signal that the meeting has gotten off to a good start.
3. **Sincere natural smile** – helps break the ice and expresses a relaxed confidence.
4. **Firm Handshake** – helps to give confidence about you to your listeners.
5. **Use mirroring techniques** – Make a subtle effort to reproduce the positive signals your interviewer/ client sends. (You should never mirror negative body signals.)
6. **Avoid staring** – Occasionally look confidently and calmly to the right or left; never look down.
7. **Do not hurry any movement.**

Active listening

Many of us are good speakers, but.... Poor listeners.

We always listen to respond, rarely listen to understand.

Improving your active listening skills can significantly enhance your communication and relationships in both personal and professional settings. Here are some effective strategies to help you become a better active listener:

1. **Be Fully Present**
   Give your full attention to the speaker. This means putting away distractions like your phone and focusing entirely on the conversation.

2. **Maintain Eye Contact**

   Maintain appropriate eye contact to show that you are engaged and interested in what the speaker is saying.

3. **Pay Attention to Non-Verbal Cues**

   Observe non-verbal signals such as body language, facial expressions, and tone of voice. These cues can provide additional context to the speaker's message.

4. **Avoid Interrupting**

   Let the speaker finish their thoughts before you respond. Interrupting often, can disrupt their flow and make them feel unheard.

5. **Ask Open-Ended Questions**

   Encourage further discussion by asking open-ended questions. This shows that you are interested in understanding more about their perspective.

6. **Paraphrase and Reflect**

   Summarize what the speaker has said in your own words to ensure you have understood correctly. This also shows the speaker that you have actively listened.

7. **Provide Feedback**

   Offer constructive feedback when appropriate. This can include nodding, smiling, or verbally acknowledging points made by the speaker.

8. **Withhold Judgment**

   Listen without forming immediate judgments or opinions. This allows you to fully understand the speaker's point of view before responding.

9. **Respond Appropriately**

   Respond in a way that is respectful and relevant to the conversation. This always helps in maintaining a positive and productive dialogue.

10. **Practice Empathy**
    Try to understand the speaker's emotions and perspectives. Empathy can help in building a deeper connection and trust.
    By incorporating these proven techniques into your daily interactions, you can become a more effective and empathetic listener.

Barriers to effective listening

Effective listening can be hindered by various barriers.

1. **Physical Barriers**
   Noise and Distractions: External sounds, poor acoustics, or visual distractions can impede listening
   Solution: Find a quiet place and minimize distractions.
2. **Emotional Barriers**
   Stress and Anxiety: High stress or emotional turmoil can make it difficult to focus.
   Solution: Practice stress management techniques and take deep breaths to calm your mind.
3. **Psychological Barriers**
   Preconceived Notions: Judging or assuming what the speaker will say can block effective listening.
   Solution: Keep an open mind and listen without forming immediate judgments.
4. **Environmental Barriers**
   Poor Environment: Inadequate lighting, uncomfortable seating, or extreme temperatures can distract you.
   Solution: Ensure the environment is conducive to listening by adjusting lighting, seating, and temperature.
5. **Cultural Barriers**
   Cultural Differences: Different communication styles and cultural norms can lead to misunderstandings.

Solution: Educate yourself about diverse cultures and be respectful of diverse communication styles.

6. **Information Overload**

    Too Much Information: Receiving too much information at once can be overwhelming.

    Solution: Break down information into manageable chunks and take notes if necessary.

7. **Lack of Interest**

    Disinterest in the Topic: If the topic is not engaging, it can be hard to listen attentively.

    Solution: Find aspects of the topic that interest you or relate it to something you care about.

8. **Personal Biases**

    Biases and Stereotypes: Personal biases can cloud your judgment and affect how you listen.

    Solution: Be aware of your biases and strive to listen objectively.

9. **Technological Barriers**

    Poor Technology: Issues with technology, such as bad connections during virtual meetings, can hinder listening.

    Solution: Ensure your technology is functioning properly and have backups ready.

10. **Lack of Feedback**

    No Feedback Mechanism: Without feedback, it is hard to know if you are listening effectively.

    Solution: Ask for feedback from others to improve your listening skills.

By recognizing and addressing these barriers, you can enhance your listening skills and improve your overall communication.

Feedback – Giving and receiving

Feedback is a crucial part of professional growth and organizational development. Here is a detailed explanation of the process:

1. **Purpose of Feedback:** Feedback in a corporate environment is intended to provide employees with an understanding of what they are doing well, what needs improvement, and what steps can be taken to improve performance. It is a tool for continued learning and for boosting employee engagement and job satisfaction.
2. **Types of Feedback:** There are two main types of feedback: **Positive** and **Constructive**.
   (I would like to avoid the term **Negative feedback**)
   Positive feedback acknowledges a job well done and reinforces those actions. Constructive feedback, on the other hand, is future-focused and provides suggestions for improvement.
3. **Giving Feedback:** When giving feedback, it is important to be:
   Specific: Avoid vagueness and be clear about which behavior or outcome you are discussing.
   Timely: Give feedback as close to the event as possible.
   Balanced: Provide both positive reinforcement and constructive criticism.
   Respectful: Feedback should be given in a respectful and honest manner, focusing on the behavior and not the person.
4. **Receiving Feedback:** When receiving feedback, one should:
   Listen Actively: Understand the perspective of the person giving feedback.
   Ask Questions: If something is not clear, ask for clarification.
   Be Open and Receptive: Even if the feedback is tough, it is important to take it in a constructive manner.
   Take Action: Implement the feedback received to improve performance.

5. **Feedback Sessions:** Feedback should be a regular part of the corporate culture. Regular feedback sessions (like one-on-ones and performance reviews) should be held where feedback is shared in a formal, structured environment.

   Remember, the goal of feedback is to improve performance and achieve desired outcomes. It is a two-way street that involves both giving and receiving. It is all about learning, growing, and creating a better work environment.

Positive and constructive feedback

Let us look at a few examples first.

Positive Feedback: "Hi Alex, I wanted to congratulate you on your presentation in yesterday's team meeting. Your thorough research on our competitors was evident and the way you articulated our company's strengths was very persuasive. The visuals you used made the information easy to digest. Keep up the splendid work!"

Constructive Feedback: "Hello Sam, I appreciate your wonderful efforts on the recent project. You have shown great initiative in taking on extra tasks. However, I noticed that there were a few errors in the report, which might be due to the workload. Let us work on improving the accuracy of the data. Perhaps we can discuss strategies for managing workload or using some tools for double-checking the data. I am confident that you can improve in this area."

In both examples, the feedback is specific, timely, and respectful. It focuses on the behavior, not the person, and provides clear direction on what was done well or what needs improvement. Remember, the goal of feedback is to encourage positive behaviors and correct any issues, helping individuals to grow professionally.

Constructive feedback and how to manage it gracefully

Constructive feedback, often referred to as constructive feedback, is information about an individual's performance that aims to improve or correct their actions. It is not meant to criticize or discourage, but to help the individual grow and improve their skills and performance. Here is how to handle it gracefully:

1. **Be Specific and Clear:** Clearly state the issue that needs improvement. Avoid generalizations and be specific about what behavior or action was not up to the mark.
2. **Focus on the Behavior, Not the Person:** Make sure to focus on the actions or behavior, not the individual. This helps to prevent the person from feeling personally attacked.
3. **Use a Positive Tone:** The tone of your feedback can significantly impact how It is received. Try to maintain a positive and respectful tone, even when discussing areas for improvement.
4. **Provide Suggestions for Improvement:** Do not just point out the problem, offer solutions. Providing suggestions or guidance on how to improve can be extremely helpful.
5. **Be Timely:** Provide feedback as soon as possible after the event. This ensures the situation is fresh in everyone's mind, making the feedback more relevant.
6. **Encourage Dialogue:** Allow the recipient to respond to your feedback. They may have valuable input or explanations that you were not aware of.

Here is an example of how constructive feedback is given gracefully:

"Hi Joe, I noticed in our last project that the deadlines were missed a couple of times. I understand that the workload was heavy, but meeting deadlines is crucial for the team's success. Let us work together on improving your time management skills. Perhaps we can break down the tasks into smaller parts and set mini-deadlines for each. I believe this could help in managing the workload more effectively."

Remember, the goal of feedback, including negative feedback, is to help the individual improve, not to discourage or demotivate them. It is all about fostering growth and development.

Frequency of feedback

The frequency of feedback can vary depending on the nature of the work, the individual's role, and the organization's culture. However, here are some general guidelines:

1. **Immediate Feedback:** If you notice something worth praising or a behavior that needs correction, immediate feedback can be highly effective. It ensures the situation is fresh in everyone's mind, making the feedback more relevant.
2. **Regular One-on-One Meetings:** These can be weekly, bi-weekly, or monthly, depending on the role and level of the employee. These meetings are a good opportunity to provide feedback on recent work and discuss any issues or challenges.
3. **Performance Reviews:** These are typically conducted annually or semi-annually and are a more formal opportunity to discuss an employee's overall performance, set goals for the future, and discuss any long-term concerns or opportunities for growth.
4. **Project or Task Completion:** It is beneficial to provide feedback at the end of a significant task or project. This allows you to discuss what went well and what could be improved in the future.

Remember, feedback is most effective when it is given regularly, not just at annual reviews. Regular feedback can help employees feel more engaged and motivated, knowing that their work is being noticed and appreciated. It also helps to address any issues or challenges promptly, allowing for quicker resolution and improvement.

360° Feedback

360-degree feedback, also known as multi-rater feedback, is a system in which employees receive confidential, anonymous feedback from the people who work around them. This typically includes the employee's manager, peers, and direct reports. It can also include external stakeholders like customers and suppliers or other interested parties.

Here is a breakdown of the process:

1. **Gathering Feedback:** Questionnaires are distributed to the manager, peers, and direct reports. They are asked to rate the individual on various aspects of their job performance and behavior. The feedback is anonymous to encourage honest and constructive feedback.
2. **Analyzing Feedback:** The feedback is collected and analyzed. It is typically presented in a format that helps the recipient understand the various perceptions of their performance.
3. **Discussing Feedback:** The individual then has a meeting with their manager or a HR representative to discuss the feedback and develop an action plan.
4. **Action Plan:** The individual creates a development plan with specific goals based on the feedback. They may also seek coaching or training to improve in certain areas.

The goal of 360-degree feedback is to provide a well-rounded view of an individual's performance and behavior. It is a powerful tool for personal and professional development, as it helps individuals understand how their effectiveness as an employee, coworker, or staff member is viewed by others. It is important to note that 360-degree feedback should be used constructively to guide performance and development, and not as a sole tool for performance appraisal.

Role of AI (Artificial Intelligence) in communication

AI plays a significant role in enhancing effective communication across various domains.

1. **Automation of Routine Tasks**
   Streamlining Workflows: AI can automate repetitive tasks such as scheduling meetings, sending reminders, and managing emails, freeing up time for more strategic activities.
2. **Personalization**
   Tailored Messaging: AI can analyze data to create personalized communication, ensuring messages are relevant and engaging for the recipient.
3. **Real-Time Assistance**
   Chatbots and Virtual Assistants: AI-driven chatbots provide instant responses and support, simulating human-like conversations and improving customer service.
4. **Data Analysis**
   Insights and Recommendations: AI can analyze vast amounts of data to provide insights and recommendations, helping organizations make informed decisions and improve communication strategies.
5. **Language Translation**
   Breaking Language Barriers: AI-powered translation tools can translate text and speech in real-time, facilitating communication across different languages and cultures.
6. **Crisis Management**
   Proactive Issue Management: AI can monitor social media and other platforms to detect potential issues early, allowing organizations to address them proactively and manage crises effectively.
7. **Enhanced Accessibility**
   Inclusive Communication: AI tools can assist individuals with disabilities by providing features like speech-to-text, text-to-speech, and other accessibility options.

8. **Improved Targeting**
   Audience Segmentation: AI can segment audiences based on behavior and preferences, enabling more targeted and effective communication campaigns.
9. **Content Creation**
   Assisting Creators AI tools can help in drafting content, ensuring consistency in tone and style, and optimizing for search engines, thus enhancing the quality and reach of communication.

   By leveraging these capabilities, AI can significantly enhance the efficiency, effectiveness, and inclusivity of communication in various settings.

AI tools for effective communication

Here are some popular AI-powered communication tools that can enhance various aspects of communication:

1. **Grammarly**
   Purpose: Enhances writing by checking grammar, spelling, punctuation, and style.
   Features: Provides genre-specific writing suggestions, plagiarism detection, and integrates with platforms like Microsoft Office and web browsers[1].
2. **ChatGPT**
   Purpose: Generates human-like text for various applications, including customer service, content creation, and more.
   Features: Uses natural language processing to create conversational dialogue, offers multilingual support, and personalizes responses based on user preferences.
3. **Jasper**
   Purpose: Assists in content generation for marketing, social media, and other writing tasks.

Features: Generates high-quality text, provides templates for different content types, and integrates with various platforms.

4. **Otter.ai**

   Purpose: Transcribes meetings, interviews, and lectures in real-time.

   Features: Provides accurate transcriptions, allows for collaboration, and integrates with tools like Zoom.

5. **Wordtune**

   Purpose: Enhances writing by suggesting alternative phrasings and improving clarity.

   Features: Offers real-time suggestions, integrates with popular writing platforms, and helps refine tone and style.

6. **Beautiful.ai**

   Purpose: Creates visually appealing presentations with ease.

   Features: Uses AI to design slides, offers templates, and ensures consistency in design.

7. **Copy.ai**

   Purpose: Generates marketing copy, social media posts, and other written content.

   Features: Provides templates, generates ideas, and helps streamline content creation.

8. **Synthesia**

   Purpose: Creates AI-generated videos for training, marketing, and communication.

   Features: Allows for customization, supports multiple languages, and integrates with various platforms.

9. **TryEllie**

   Purpose: Enhances email communication by suggesting improvements and automating responses.

   Features: Provides real-time suggestions, automates routine email tasks, and integrates with email platforms.

10. **Hemingway Editor**

    Purpose: Improves writing by highlighting complex sentences and suggesting simpler alternatives.

    Features: Analyzes readability, highlights passive voice, and provides real-time feedback.

    (Source: Internet)

    These tools can significantly enhance your communication efficiency and effectiveness.

For your information

Office etiquettes

Dressing:
Dressing is the most essential thing in any office. Dressing creates an impression and confidence.

Smiling:
Keeping a smiling face at office and being approachable.

Time discipline:
Keep up one's time and respect and value other's time.

Mannerisms:
Develop some good mannerisms and avoid bad mannerisms at office.

Use of mobile phone:
Keeping the mobile phone either vibrate or silent at office is encouraged. To attend any personal call, it is a good practice to move away from workplace and not to disturb other employees.

Social media use:
As far as possible using social media at office should be avoided. At the least using company assets should be avoided.

Meetings:
Be on time, attentive, and respond during meeting. Take notes.

Lunch time:
Socialize during lunch time but maintain the timing.

CHAPTER 3

INTERPERSONAL SKILL

*I*nterpersonal skills are the abilities we use to interact and communicate effectively with others. These skills are crucial in both personal and professional settings as they help build and maintain relationships, facilitate teamwork, and enhance communication.

Examples of Interpersonal Skills

Some common interpersonal skills include:

- **Communication**: Clearly conveying information and ideas.
- **Active Listening**: Fully concentrating, understanding, and responding thoughtfully to others.
- **Empathy**: Understanding and sharing the feelings of others.
- **Conflict Resolution**: Addressing and resolving disagreements in a constructive manner.
- **Teamwork**: Working effectively and harmoniously with others.
- **Leadership**: Guiding and motivating a group towards a common goal.
- **Negotiation**: Reaching mutually beneficial agreements through discussion.
- **Emotional Intelligence**: Recognizing and managing your own emotions and those of others.

Importance of Interpersonal Skills

Interpersonal skills are vital for several reasons:

1. **Building Relationships**: They help in forming and nurturing personal and professional relationships.
2. **Effective Communication**: Good interpersonal skills ensure clear and effective communication, reducing misunderstandings.
3. **Conflict Management**: They enable you to handle conflicts and disagreements constructively.
4. **Team Collaboration**: These skills are essential for working well in teams, fostering a cooperative and productive environment.
5. **Career Advancement**: Strong interpersonal skills can enhance your career prospects by making you a more effective and likable colleague or leader.
6. **Personal Well-being**: They contribute to better mental health and overall well-being by improving your interactions and relationships with others.

How to develop interpersonal skills

Building Genuine Relationships

- **Show Genuine Interest**: Ask people about their interests, listen actively, and remember details about their lives.
- **Smile**: A simple smile can make a significant difference in how others perceive you and can create a positive atmosphere.

Effective Communication

- **Be Clear and Concise**: When communicating, be clear about your message and avoid unnecessary jargon.
- **Use Names**: Remembering and using people's names in conversation shows respect and helps build rapport.

Empathy and Understanding

- **Listen Actively**: Pay full attention when others are speaking and show that you understand by nodding or giving verbal acknowledgments.
- **Put Yourself in Their Shoes**: Try to understand situations from others' perspectives to build empathy.

Positive Attitude

- **Express Appreciation**: Regularly acknowledge and appreciate others' efforts and contributions.
- **Stay Positive**: Focus on positive aspects in conversations and avoid complaining or criticizing.

Handling Criticism and Complaints

- **Stay Calm**: When receiving criticism, stay calm and listen without interrupting.
- **Seek Solutions**: Focus on finding solutions rather than dwelling on the problem.

Influence and Leadership

- **Lead by Example**: Demonstrate the behaviors and attitudes you want to see in others.
- **Encourage and Inspire**: Motivate others by recognizing their strengths and encouraging their efforts.

Daily Practices

- **Morning Reflection**: Spend a few minutes each morning reflecting on how you can apply these principles throughout your day.
- **Set Goals**: Set specific, achievable goals for improving your interpersonal skills, such as complimenting a colleague or actively listening during meetings.

- **Seek Feedback**: Ask for feedback from friends, family, or colleagues on how you can improve your interactions.

Transactional Analysis

Remember the Preface of this book wherein I have mentioned the three qualities of a human being (Tri gunas), and these qualities play a vital role during interpersonal relationships. We meet different types of people in our daily life.

First, let us try to understand the age-old theory called *"Transactional Analysis"*

Transactional Analysis (TA) is a psychoanalytic theory and method of therapy developed by Eric Berne in the 1950s. It focuses on analyzing social interactions, or "transactions," to understand the ego states of the communicators involved. These ego states are categorized into three types:

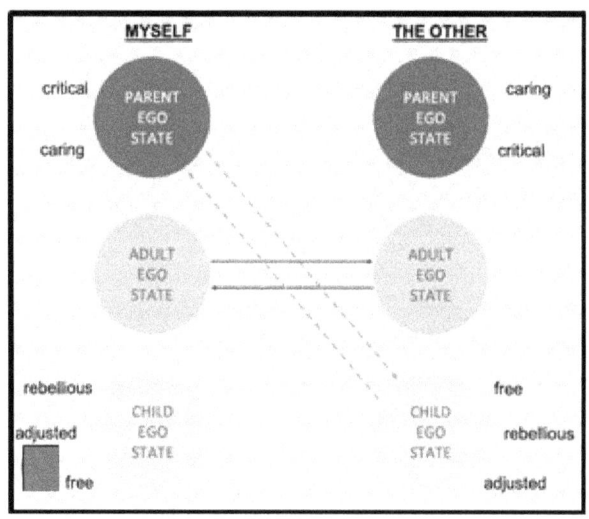

Parent, Adult, and Child.

Key Concepts of Transactional Analysis

Ego States:

Parent: This state contains the attitudes and behaviors incorporated from external sources, primarily parents. It can be nurturing or critical.

Adult: This state is based on direct responses to the here and now. It is rational and objective.

Child: This state is a set of behaviors, thoughts, and feelings replayed from childhood. It can be free and natural or adapted and compliant.

Transactions:

Transactions are the communication exchanges between people. Each transaction involves a stimulus and a response, which can come from any of the three ego states.

Life Scripts:

These are unconscious life plans developed in childhood, influenced by parental messages and early decisions. They guide how individuals live their lives and interact with others.

Games:

These are repetitive, unconscious patterns of behavior that people play out in their interactions. They often result in negative feelings and reinforce life scripts.

Applications of Transactional Analysis

TA is used in various fields, including psychotherapy, counseling, education, and organizational development. It helps individuals understand their own behavior and improve their communication and relationships with others.

TA can be highly beneficial for both *individual and organizational development*. Here is how:

Individual Development

Self-Awareness:

TA helps individuals understand their own behavior and the underlying ego states (Parent, Adult, Child) that drive their actions. This self-awareness can lead to more conscious and intentional behavior.

Improved Communication:

By recognizing and analyzing transactions, individuals can improve their communication skills, making interactions more effective and reducing misunderstandings.

Personal Growth:

TA encourages individuals to identify and challenge negative life scripts and games, promoting healthier and more fulfilling life choices.

Emotional Intelligence:

Understanding the emotional aspects of the Child ego state and the rational aspects of the adult ego state can enhance emotional intelligence, helping individuals manage their emotions better.

Organizational Development

Enhanced Team Dynamics:

TA can improve team interactions by fostering better understanding and communication among team members. This leads to more cohesive and effective teams.

Conflict Resolution:

By identifying crossed transactions and underlying issues, TA can help resolve conflicts more effectively, promoting a healthier work environment.

Leadership Development

Leaders can use TA to understand their own leadership style and its impact on others. This can lead to more adaptive and effective leadership practices.

Organizational Culture:

TA can contribute to building a positive organizational culture by promoting open communication, mutual respect, and understanding.

Change Management

TA provides tools for managing change by helping individuals and teams understand and navigate the emotional and psychological aspects of change.

By applying the principles of TA, both individuals and organizations can achieve greater self-awareness, improved communication, and more effective interactions, leading to overall growth and development.

TA offers several techniques to help individuals understand and improve their interactions. Here are some common techniques used in TA:

1. Ego State Analysis

- **Identify Ego States**: Recognize whether interactions are coming from the Parent, Adult, or Child ego state. This helps in understanding the dynamics of communication and adjusting responses accordingly.

2. Transactional Analysis Proper

- **Analyze Transactions**: Examine the exchanges between individuals to identify complementary, crossed, or ulterior transactions. This helps in understanding and improving communication patterns.

3. Script Analysis

- **Uncover Life Scripts**: Identify and analyze the unconscious life scripts that guide behavior. This involves understanding decisions made in childhood that affect current behavior and working to change unhelpful scripts.

4. Game Analysis

- **Identify Psychological Games**: Recognize and analyze repetitive, manipulative interactions (games) that lead to negative outcomes. Understanding these games helps in breaking unhealthy patterns.

5. Stroke Economy

- **Manage Positive and Negative Strokes**: Strokes are units of recognition. This technique involves understanding how individuals give and receive positive and negative strokes and working towards a healthier balance.

6. Contracting

- **Set Clear Agreements**: Establish clear, mutual agreements (contracts) between individuals or within therapy sessions to ensure goals and expectations are understood and agreed upon.

Practical Application

- **Self-Reflection**: Regularly reflect on your interactions to identify which ego states you and others are operating from.
- **Mindful Communication**: Practice being aware of your transactions and aim for complementary transactions to improve communication.

- **Challenge Scripts**: Work on identifying and challenging unhelpful life scripts that may be influencing your behavior.

By using these techniques, you can gain deeper insights into your interactions and work towards more effective and fulfilling communication.

Games People play (Eric Berne)

In TA, "games" refer to repetitive, unconscious patterns of behavior that people engage in during social interactions. These games often have hidden motives and predictable outcomes, which can be detrimental to relationships. Here are some common games identified by Eric Berne in his book "Games People Play":

1. "Yes, But…"

- **Description**: One person presents a problem and asks for advice. However, they counter every suggestion with "Yes, but…" to show why it will not work.
- **Outcome**: The advice-giver feels frustrated, and the problem remains unsolved.

2. "Why Do not You – Yes But"

- **Description**: Similar to "Yes, but…," this game involves a group where one person presents a problem, and others offer solutions. The problem-presenter dismisses each suggestion with "Yes, but…"
- **Outcome**: The group feels frustrated, and the problem-presenter gains attention without resolving the issue.

3. "If It Weren't for You"

- **Description**: One person blames their lack of success or happiness on another person or external circumstances.
- **Outcome**: The blamer avoids taking responsibility for their own actions and remains stuck.

4. "Ain't It Awful"

- **Description**: Participants complain about their problems or the state of the world, reinforcing each other's negative views.
- **Outcome**: The participants bond over shared negativity but do not take steps to improve their situations.

5. "See What You Made Me Do"

- **Description**: One person blames another for their own mistakes or failures.
- **Outcome**: The blamer avoids responsibility, and the blamed person feels guilty or defensive.

6. "Blemish"

- **Description**: One person finds faults in others to feel superior.
- **Outcome**: The faultfinder feels a temporary boost in self-esteem, while others feel criticized and demoralized.

7. "Now I've Got You, You Son of a B**"**

- **Description**: One person waits for another to make a mistake and then aggressively confronts them.
- **Outcome**: The aggressor feels justified in their anger, while the other person feels attacked and defensive.

8. "I'm Only Trying to Help"

- **Description**: One person offers unsolicited help or advice, often in a way that makes the recipient feel incompetent.
- **Outcome**: The helper feels superior, while the recipient feels undermined.

Practical Steps to Avoid Games

- **Awareness**: Recognize when you or others are engaging in these games.

- **Adult Ego State**: Respond from the Adult ego state, focusing on rational and constructive communication.
- **Set Boundaries**: Politely set boundaries if someone tries to engage you in a game.
- **Seek Solutions**: Focus on finding practical solutions rather than getting caught up in the game dynamics.

Understanding these games can help you avoid unproductive interactions and foster healthier, more authentic relationships.

Life Scripts

Life scripts are a central concept in TA, developed by Eric Berne. They refer to unconscious life plans formed in childhood, which influence our behavior, thoughts, and interactions throughout our lives. Here is a deeper look into life scripts:

Formation of Life Scripts

- **Early Childhood**: Life scripts are typically formed during early childhood through interactions with primary caregivers and significant others. These scripts are influenced by the messages we receive about ourselves and the world around us.
- **Unconscious Patterns**: These scripts operate unconsciously, shaping our expectations, behaviors, and decisions without us being fully aware of their influence.

Components of Life Scripts

- **Physiological Reactions**: Scripts can be based on physiological survival reactions to stress and relational disruptions.
- **Implicit Conclusions**: They include implicit experiential conclusions drawn from repeated experiences and interactions.

- **Explicit Decisions**: Scripts also involve explicit decisions made in response to noteworthy events or messages received during development.

Impact of Life Scripts

- **Behavior and Choices**: Life scripts influence our behavior, choices, and how we perceive and respond to situations. For example, a script formed from constant criticism might lead to a belief that "I am not enough," affecting self-esteem and relationships.
- **Relational Patterns**: They shape our relational patterns, determining how we interact with others and what we expect from relationships.

Identifying and Changing Life Scripts

- **Self-Awareness**: Recognizing and understanding your life script is the first step towards change. This involves introspection and identifying recurring patterns in your thoughts and behaviors.
- **Therapeutic Work**: Collaborating with a therapist trained in TA can help uncover and reframe these scripts, allowing for healthier and more adaptive behaviors.
- **Rewriting Scripts**: By challenging and changing the underlying beliefs and decisions that form your script, you can create a new, more positive narrative for your life.

Practical Steps

- **Reflect on Childhood Messages**: Consider the messages you received from caregivers and significant others during your childhood.
- **Identify Patterns**: Look for recurring themes in your behavior and relationships that might be influenced by your script.
- **Challenge Negative Beliefs**: Actively challenge and reframe negative beliefs and decisions that are part of your script.

- **Seek Support**: Consider collaborating with a therapist to explore and change your life script.

Understanding and changing life scripts can lead to greater self-awareness, improved relationships, and a more fulfilling life.

How to identify your own script?

Identifying your own life script involves introspection and understanding the unconscious patterns that guide your behavior and interactions. Here are some steps and techniques to help you uncover your life script:

1. **Reflect on Childhood Messages**

- **Parental Messages**: Consider the explicit and implicit messages you received from your parents or caregivers. These could be direct statements or behaviors that conveyed certain expectations or beliefs.
- **Significant Events**: Reflect on noteworthy events from your childhood and how they might have shaped your beliefs and decisions.

2. **Identify Recurring Patterns**

- **Behavioral Patterns**: Look for recurring behaviors or situations in your life. For example, do you often find yourself in similar conflicts or relationships?
- **Emotional Responses**: Notice your emotional responses to different situations. Are there patterns in how you feel and react?

3. **Analyze Your Beliefs**

- **Core Beliefs**: Identify core beliefs about yourself, others, and the world. These beliefs often stem from your life script.

- **Life Positions**: Consider which of the four life positions you most identify with:
  - "I'm OK, You're OK"
  - "I'm OK, You're not OK"
  - "I'm not OK, You're OK"
  - "I'm not OK, You're not OK"

4. **Use Script Analysis Techniques**

- **Script Questions**: Ask yourself questions to uncover your script, such as:
  - What do I believe about myself?
  - What do I believe about others?
  - What do I believe about the world?
- **Dreams and Fantasies**: Pay attention to your dreams and fantasies, as they can reveal underlying script beliefs.

5. **Seek Professional Help**

- **Therapy**: Collaborating with a therapist trained in TA can provide deeper insights and guidance in identifying and changing your life script.
- **Workshops and Courses**: Consider attending workshops or courses on TA to gain a better understanding of life scripts and how to analyze them.

Practical Steps

- **Journaling**: Keep a journal to document your thoughts, feelings, and recurring patterns. This can help you identify and reflect on your life script.
- **Mindfulness**: Practice mindfulness to become more aware of your thoughts and behaviors in the present moment.

- **Feedback**: Seek feedback from trusted friends or family members about patterns they notice in your behavior.

By taking these steps, you can gain greater self-awareness and begin to understand the unconscious patterns that influence your life. This awareness is the first step towards making positive changes and rewriting your life script.

Some common life scripts

Life scripts are unconscious life plans formed in childhood that influence our behavior and interactions throughout life. Here are some common life scripts and their potential effects:

1. "I'm Not OK, You're OK"

- **Description**: This script involves a belief that others are competent and worthy, but the individual feels inadequate or unworthy.
- **Effects**: This can lead to low self-esteem, dependency on others for validation, and difficulty asserting oneself.

2. "I'm Not OK, You're Not OK"

- **Description**: This script reflects a belief that both the individual and others are inadequate or unworthy.
- **Effects**: It can result in feelings of hopelessness, depression, and difficulty forming healthy relationships.

3. "I'm OK, You're Not OK"

- **Description**: In this script, the individual feels competent and worthy, but views others as inadequate or unworthy.
- **Effects**: This can lead to arrogance, difficulty in teamwork, and strained relationships due to a lack of empathy.

4. "I'm OK, You're OK"

- **Description**: This is the healthiest script, where the individual believes both they and others are competent and worthy.
- **Effects**: It fosters positive self-esteem, healthy relationships, and effective communication.

5. "If It Weren't for You"

- **Description**: This script involves blaming others for one's own lack of success or happiness.
- **Effects**: It can lead to a lack of personal responsibility, resentment, and stagnant personal growth.

6. "After"

- **Description**: This script involves a belief that happiness or success will come only after a certain condition is met (e.g., "I'll be happy after I get a promotion").
- **Effects**: It can result in perpetual dissatisfaction and a tendency to postpone happiness.

7. "Never"

- **Description**: This script involves a belief that certain positive outcomes will never happen (e.g., "I'll never be successful").
- **Effects**: It can lead to self-sabotage, low motivation, and a defeatist attitude.

8. "Always"

- **Description**: This script involves a belief that certain negative outcomes will always happen (e.g., "I always fail at relationships").
- **Effects**: It can result in a self-fulfilling prophecy, where the individual unconsciously ensures the negative outcome.

Practical Steps to Change Life Scripts

- **Self-Awareness**: Reflect on your beliefs and behaviors to identify your life script.
- **Challenge Negative Beliefs**: Actively challenge and reframe negative beliefs that are part of your script.
- **Seek Support**: Consider collaborating with a therapist to explore and change your life script.
- **Set Positive Goals**: Focus on setting and achieving positive, realistic goals to create a new, healthier script.

Understanding and changing your life script can lead to greater self-awareness, improved relationships, and a more fulfilling life.

How to rewrite your negative life script?

Rewriting a negative life script involves several steps aimed at increasing self-awareness, challenging old beliefs, and adopting new, healthier patterns. Here is a guide to help you through the process:

1. Self-Awareness and Reflection

- **Identify Your Script**: Reflect on recurring patterns in your behavior and relationships. Consider the messages you received in childhood and how they might have shaped your beliefs.
- **Journal**: Keep a journal to document your thoughts, feelings, and behaviors. This can help you identify patterns and triggers.

2. Understand the Components of Your Script

- **Injunctions and Drivers**: Identify the prohibitions (injunctions) and behavioral signposts (drivers) that influence your script. For example, an injunction might be "Do not succeed," while a driver could be "Be perfect".

- **Life Positions**: Determine which life position you most identify with (e.g., "I'm not OK, You're OK") and how it affects your interactions.

3. Challenge Negative Beliefs

- **Question Your Beliefs**: Actively challenge the negative beliefs that are part of your script. Ask yourself if these beliefs are truly valid or if they are based on outdated information.
- **Reframe**: Reframe negative beliefs into positive ones. For example, change "I always fail" to "I am capable of learning and improving."

4. Make Conscious Redecision

- **Redecision Therapy**: Work with a therapist trained in TA to make a conscious Redecision about your life script. This involves revisiting past decisions made in childhood and choosing new, healthier ones.
- **Affirmations**: Use positive affirmations to reinforce new beliefs. For example, "I am worthy of success and happiness."

5. Practice New Behaviors

- **Set Goals**: Set specific, achievable goals that align with your new script. This helps in reinforcing new patterns of behavior.
- **Mindfulness**: Practice mindfulness to stay aware of your thoughts and behaviors in the present moment. This can help you catch and change old patterns as they arise.

6. Seek Support

- **Therapy**: Consider collaborating with a therapist to explore and change your life script. Therapy can provide a safe space to understand and reframe your beliefs.
- **Support Groups**: Join support groups or workshops focused on personal growth and TA. Sharing experiences with others can provide additional insights and encouragement.

7. **Practical Exercises**
- **Visualization**: Visualize yourself living according to your new script. Imagine how you would think, feel, and behave differently.
- **Role-Playing**: Practice new behaviors through role-playing exercises. This can help you become more comfortable with your new script in real-life situations.

By following these steps, you can begin to rewrite your negative life script and create a more positive and fulfilling narrative for your life.

Positive affirmations

Positive affirmations are short, powerful statements that can help you challenge and overcome negative thoughts. Here are some common examples of positive affirmations:

General Affirmations

- I am worthy of love and respect.
- I am capable of achieving my goals.
- I am confident and self-assured.
- I am in control of my thoughts and emotions.
- I am deserving of happiness and success.

Affirmations for Self-Esteem

- I believe in myself and my abilities.
- I am proud of who I am.
- I accept myself unconditionally.
- I am enough just as I am.
- I am growing and improving every day.

Affirmations for Stress and Anxiety

- I am calm and at peace.
- I trust in the process of life.

- I release all tension and stress.
- I am safe and secure.
- I handle challenges with grace and ease.

Affirmations for Health and Well-Being

- I am healthy, strong, and vibrant.
- I take care of my body and mind.
- I am grateful for my health.
- I nourish my body with healthy choices.
- I am full of energy and vitality.

Affirmations for Relationships

- I attract positive and loving relationships.
- I communicate openly and honestly.
- I am surrounded by supportive and caring people.
- I give and receive love freely.
- I am a good friend and partner.

Affirmations for Success and Abundance

- I am successful in everything I do.
- I attract abundance into my life.
- I am open to new opportunities.
- I am confident in my ability to succeed.
- I am grateful for the abundance I have.

How to Use Affirmations

- **Daily Practice**: Repeat your affirmations daily, either in the morning or before bed.
- **Write Them Down**: Write your affirmations in a journal or on sticky notes placed around your home.
- **Visualize**: As you say your affirmations, visualize them coming true.

- **Believe**: Honestly believe in the words you are saying and feel the positive emotions associated with them.

Using positive affirmations regularly can help rewire your brain, reduce negative self-talk, and promote a more positive mindset.

Positive work-life-related affirmations

Career-related affirmations can help boost your confidence, motivation, and overall mindset towards your professional goals. Here are some examples:

General Career Affirmations

I am creating my dream career.
- I am achieving my career goals.
- I am open to new and exciting opportunities.
- I am confident in my abilities and skills.
- I am successful in everything I do.

Affirmations for Job Search

- I am completely energized to find my perfect job.
- I am open to new and exciting opportunities to find my ideal work.
- I see myself in my dream job.
- I am confident and calm in interviews.
- Every interview takes me closer to my dream job.

Affirmations for Career Growth

- I am attracting amazing career opportunities.
- I am a valuable member of my team.
- I am confident to speak up and share my ideas and talent.
- I am always learning and growing in my career.
- I deserve to be happy and successful in my career.

Affirmations for Workplace Confidence

- I am a valued person at my workplace and my voice is always heard respectfully.
- I am grateful for all that I learn at my job.
- I handle challenges with grace and ease.
- I am resourceful and take initiative.
- I am full of great ideas and contribute positively to my team.

Affirmations for Work-Life Balance

- I am able to balance my career with my family life so that both are in harmony.
- I am creating a fulfilling and meaningful career.
- I give myself time to understand what works for me.
- I am brave enough to make choices that take me closer to my ideal career.
- I am grateful for the moments when I realize what is meant for me.

Using these affirmations regularly can help you maintain a positive mindset and stay motivated in your career journey.

Johari Windows

How can we establish and enhance our interpersonal relationships?

Johari Windows:

The American Psychologists, Joseph Luft and Harry Ingham first introduced the concept IN 1955 during a research in Los Angeles, California.

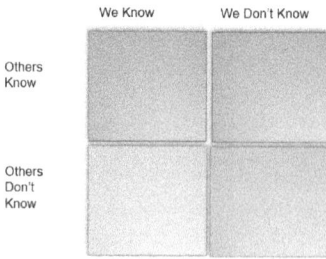

The **Johari Window** is a psychological model developed by Joseph Luft and Harry Ingham in 1955. It helps individuals understand their interpersonal communication and relationships. Here is how it works:

Open Area (Arena): This quadrant represents aspects of ourselves that both we and others can see. It includes our attitudes, behavior, motivation, values, and lifestyle. We move freely within this area, like "open books."

Hidden Area (Facade): Adjectives selected by the subject but not by peers go here. These are things peers are unaware of or that are untrue but claimed by the subject.

Blind Spot: Adjectives not selected by the subject but chosen by peers go here. These represent what others perceive but the subject does not.

Unknown Area: Adjectives that neither the subject nor peers selected go here. They represent the subject's behaviors or motives that no one recognizes due to ignorance or lack of applicability.

The Johari Window aims to improve self-awareness, communication, and trust in relationships. It is fascinating how it can be used for personal development and better understanding within groups!

> **For your information**
>
> **Pure perseverance**
>
> **Putting pure perseverance into action**
>
> The ability to endure setbacks, push through challenges, and maintain focus on the big goal ultimately differentiates successful people from unsuccessful ones. Here are a few pointers to keep in mind:
>
> **1. Embrace failure as part of the journey:**
>
> Failure is not the end; it is a step on the path to success. Learn from it, adapt, and keep moving forward.
>
> **2. Develop a resilient mindset:**
>
> Expect challenges and be prepared to face them head-on. Cultivate a mindset that views obstacles as opportunities to grow and improve.
>
> **3. Stay passionate:**
>
> Find what you are passionate about and let that passion fuel your perseverance.
>
> When you are doing something, you love, the journey becomes more bearable, and the rewards are that much sweeter.
>
> **4. Surround yourself with support:**
>
> Entrepreneurship can be a lonely journey. Surround yourself with mentors, peers, and support system that can help you stay motivated and resilient.
>
> **5. Focus on the long-term vision:**
>
> Keep your eyes on the big picture. The road may be rough, but staying focused on your ultimate goal will help you navigate the ups and downs.
>
> **Take the above 'Steve jobs' advice to heart. Never lose sight of your vision. It is not an easy journey, but it can lead to incredible rewards if you are willing to stay the course.**

CHAPTER 4

CONFLICT MANAGEMENT

*C*onflict is difficult to define because it occurs in many different settings. The essence of conflict is disagreement, contradiction, or incompatibility.

Conflict is a "process that begins when one party perceives that another party has negatively affected something that the first party cares about."

Five traits of personality

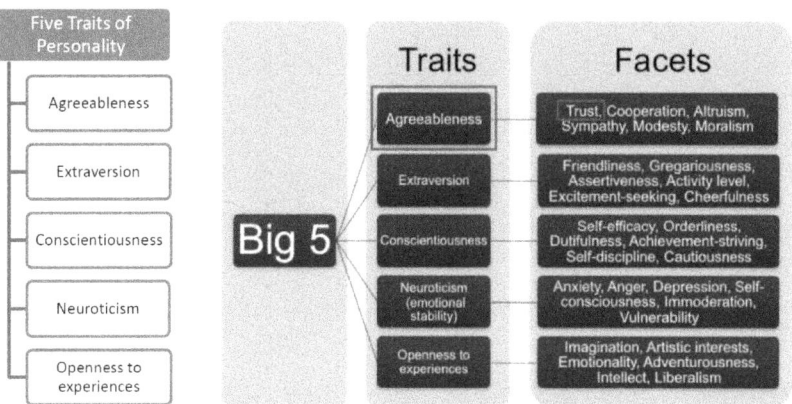

Agreeableness:

It applies to one person's willingness to have a good relationship with others. The trait is characterized by confidence, collaboration, compassion, and empathy. Those who are highly agreeable value harmony more than just having a say or a way. They are cooperative and trust other people. People who concentrate more on their own needs than on acceptability needs of those who are weak.

Extroversion:

It represents the degree of comfort a person has with relationships. Extroverts are sociable, talkative, assertive, and open to new relations. Introverts are less sociable, less talkative, less assertive, and more reticent about beginning new relationships.

Conscientiousness:

This trait refers to the number of targets a person is focusing on. At one point, a person of high conscience focuses on very few goals. Such individuals are believed to appear to be well-organized, cautious, responsible, self-disciplined, and centered. A person with low conscientiousness tends to be less concentrated, and at one time may seek to accomplish several goals.

Neuroticism or Emotional stability:

This personality trait centers on the ability of an individual to cope with stress. Emotionally stable individuals tend to be calm, enthusiastic, and secure. The emotionally unstable person, on the contrary, appears to be anxious and deprived with insecurities.

Openness to Experiences:

Creativity and innovation intrigue especially transparent humans. They're willing to listen to innovative ideas in reaction to new knowledge and change their own ideas, beliefs, and attitudes. On the other hand, those with low levels of transparency tend to be less inclined towards innovative ideas and less likely to change their minds, respectively. These do seem to be less adventurous and have fewer focused interests.

The "Big Five" framework is considered valuable for managers as the study of these personality dimensions gives them the power to predict the behavior of individuals in certain situations.

However, there are many demographic, cultural, and environmental factors that influence the Big Five traits. These factors should be taken into consideration while making decisions based on The Big Five Personality dimensions.

Some more traits which are useful to understand a person

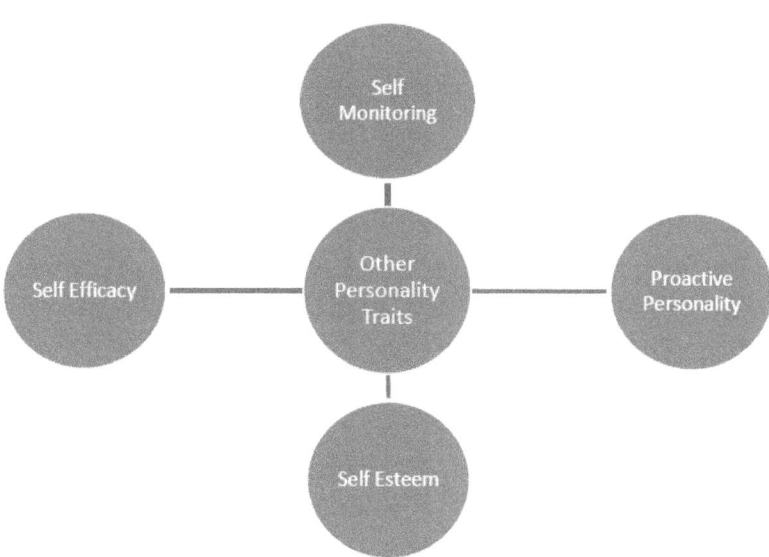

Self-Monitoring:

It refers to the degree to which a person is capable in social contexts of controlling his or her behavior and appearance. "People who are social monitors are social chameleons who understand what the situation demands and act accordingly, while low social monitors tend to act the way they feel.

Proactive personality:

This refers to the desire of a person to correct what is wrong, to change things, and to use initiative to overcome problems. Rather than waiting to be told what to do, positive people are taking steps to bring about real change through the barriers that they face along the way. Proactive individuals tend to be more effective in both work searches and career paths.

Self-esteem:

It is the degree to which a person has positive feelings about himself or herself overall. People with high self-esteem take a positive view of themselves are confident and respect themselves. Those with low self-esteem, by comparison, experience elevated levels of self-doubt and challenge their self-worth. High self-esteem is linked to higher levels of work satisfaction and higher levels of performance on the job.

Self-efficacy:

It is a belief that one can perform a specific task successfully. Evidence indicates the assumption that anything we can do is a strong indicator of how we can actually do it. Self-efficacy varies from other personality characteristics since it is unique to the task. You may have a high degree of self-efficacy in being academically effective but low self-efficacy with respect to your ability to repair your car.

Perception

Having understood about personality traits, not one need to understand the perception.

What is perception?

"Perception is an active psychological process by which individuals organize and interpret their sensory impressions in order to give meaning to their environment."

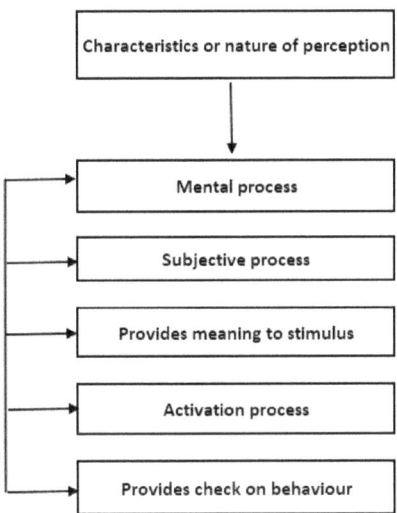

Process of perception

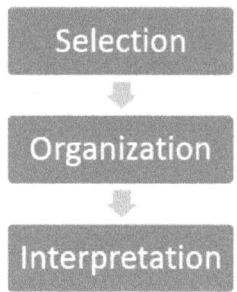

Selection

The world around us was packed with endless stimuli that we should follow, but our brains did not have the energy to pay attention to everything. And the first decision stage is to decide what we want. When we pick one object in our universe, whether it is a smell, a feeling, a sound, or something else, it is the stimulus that is being attended to.

Selecting is the first aspect of the perception process, where we concentrate our attention on the sensory feedback that is coming in. In selection, we choose stimuli which attract our attention. We focus on those that distinguish our senses (seeing, sound, smell, taste, and touch).

Organization

When we have chosen to take care of stimuli in the world, the option sets in our brain a sequence of reactions. This neural process starts when our sensory receptors (touch, taste, smell, sight, and hearing) are triggered.

Organizing is the second part of the process of perception in which we sort and categorize information we perceive based on cognitive patterns that are innate and learned. Through using proximity, similarity, and difference (Stanley, mo.), we sort items into patterns in three ways.

Interpretation

Having attended to a stimulus and having obtained and arranged the information from our minds, we perceive it in a way that makes sense using our current knowledge.

The word Interpretation means we are taking the information we have sensed and organized and turning it into something we can classify. We can better understand and react to the world around us by putting different stimuli into the categories. Other experiences include sensing, arranging, and processing details about people and what they are doing and doing.

The feeling is a primary function of perception because it relates to external information. First of all, the perceiver will pick what will be experienced in the perceptual phase. Instead, as listeners recognize the type of sound and equate it with other sounds heard in the past, the organization is retained.

Interpretation and categorization are generally the most subjective areas of perception since they involve decisions as to whether listeners like what they hear and want to continue listening. We conduct instant assessments that cause unconscious conclusions of positive and negative reactions to others outside of our consciousness.

Selection, organization, and interpretation of perceptions can differ from one person to another. Based on these, the perceptual performance of the perceiver implies varying beliefs, attitudes, behaviors, etc. Therefore, when people react differently in a situation, by examining their perceptual process, they can explain part of their behavior, and how their perceptions lead to their responses.

"Mind" through the lens of Hinduism

I will be sharing with you here how the mind functions, through the lens of Hindu philosophy. We will look at the six means of knowledge, known as *pramanas,* and how they can help you understand your Self in any given situation.

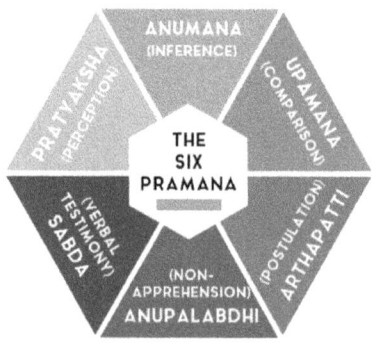

The Six Pramana

The following six pramana are said to be the only reliable and accurate means of knowledge available to us.

1. Pratyaksha (Perception)

Split into two types, internal and external, *pratyaksha* refers to acquiring knowledge based on direct experience.

It is important that knowledge acquired through pratyaksha is from your own perception, not having accepted someone else's.

External pratyaksha involves using the five senses, whereas internal pratyaksha relies on intuition and cognition of remembered feelings such as pain, love, danger, or anger.

2. **Anumana (Inference)**

   Anumana involves applying reason and prior knowledge to one or more observations in order to reach a new conclusion. A common example of Anumana is inferring fire after observing smoke.

3. **Upamana (Comparison and Analogy)**

   Upamana is a process by which conclusions are drawn from either observing similarities or understanding analogies of a similar word, object, or situation.

   Similes and metaphors can help us to acquire knowledge through *upamana*.

4. **Arthapatti (Postulation)**

   Arthapatti is a presumption or supposition of a fact derived from circumstance or an already established fact. In this sense, arthapatti can be considered the junction between common sense and conjecture.

5. **Anupalabdhi (Non-apprehension)**

   Anupalabdhi is using existing knowledge of a negative as cognitive proof to derive further knowledge. By non-perception, it is possible to prove the non-existence of something.

6. **Sabda (Verbal Testimony)**

   Sabda is the relying on the spoken and written word of past or present experts. This is considered an important and authentic means of knowledge since we each have only limited time and energy available to learn truths directly.

   Whilst each pramana operates as a clear and distinct means of knowing, they also each have a rather limited scope. As such, it is important not only to observe how they interact with one another but to try and become conscious of which pramana to resort to and when.

   Understanding how we may interpret knowledge based on the theory of pramana helps us to understand how we react and respond in various situations.

Perception errors

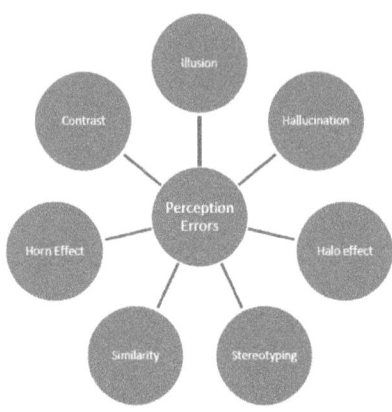

Illusion

False thinking is delusion. The individual is going to botch an improvement here and see it wrongly. In darkness, for example, a rope is mixed up like a snake, or the other way around. An unknown individual's voice is mixed up like the voice of a friend. A person who remains a way off and who may not be seen as a recognized entity.

Hallucination

Wherever the individual sees any stimuli, it cannot be present in any situation. This mystery is called Hallucination. The person may see an object, a person, and so on, or he may hear some voice out, but there are actually no articles and sounds.

Halo effect

Individuals are evaluated on the basis of apparent positive quality, aspect, or function. A corona impact works when we draw a general impression about a person based. For example, on a solitary trademark, knowledge, friendliness, or appearance. At the end of the day, that is the tendency to score a man consistently high or low in different characteristics on the off chance that he is exceedingly high or low in one specific attribute: if a worker does not have several unfortunate shortcomings, his boss will award him a high rating in any other region of work.

Stereotyping

Individuals will typically fall into a general class based on physical or social characteristics in either situation or then they are assessed. We use the simple route called stereotyping at the point where we judge others based on our understanding of the gathering that the individual has a place to.

Similarity

Frequently, individuals will in general search out and rate all the more emphatically the individuals who are like themselves. This propensity to affirm comparability may make evaluators give better appraisals to representatives who show similar interests, work techniques, perspectives, or models.

Horn Effect

At the point where the person is judged solely on the basis of an obvious negative attribute or highlight. These findings are lower than an acceptable rate in a general ranking. He cannot spruce up in the office, which is why he could possibly grind away too.

Contrast

The propensity to rate an individual's comparative with others instead of to the individual execution the individual is doing. Or maybe will assess a representative by contrasting that worker's exhibition and different workers.

Types of Conflict

CONFLICT refers to any situation in which there are incompatible Goals, Cognitions, or Emotions within or between individuals or groups that lead to opposition or antagonistic interaction.

The definition recognizes three basic types of conflict:

Goal conflict is a situation in which desired end states or preferred outcomes appear to be incompatible.

Cognitive Conflict is a situation in which ideas or thoughts are inconsistent.

Affective Conflict is a situation in which feelings or emotions are incompatible; that is, people literally become angry with one another. Conflict is quite common in organizational settings. This is not necessarily a negative feature; the resolution of conflict often leads to constructive problem solving.

Conflict exists in many forms other than the form that can result from competition, and managers should understand the different ways of conflict resolution.

Let us examine conflict from a variety of viewpoints.

- First considering the positive and negative aspects of conflict.
- Next, discussing the levels of conflict that can occur within organizations.
- Finally, identifying some of the basic strategies for managing conflict.

Levels of conflict

There are basically five levels of conflicts as follows:

    I. Intrapersonal (within an individual),
    II. Interpersonal (between individuals),
    III. Intragroup (within a group),

IV. Intergroup (between groups), and
V. Intraorganizational (within organizations).

Intrapersonal Conflict

Intrapersonal Conflict, which occurs within an individual, often involves some form of goal conflict or cognitive conflict. Goal conflict exists for individuals when their behavior will result in outcomes that are mutually exclusive or have compatible elements (both positive and negative outcomes).

Approach-approach conflict is a situation in which a person has a choice between two or more alternatives with positive outcomes; for example, a person can choose between two jobs that appear to be equally attractive.

Avoidance – avoidance conflict is a situation in which a person must choose between two or more alternatives, and they all have negative outcomes. For example, employees may be threatened with punishment in the form of demotion unless they do something they dislike spend much time traveling on their job, for example.

Approach-avoidance conflict is a situation in which a person must decide whether to do something that has both positive and negative outcomes, for example, being offered a decent job in a bad location.

Interpersonal Conflict

Interpersonal conflict involves two or more individuals rather than one individual. Two managers competing for the same promotion, and two executives maneuvering for a larger share of corporate capital examples of conflict between individuals are legion and quite familiar.

Probable reasons

Personality differences: Some people have difficulty having a good relationship with each other. This is purely a psychological problem, and it has nothing to do with their job requirements or formal interactions.

Perceptions: Varied backgrounds, experiences, education, and training result in individuals developing different perceptions of similar realities; the result being an increase in the likelihood of interpersonal conflict.

Clashes of values and interests: Conflict that so commonly develops between engineering and manufacturing personnel shows how differences in values might underlie conflict. Members of the engineering department might place a premium on quality, sophisticated design, and durability while members of the manufacturing department might value simplicity and low manufacturing costs.

Power and status differences: "Organizations are political structures." They operate by distributing authority and setting a stage for the exercise of power. Similarly, status inconsistencies lead to conflict.

Scarce resource: Interpersonal conflict is almost automatic anytime there is scarcity. Conflicts over scarce resources are exceedingly common in organizations. Where the scarcity is absolute (the resource level cannot be enhanced) it is exceedingly difficult to manage interpersonal conflicts.

For example, if three qualified individuals i.e., for superior positions in the organization and there is only one such position, interpersonal conflict may develop to an unmanageable level.

Intragroup Conflict

A group experiencing intragroup conflict may eventually resolve it, allowing the group to reach a consensus. Or the group may not resolve the conflict, and the group discussion may end in disagreement among the members.

A study of a large number of groups engaged in business and governmental decision-making, tried to identify some of the conditions that lead to

- the successful resolution of conflict (consensus)
- the failure to resolve conflict (disagreement).

This study showed that conflict within groups is not a simple, single phenomenon. Instead, intragroup conflict seems to fall into two distinct categories :

- substantive conflict
- affective conflict.

Substantive conflict refers to conflict based on the nature of the task or to "content" issues. It is associated with intellectual disagreements among the group members.

In contrast, affective conflict derives primarily from the group's interpersonal relations. It is associated with emotional responses aroused during interpersonal clashes.

Inter-Group Conflict

An organization is a collection of individuals and groups. As the situation and requirements demand, the individuals form various groups.

The success of the organization as a whole depends upon the harmonical relations among all interdependent groups, even though some intergroup conflicts in organizations are inevitable.

The idea is to study intergroup behaviors within an organization so that any conflict can be recognized and dealt with by the management.

Intra-Organizational Conflict

Four types of intra-organizational conflict exist:

- vertical conflict
- horizontal conflict
- line-staff conflict and
- role conflict.

Although these types of conflict can overlap, especially with role conflict, each has distinctive characteristics.

Vertical Conflict: Vertical conflict refers to any conflict between levels in an organization; superior-subordinate conflict is one example. Vertical conflicts usually arise because superiors attempt to control subordinates and subordinates.

Horizontal Conflict: Horizontal Conflict refers to conflict between employees or departments at the same hierarchical level in an organization.

Line-Staff Conflict: Most organizations have staff departments to assist the line departments.

The line-staff relationship frequently involves conflict. Staff managers and line managers typically have different personal characteristics. Staff employees tend to have a higher level of education, come from diverse backgrounds, and are younger than line employees. These different personal characteristics are frequently associated with different values and beliefs, and the surfacing of these different values tends to create conflict.

Role Conflict: A role is the cluster of activities that others expect individuals to perform in their position. A role frequently involves conflict.

Managing Conflict

Five Methods for Managing Conflict

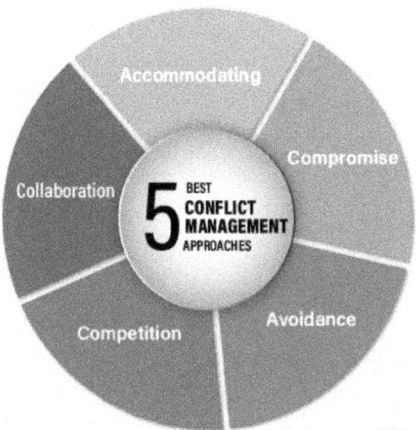

The conflict has many sources in the workplace. It is born out of differences and will arise in any situation where people are required to interact with one another.

Dealing with conflict effectively is a key management skill. This section outlines five different approaches to conflict management and the situations they are most appropriate for.

Accommodating

This is a lose/win situation. The accommodation approach is generally used when one party is willing to forfeit their position. It is best used in situations where:

- One party wishes to indicate a degree of fairness.
- People wish to encourage others to express their own opinions.
- The issue or problem is more important to the other party concerned.
- It is more important to safeguard the relationship rather than argue about the issue.

Compromise

This is a win/lose – win/lose situation, i.e., everyone involved either gains or loses through negotiation and flexibility.

Each will win some of what they desire while at the same time giving something up. The main goal of this approach is to find common ground and maintain the relationship. Compromise is best used:

- To achieve an agreement when all parties have equal power.
- To reach a temporary resolution in more complicated matters.
- To achieve a settlement when time or other circumstances are constrained.

Avoidance

This is a lose/lose situation. Neither party takes action to address the issues involved in the conflict, meaning that it will remain unresolved. This approach is best used:

- If all concerned feel that the issue is a minor one and will be resolved in time without any fuss.
- When the parties need a chance to cool down and spend time apart.
- If other people can resolve the conflict more effectively than the parties concerned.
- When more time is needed before thinking about dealing with the issues.
- If the impact of dealing with the situation may be damaging to all parties involved.

Competition

This is a win/lose situation. One party attempt to win the conflict through dominance and power. This approach is best used:

- When all other methods have been tried (and failed).

- In emergency situations when quick, immediate, and decisive action is called for.
- In situations where unpopular changes need to be applied and discussion is not appropriate.

Collaboration

This is a win/win situation. It is the most effective but most difficult way of managing differences. It requires trust and commitment on all sides to reach a resolution by getting to the heart of the problem. All parties need to be willing to empathize and try to understand each other's situation. Collaboration is most appropriate:

- When all parties are willing to investigate alternative solutions together that they may not necessarily have thought of on their own.
- When trying to get to the source of problems that have continued for a long time.
- When upholding objectives that cannot be compromised on any side while still preserving the relationship. • When parties from diverse backgrounds and experiences are involved.

Except in very few situations where the conflict can lead to competition and creativity so that in such situations the conflict can be encouraged, in all other cases where conflict is destructive in nature, it should be resolved as soon after it has developed as possible, but all efforts should be made to prevent it from developing.

Handling the conflict

Handling conflicts constructively is essential for maintaining healthy relationships and a positive environment. Here are some effective strategies:

1. **Stay Calm and Composed**
   - **Take Deep Breaths**: Before responding, take a moment to calm yourself.
   - **Maintain a Neutral Tone**: Avoid raising your voice or using aggressive language.

2. **Listen Actively**
   - **Give Full Attention**: Listen to the other person's perspective without interrupting.
   - **Show Understanding**: Use phrases like "I understand" or "I see your point" to show you are listening.

3. **Communicate Clearly**
   - **Use "I" Statements**: Express your feelings and needs without blaming others. For example, "I feel upset when meetings start late because it affects my schedule."
   - **Be Specific**: Clearly state the issue and avoid generalizations.

4. **Seek Common Ground**
   - **Identify Shared Goals**: Focus on what both parties want to achieve.
   - **Find Compromises**: Look for solutions that satisfy both parties' needs.

5. **Stay Respectful**
   - **Avoid Personal Attacks**: Focus on the issue, not the person.
   - **Acknowledge Emotions**: Recognize and validate the other person's feelings.

6. **Problem-Solving Approach**
   - **Brainstorm Solutions**: Collaborate to produce workable solutions.
   - **Evaluate Options**: Discuss the pros and cons of each solution and agree on the best course of action.

7. **Follow Up**
   - **Check In**: After resolving the conflict, follow up to ensure the solution is working.
   - **Adjust if Necessary**: Be open to making adjustments if the initial solution is not effective.

Practical Tips

- **Take Breaks if Needed**: If emotions run high, suggest taking a break and revisiting the discussion later.
- **Seek Mediation**: If the conflict is complex, consider involving a neutral third party to mediate.

By applying these strategies, you can handle conflicts in a way that promotes understanding, cooperation, and positive outcomes.

Resolving Behavioral Conflict

Various researchers have identified five primary strategies for dealing with and reducing the impact of behavioral conflict. Even though different authors have given different terminology to describe these strategies, the basic content and approach of these strategies remain the same.

Ignoring the conflict

In certain situations, it may be advisable to take a passive role and avoid it altogether. From the manager's point of view, it may be especially necessary when getting involved in a situation would provoke further controversy or when conflict is so trivial in nature that it would not be worth the manager's time to get involved and try to solve it.

It could also be that the conflict is so fundamental to the position of the parties involved that it may be best either to leave it to them to solve it or to let events take their own course. The parties involved in the conflict may themselves prefer to avoid conflict, especially if they are emotionally upset by the tension and frustration created by it.

People may intrinsically believe that conflict is fundamentally evil, and its final consequences are never good. Thus, people may try to get away from conflict-causing situations.

Smoothing

Smoothing simply means covering up the conflict by appealing to the need for unity rather than addressing the issue of the conflict itself.

An individual with internal conflict may try to "count his blessings" and forget about the conflict. If two parties have a conflict within the organization, the supervisor may try to calm things down by being understanding and supportive to both parties and appealing to them for co-operation.

The supervisor does not ignore or withdraw from the conflict, nor does he try to address and solve the conflict but expresses hope that "everything will work out for the best of all." Since the problem is never addressed, the emotions may build up further and suddenly explode.

Thus, smoothing provides only a temporary solution and conflict may resurface again in the course of time. Smoothing is a more sensitive approach than avoiding in that as long as the parties agree that not showing conflict has more benefits than showing conflicts, the conflict can be avoided.

Compromising

A compromise in the conflict is reached by balancing the demands of the conflicting parties and bargaining in a give-and-take position to reach a solution. Each party gives up something and also gains something.

This technique of conflict resolution is quite common in negotiations between the labor unions and management. It has become customary for the union to ask for more than what they are willing to accept and for management to offer less than what they are willing to give in the initial stages. Then through the process of negotiating and bargaining, mostly in the presence of arbitrators, they reach a solution by compromising. This type of compromise is known as integrative bargaining in which both sides win in a way.

Compromising is a useful technique, particularly when two parties have relatively equal power, thus no party can force its viewpoints on the other and the only solution is to compromise. It is also useful when there are time constraints. If the problems are complex and many faceted, and the time is limited to solve them, it might be in the interest of conflicting parties to reach a compromise.

Forcing

As someone puts it, "The simplest conceivable resolution is the elimination of the other party – to force opponents to flee and give up the fight – or slay them."

This is a technique of domination where the dominator has the power and authority to enforce his own views over the opposing conflicting party.

This technique is potentially effective in situations such as a president of a company firing a manager because he is considered a troublemaker and conflict creator.

This technique always ends up in one party being a loser and the other party being a clear winner. Many professors in colleges and universities have lost promotions and tenured re-appointments because they could not get along well with their respective chairpersons of the departments and had conflicts with them.

This approach causes resentment and hostility and can backfire. Accordingly, management must look for better alternatives if these become available.

Problem solving

This technique involves "confronting the conflict" in order to seek the best solution to the problem.

This approach objectively assumes that in all organizations, no matter how well they are managed, there will be differences of opinions which must be resolved through discussions and respect for differing viewpoints.

In general, this technique is especially useful in resolving conflicts arising out of semantic misunderstandings. It is not so effective in resolving non-communicative types of conflicts such as those that are based on differing value systems, where it may even intensify differences and disagreements. In the long run, however, it is better to solve conflicts and take such preventive measures that would reduce the likelihood of such conflicts surfacing again.

If there is a single contributory factor that helps in reducing and eliminating negative conflict, it is **"trust"**.

Our ability to trust each other has a significant impact on our working lives, on our family interactions and our achievement of personal and organizational goals.

In order to create trust and be trustworthy, it is necessary to avoid aggressive behaviors and at the same time develop supportive behaviors where people are respected for what they are or what they believe in and are treated equally without bias or prejudice. In case, a conflict develops at any level, it should be resolved with mutual benefit in mind.

Preventing conflicts

Every organization needs to take some steps to prevent conflicts. Some of the effective tools are:

Goal structure: Goals should be clearly defined and the role and contribution of each unit towards the organizational goal must be clearly identified. All units and the individuals in these units must be aware of the importance of their role and such importance must be fully recognized.

Reward System: The compensation system should be such that it does not create individual competition or conflict within the unit. It should be appropriate and proportionate to the group effort and reflect the degree of interdependence among units where necessary.

Trust and communication: The greater the trust among the members of the unit, the more honest and open the communication among them would be. Individuals and units should be encouraged to communicate openly with each other so that they can all understand each other, understand each other's problems, and help each other when necessary.

Co-ordination: Co-ordination is the next step to communication. Properly coordinated activity reduces conflict. Wherever there are problems in co-ordination, a special liaison office should be established to assist such co-ordination.

Culture: Creating a culture of openness, equality, and merit within the organization are essential to prevent conflicts.

> **For your information**
>
> **Personal identity theft**
>
> Personal identity theft in the cyber realm, often referred to as cyber identity theft, is when the cybercriminal gains unauthorized access to one's personal information, such as your name, social security number, or credit card details.
>
> They may use these information to commit fraud, such as opening new bank accounts, buying SIM cards, making purchases, etc.
>
> To safeguard against cyber identity theft, it is crucial to adopt a proactive and vigilant approach.
>
> Here are some key pointers to note:
>
> Use Strong passwords and change them regularly.
>
> Enable multi-factor authentication, which is an extra layer of security.
>
> Be cautious about the information you share on social media and other online platforms.

CHAPTER 5

STRESS MANAGEMENT

*A*s per physics, stress is the force acting on the unit area of a material. The effect of stress on a body is called strain. Stress can deform the body. How much force material experience can be measured using stress units?

There are basically two types of stress:

Longitudinal stress and bulk stress.

Hold on, I am not deviating from the subject.

The above definition is purely science and the same can applied to the human body.

When somebody is put under tremendous pressure, stress develops. And this stress can influence our body and mind. (Both positive as well as negative.)

No one in this world is living without stress, only the level varies. Stress cannot be avoided but can be managed.

Stress is the natural reaction your body has when changes or challenges occur. It can result in many different physical, emotional, and behavioral responses. Everyone experiences stress from time to time. You cannot avoid it. But stress management techniques can help you deal with it.

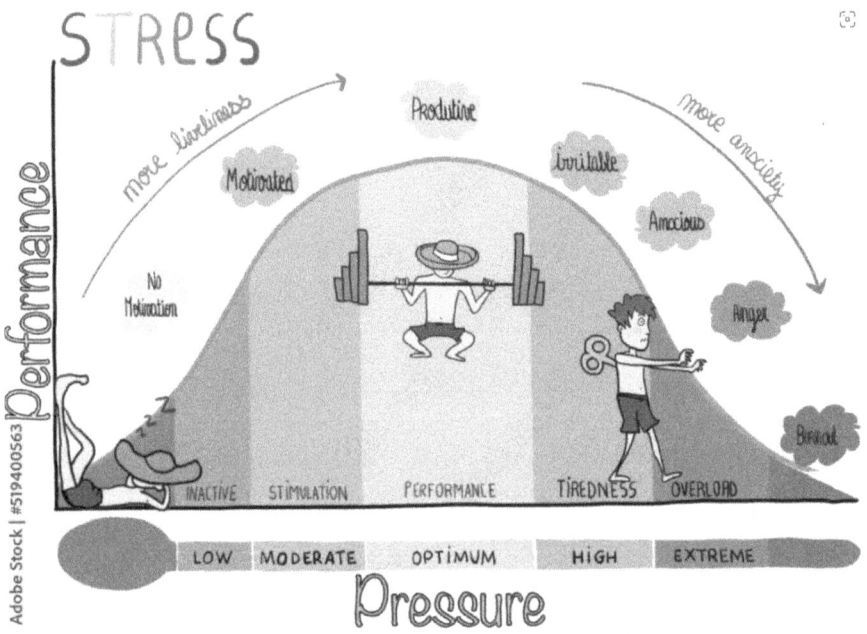

Stress management

Managing stress effectively is crucial for maintaining productivity and well-being, especially for busy professionals. Here are some techniques that might help:

Mindfulness and Meditation: Regular practice of mindfulness and meditation can help reduce stress and anxiety, improve focus, and promote a sense of calm. Even a few minutes a day can make a difference.

Physical Activity: Regular exercise is a powerful stress reliever. It can boost your mood, serve as a distraction from worries, and improve your overall health.

Balanced Diet: Eating a healthy diet can help you better cope with stress. Try to incorporate a variety of fruits, vegetables, lean proteins, and whole grains into your meals.

Adequate Sleep: Lack of sleep can contribute to stress and impact your productivity. Aim for 7-9 hours of quality sleep each night.

Deep Breathing Exercises: Deep, controlled breathing can help lower stress levels by slowing the heart rate and lowering blood pressure.

Time Management: Effective time management can help reduce feelings of stress and overwhelm. Prioritize your tasks, break them down into manageable parts, and avoid procrastination.

Positive Social Interactions: Connecting with others can help reduce stress. This could be a quick chat with a colleague, a call to a friend, or spending time with family.

Professional Help: If stress becomes overwhelming, do not hesitate to seek help from a mental health professional. They can provide strategies and tools to manage stress effectively.

Remember, it is important to find what techniques work best for you and incorporate them into your routine. Everyone is different, so what works for one person might not work for another. The key is to be consistent and make stress management a part of your daily routine.

Symptoms of stress

Symptoms of stress fall into three general, but interrelated, categories—physical, mental, and emotional. Review this list carefully. If you find yourself frequently experiencing these symptoms, you are likely feeling distressed:

- Headaches
- Fatigue

- Gastrointestinal problems
- Hypertension (high blood pressure)
- Heart problems, such as palpitations
- Inability to focus/lack of concentration
- Sleep disturbances, whether it is sleeping too much or an inability to sleep
- Sweating palms/shaking hands
- Anxiety
- Sexual problems.

Even when you do not realize it, stress can cause or contribute to serious physical

disorders. It increases hormones such as adrenaline and corticosterone, which affect your metabolism, immune reactions, and other stress responses. That can lead to increases in your heart rate, respiration, blood pressure, and physical demands on your internal organs.

Behavioral changes are also expressions of stress. They can include:

- Irritability
- Disruptive eating patterns (overeating or undereating)
- Harsh treatment of others
- Increased smoking or alcohol consumption
- Isolation
- Compulsive shopping

A sustained elevated level of stress is no laughing matter. It can affect every area of your life—productivity in the workplace and classroom, increased health risks, and relationships, to name just a few.

Managing the stress

Managing stress is a skill that can be learned. The initial step involves gaining a deeper understanding of yourself—how you respond in various situations, what triggers your stress, and how you behave when stressed. Once you have this self-awareness, consider the following steps:

Set Priorities: Utilize the time-management strategies discussed in this book. Create a To-Do list, identifying what needs to be accomplished today and what can be deferred. This approach ensures you focus on your most immediate priorities, alleviating the stress of trying to remember your tasks.

Practice Facing Stressful Moments: Anticipate upcoming events or situations and rehearse your responses. Find opportunities to practice handling these challenges. For instance, if public speaking intimidates you, practice with a trusted friend or colleague. If test anxiety is an issue, purchase practice tests and work on them in a relaxed setting.

Examine Your Expectations: Set realistic goals. While it is beneficial to strive for excellence, ensure your expectations are attainable. Be wary of perfectionism. Aim to do your best, recognizing that no one is perfect—not you, not your peers.

Embrace Mistakes as Learning Opportunities: Allow yourself and others the freedom to make mistakes, understanding that they can be valuable teachers.

Live a Healthy Lifestyle: Engage in regular exercise, consume nutritious foods, and allocate time for rest and relaxation. Discover a relaxation technique that suits you, such as prayer, yoga, meditation, or breathing exercises.

Find Humor and Enjoy Life: Seek out the humor in life and take time to enjoy yourself.

Accept Change: Recognize that change is an inherent part of life.

Develop a Support System: Cultivate a network of friends and family members with whom you can share your thoughts and feelings.

Believe in Yourself: Have confidence in your abilities and potential. Remember that many individuals from disadvantaged backgrounds have achieved remarkable success.

Avoid Harmful Activities: Steer clear of activities that falsely promise stress relief but actually exacerbate it, such as consuming alcohol, caffeine, smoking, using narcotics (including marijuana), and overeating. These habits add to the body's stress and have other detrimental effects.

Additional strategies for managing stress include:

Schedule Leisure Time: Plan vacations, breaks, hobbies, and enjoyable activities.

Ensure Uninterrupted Work Time: Arrange periods of uninterrupted time to focus on tasks requiring concentration. Also, schedule leisure activities that you genuinely enjoy.

Avoid Over-Scheduling: Prevent back-to-back appointments, meetings, and classes. Allow for breaks to catch your breath. Practice deep breathing exercises to calm yourself.

Master Time Management: Read books, watch videos, and attend seminars on time management. Reducing time-wasting activities will free up time for recharging.

Learn to Say "No": Setting boundaries can reduce stress. Focus on your primary responsibilities and priorities rather than letting others dictate your time.

Exercise Regularly: Regular physical activity reduces muscle tension and promotes a sense of well-being.

Utilize Your Support Network: Lean on family, friends, and social groups when facing stressful events.

"Buddha" on stress management

Buddhism offers valuable strategies for coping with stress. Here are some ways in which Buddhist teachings address stress:

Meditation: Focusing on a structured aspect of a situation (such as the breath or a mantra) in a relaxed, nonjudgmental way.

Mindfulness: Cultivating nonjudgmental awareness and acceptance of the present moment.

Lovingkindness: Being compassionate and kind to oneself and others.

Morality: Practicing right speech, right action, and right livelihood with good intentions.

Impermanence: Recognizing that nothing lasts forever.

Comprehensive Karma: Acknowledging that past, present, and future actions have consequences and that we can control our current actions.

Fatalistic Karma: Feeling a sense of helplessness due to past actions, leading to the current state.

Buddhism does not solely focus on stress management; it encompasses much more. However, these teachings can help alleviate stress and promote well-being.

As the Buddha said, he taught one thing: suffering and how to transcend it.

Remember, stress can also spark inner strength and courage, allowing us to overcome challenges.

Some positive effects of stress

"Consider a life devoid of worry or suffering, where only positive events unfold. While this idyllic existence may seem appealing, it could potentially lack enjoyment and become monotonous. Life, with its interplay of positives and negatives, ultimately hinges on individual perception."

Stress, often perceived as negative, can indeed have positive effects on human beings. Here are a few ways in which stress can be beneficial:

Eustress: This is positive stress, which motivates and energizes us. It helps us perform better, stay alert, and achieve goals. For example, the excitement before a challenging task or a competition can enhance performance.

Adaptation: Stress triggers our body's fight-or-flight response, preparing us to face threats. Over time, this adaptation strengthens our resilience and ability to cope with future stressors.

Growth: Some stressors, such as overcoming obstacles or learning new skills, lead to personal growth. They push us out of our comfort zones and encourage development.

Immune Response: Short-term stress can boost our immune system by increasing white blood cell production. This helps us fight infections and heal faster.

Social Bonds: During stressful times, humans often seek social support. This strengthens relationships and fosters a sense of community.

However, it is essential to recognize that chronic or excessive stress can harm physical and mental health. Balancing stress with relaxation techniques, self-care, and mindfulness is crucial for overall well-being.

Stress Busters

Here are **several effective stress-busting strategies** you can try:

Be Active: Regular exercise, such as walking, swimming, or yoga, can reduce emotional intensity and help you deal with stress.

Take Control: Empower yourself by addressing problems directly. Feeling in control is crucial for well-being.

Connect with People: A strong support network of friends and family can provide perspective and relaxation.

Prioritize "Me Time": Set aside moments for relaxation, socializing, or exercise away from work.

Challenge Yourself: Pursue goals and new experiences to build confidence and manage stress.

Avoid Unhealthy Habits: Relying on alcohol, smoking, or caffeine will not solve stress; tackle the root cause instead.

Help Others: Volunteering or small acts of kindness can enhance resilience.

Work Smarter: Prioritize tasks that truly matter and accept that you cannot do everything.

Remember, a positive outlook and balanced lifestyle contribute to effective stress management.

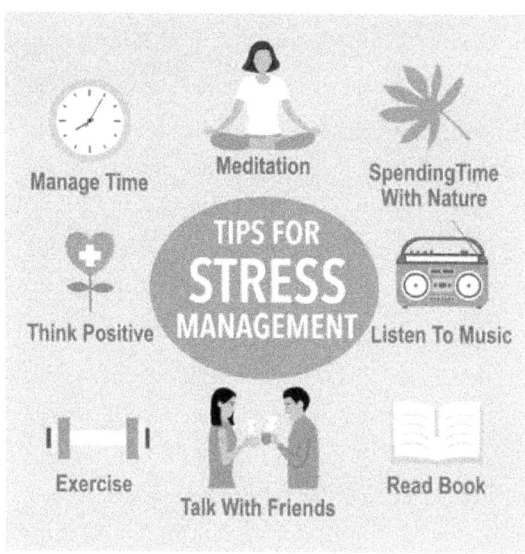

MINDFUL WALKING – wonderful stress buster

Mindful walking aligns awareness with movement and thus enhances the effect of walking on different muscles. In this way, mindful walking can double up on the benefits of walking.

In mindful walking, you pay full attention to walking by being conscious of every step and its sensations; breathing in time; and noticing all of the surroundings. It teaches you to be in the moment while not merely rushing between A and B and experiencing and enjoying each stride.

Mindful walking promotes deep, rhythmic breathing. Walking mindfully keeps one's breath in sync with their gait, so one feels a flow of more oxygen through the body. Because it channels the energy making you feel rejuvenated, the walking experience becomes more fun than just a workout.

Regular exercises, including mindful walking, improve your immunity. Walking enhances blood circulation, which ensures the free distribution of immune cells through the body. Coupled with mindfulness, this type of activity reduces stress.

Mental and emotional benefits of mindful walking

Mindful walking connects and touches different aspects beyond just moving your body. Walking mindfully contributes a lot to mental and emotional well-being, further helping you improve the quality of your life by leading you to peace and clarity.

Mindfulness walks allow you the ability to connect with your surroundings in a peaceful manner. Gaining insight into your breath and the sensations of walking ground you, therefore helping with anxiety and stress. This is a form of meditation, creating much-needed respite from daily pressures.

In addition, walking releases endorphins, natural mood elevators in the body. Add mindfulness to this, and the outcome is a complete brain stimulator.

How to walk mindfully?

It doesn't have to be complicated to learn mindful walking. Here are a few simple steps to get started:

Pick a location that inspires you whether it's a park, nature trail, or even a quiet street. The beauty of your surroundings can enhance your mindfulness practice.

For your information

Tools for business analysis

SWOT analysis is a widely used strategic planning tool that help businesses, assess their internal strengths and weaknesses, as well as external opportunities and threats.

However, there are several alternatives to SWOT analysis that offer unique perspectives and additional insight in business analysis. Here are a few:

1. **SCORE Analysis:** This model focusses on action oriented steps:

Strengths (S): what you are doing well or have potential to do well'

Challenges (C): Areas where you need additional resources or capabilities to succeed.

Options (O): Opportunities and risks you face.

Responses (R): Stakeholder responses and anticipated rewards.

Effectiveness (E): How you intend to make your initiative work efficiently and reliably.

2. **SOAR Analysis:** Similar to SWOT, but emphasizes on the strengths and opportunities:

Strengths (S): Positive aspects of your organization.

Opportunities (O): External factors that can benefit you.

Aspirations (A): Goals and desired outcomes.

Results (R): The impact of your actions.

3. **PESTLE Analysis:** Examines the external factors:

Political: Government policies, stability, and regulations.

Economic: Economic conditions, inflation, and exchange rates.

Social: Cultural trends, demographics, and social attitudes.

Technological: Technological advancements and innovations.

Legal: Legal framework and compliance.

Environmental: Environmental factors and sustainability.

4. **Porter's Five forces framework:** Analyzing industry competitiveness:

Threat of new entrants: Barriers to entry.

Bargaining power of suppliers: Supplier influence.

Bargaining power of buyers: Customer influence.

Threat of substitutes: Availability of alternatives.

Rivalry among existing competitors: Intensity of competition.

CHAPTER 6

TIME MANAGEMENT

*I*t is a common misconception that time management is solely applicable to the corporate world. This, however, is far from the truth. Time management is a crucial skill that permeates every facet of our lives.

Have you ever heard someone proclaim, "Apologies, but I simply do not have the time," or "I'm just too swamped"? I find such statements hard to believe. With proper planning, everything can be managed efficiently.

Consider this: each year, on the first day of January, we are each given 525,600 minutes - the equivalent of a year's worth of time. It is entirely up to us whether we choose to invest these minutes wisely or squander them.

Let us delve into an intriguing aspect of our lives. For an individual who works in an office,

let us break down the statistics:

> **Total Number of Days in a Year: 365**
>
> - **Public Holidays:** 12
> - **Leave:** 24
> - **Weekends:** 96 (Saturdays and Sundays)
> - **Working Days:** Calculated as (8 hours for 22 days a month × 12 months) / 24 hours = 88 days (indicating that only one-fourth of the year is spent in the office).
>
> **Summary of Days:**
>
> - Public Holidays + Leave + Weekends = 132 days
> - Working Days = 88 days
>
> **Calculation:**
>
> 365 days – (132 days + 88 days) = 145 days
>
> This leaves us with 145 days remaining in the year, which are allocated to sleeping, commuting, entertainment, and other activities. Assuming an average of 8 hours of sleep per day, we are left with approximately 100 days.
>
> Thus, we have 100 days + 132 days = 232 days at our disposal to perform various activities in a given year.

From this analysis, it becomes evident that the claim "I do not have time" is a fallacy. It all hinges on how we organize our time meaningfully.

Consider this: if one were to sleep two hours less each day, they could gain an additional 30 days each year.

While I concur that entertainment, sports, and similar activities are necessary stress busters, devoting an excessive amount of time to these pursuits constitutes a sheer waste of time.

I strongly recommend taking a moment to jot down how you typically spend your time in a day, week, or month. You may be surprised to discover how much time is wasted on non-value-adding activities.

Time, after all, is the most valuable currency we possess. Let us spend it wisely.

Interludes of Time: (also called "Short Gaps")

Each of us encounters brief interludes of time throughout our typical day. But what exactly are these interludes?

For instance,

- A daily commute to work by train, which takes 40 minutes each way.
- The inevitable waiting periods we experience at various times. (For example, in a clinic, airport lounges, etc.)
- The time spent walking.
- The moments spent standing in a long queue.

If you were to add up these seemingly insignificant moments, you might find that they collectively amount to approximately two hours each day.

So, how can one make the most of these fleeting interludes?

Perhaps one could carry a favorite book to read during these moments. Alternatively, one could listen to an audiobook or music of their choice. Reciting cherished chants or hymns mentally is another option.

Regardless of the method chosen, the key is to utilize these brief interludes for activities that one typically struggles to find time for.

These moments, though fleeting, can be transformed into islands of opportunity in the ocean of our daily routines.

In the bustling local trains of Chennai and Mumbai, I have observed numerous women engaging in productive activities such as threading flowers or crafting bags from plastic tape.

Simultaneously, there are those who choose to while away their time playing video games or watching short videos on YouTube. Interestingly, these are often the same individuals who lament about their lack of time.

As for myself, I make it a point to always carry a book that I have not had the chance to read for a while and utilize these moments to delve into its pages.

Additionally, while walking, I recite hymns to keep my memory sharp and active. It is all about making the most of the time we have at our disposal.

Value-adding and non-value-adding activities

Let us delve into the concept of value-adding and non-value-adding activities:

Value-Adding Activities:

Value-adding activities are those that contribute positively to one's personal or professional growth, productivity, or well-being. They are tasks that, when completed, bring a sense of accomplishment and progress. Here are some examples:

Professional Development: This includes activities like attending workshops, webinars, or courses related to your field of work. Reading industry-related books or articles also falls into this category.

Health and Wellness: Regular exercise, a balanced diet, and adequate sleep are crucial for maintaining physical health, which in turn impacts productivity at work.

Networking: Building professional relationships can open doors to new opportunities and collaborations.

Planning and Organizing: Setting goals, making to-do lists, and scheduling tasks can greatly enhance productivity.

Non-Value-Adding Activities:

Non-value-adding activities, on the other hand, are those that do not contribute to one's personal or professional growth or productivity. They are often tasks that consume time but yield little to no benefit. Here are some examples:

Excessive Social Media Use: While social media can be a tool for networking and staying informed, excessive use can lead to procrastination and decreased productivity.

Unnecessary Meetings: Meetings that could have been emails or do not require your presence can consume a significant amount of your time.

Multitasking: While it may seem like you are getting more done, multitasking can often lead to mistakes and decreased productivity. There are a few exceptions who are good at multi-tasking.

Procrastination: Delaying tasks can lead to stress and rushed work.

Remember, the key to effective time management lies in identifying these activities and striving to maximize the value-adding ones while minimizing the non-value-adding ones. It is all about making the most of the time we have at our disposal.

How to overcome procrastination?

Breaking the habit of procrastination (meaning: postponing or delaying something) can be a challenge, but it is certainly achievable with the right strategies. Here are some steps you can take:

Set Clear Goals and Deadlines: Having a clear understanding of what you need to do and when it needs to be done can help motivate you to get started. Break down larger tasks into smaller, manageable parts and set a deadline for each.

Prioritize Tasks: Not all tasks are equally important. Determine the urgency and importance of your tasks and prioritize them accordingly. This can help you focus on what really matters and avoid wasting time on less important tasks.

Eliminate Distractions: Identify what typically distracts you and try to eliminate or reduce these distractions when you are working. This could be turning off notifications on your phone or choosing a quiet place to work.

Use Time Management Techniques: Techniques such as the Pomodoro Technique, where you work for a set amount of time (e.g., 25 minutes) and then take a short break (e.g., 5 minutes), can be highly effective in combating procrastination.

Start with the Most Challenging Task: Often referred to as "eating the frog," this strategy involves completing the most challenging task first. Once this is out of the way, you will feel more accomplished and motivated to tackle other tasks.

Practice Mindfulness and Stress Management: Procrastination can often be a way of dealing with stress and anxiety. Practices such as mindfulness and meditation can help manage stress levels and improve focus and productivity.

Seek Support: If procrastination has become a chronic issue affecting your quality of life or mental health, do not hesitate to seek support from a mental health professional.

Remember, overcoming procrastination is a gradual process and it is okay to have off days. The key is to keep trying and not be too hard on yourself. Celebrate your progress and keep moving forward!

Designating Personal Time – Daily

It is often the case that we dedicate most of our time to others. But have you ever contemplated setting aside time specifically to yourself?

If your answer is a resounding 'No,' then I encourage you to continue reading. If not, feel free to proceed to the next section.

Every day, from 8 to 9 PM, I reserve time exclusively for myself. Regardless of the circumstances, I retreat to my personal space, ensuring that I am not disturbed during this hour.

During this time, I engage in activities that I feel drawn to on that day, without any pre-planning.

Some days, I might sing, on others, I might read, or perhaps I will reach out to an old friend for a chat. The activity could be anything that deviates from my usual routine.

Why is this practice essential?

Over time, we can experience burnout due to monotonous work styles and pressures. It is crucial to remember that no office or project hinges solely on one person's contribution. No one is irreplaceable.

As time passes, our inherent creativity can wane, and we may begin to lose interest in various aspects of life. This can sometimes have detrimental effects on our health.

Therefore, dear reader, I strongly recommend allocating at least one hour each evening for yourself. Revel in this time and enjoy the activities that bring you joy and relaxation.

How to prevent "Burn out":

Maintaining well-being and preventing burnout is crucial for both personal and professional success. Here are some strategies that might help:

Regular Exercise: Physical activity can help reduce stress and improve mood. Aim for at least 30 minutes of moderate exercise most days of the week.

Balanced Diet: Eating a diet rich in fruits, vegetables, lean proteins, and whole grains can boost your energy levels and overall health.

Adequate Sleep: Quality sleep is essential for good health and well-being. Try to establish a regular sleep schedule and create a restful environment to improve your sleep.

Mindfulness and Relaxation Techniques: Practices such as yoga, meditation, and deep breathing can help reduce stress and increase your sense of well-being.

Social Connections: Spend time with family and friends. Social connections can help you feel more grounded and can provide a sense of belonging and self-worth.

Hobbies and Interests: Engage in activities you enjoy. Whether it is reading, gardening, painting, or playing a musical instrument, hobbies can provide an outlet for stress and offer a break from daily routines.

Professional Help: If stress and burnout become overwhelming, do not hesitate to seek help from a mental health professional. They can provide strategies and tools to cope with stress and improve your mental health.

Remember, it is important to listen to your body and mind and take steps to care for your physical and mental health. Everyone is different, so find what works best for you and make it a part of your routine.

THE POWER OF SOFT SKILLS

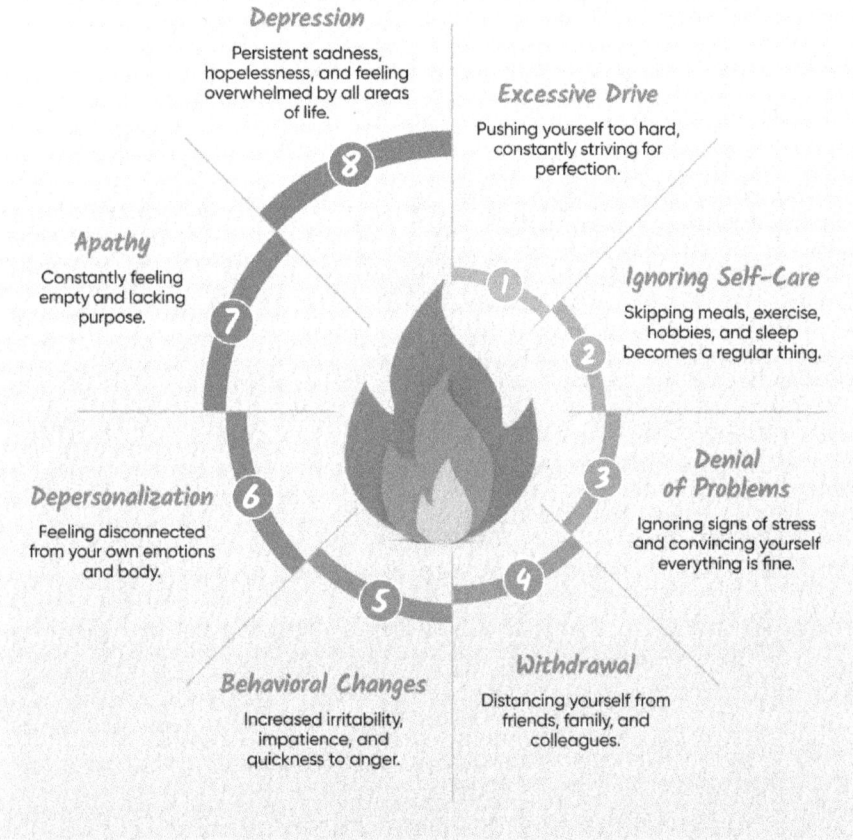

How to manage time?

Time management is the process of organizing, planning, and dividing your time between specific activities.

Good time management skills enable you to work smarter, not harder. If you work smartly, you will get more done in less time, even when time is tight, and pressures are high.

Failing to manage your time while performing a task will damage your effectiveness and cause stress.

Some of the most valuable time management skills include:

- Prioritization
- Goal setting
- Communication
- Planning
- Delegation
- Stress management

Time management skills are extremely important in any job. Because they help you structure your work in a way that allows you to achieve goals. If you have a specific time set aside to complete your tasks, you can also have extra time to think about the big picture for yourself and your company.

Urgent – Important Matrix

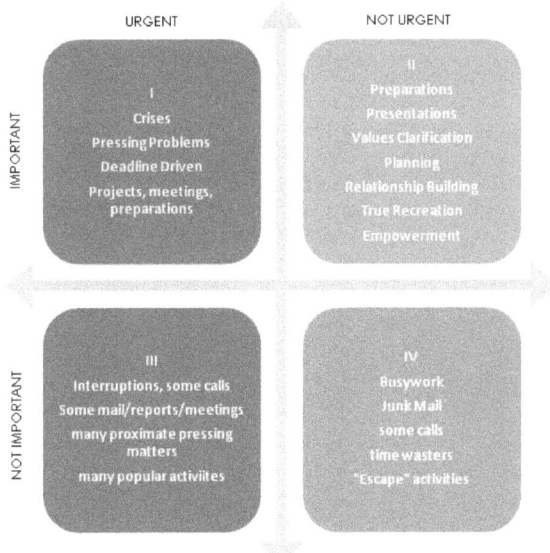

(Source: The 7 Habits of Highly Effective People)

This is a powerful tool to organize the tasks in hand based on priorities.

President Dwight Eisenhower himself developed the concept behind what would later be called the Eisenhower Matrix. He used it to help him prioritize and deal with the many high-stakes issues he faced as a US Army general, then as Supreme Allied Commander of NATO Forces, and eventually as president of the United States.

Eisenhower Matrix:

"I have two kinds of problems: the urgent and the important. The urgent are not important, and the important are never urgent."

– Dwight D. Eisenhower

It was popularized by Stephen Covey in his best-selling book, The 7 Habits of Highly Effective People. It was named after Dwight D. Eisenhower, the 34th President of the United States, known for his high output and organization. President Eisenhower is said to have arranged his obligations so that only the important and urgent matters came across his desk.

The Eisenhower Matrix uses this same principle to sort out the less urgent and important tasks on your list, which you can then delegate or not do at all.

The Eisenhower Matrix can help if you:

- Run around putting out fires all day, rather than focusing on tasks you want to complete
- Are busy, but feel like your work has little impact
- Aren't making progress on long-term goals
- Suffer from procrastination
- Struggle to say "no" when asked to do something
- Have a hard time delegating tasks

The difference between urgent and important tasks

The core principle behind the Eisenhower Matrix is the distinction between important and urgent tasks.

Urgent tasks are time-sensitive and *demand* your attention. They're tasks you feel obligated to address. Focusing on urgent tasks puts you in a *reactive* mindset, which can make you feel defensive, rushed, and narrowly focused.

Important tasks contribute to your long-term mission, values, and goals. They may not yield immediate results (making them easy to neglect). Sometimes important tasks are also urgent — but usually not. Focusing on important tasks puts you in a *responsive* mindset, which can make you feel calm, rational, and open to new ideas.

Note: If you put off important tasks long enough, they can become urgent.

People tend to believe that all urgent tasks are also important — when frequently, they are not. This misrepresentation may have to do with our preference for focusing on short-term problems and solutions.

But happiness and fulfillment come when we focus on the long-term, not the short-term and urgent.

The quadrants of the Eisenhower Matrix

The Eisenhower Matrix is divided into four parts:

- Quadrant 1: Important and urgent / Do
- Quadrant 2: Important but not urgent / Schedule
- Quadrant 3: Urgent but not important / Delegate
- Quadrant 4: Not important, not urgent / Delete

> *"The key is not to prioritize what's on your schedule, but to schedule your priorities."*
>
> **– Stephen Covey**

Pareto's Principle

The 80:20 rule, also known as the Pareto Principle, is named after the Italian economist Vilfredo Pareto.

Pareto observed that approximately 80% of the land in Italy was owned by 20% of the population. He further noticed that this distribution seemed to apply in other parts of his life, such as gardening: 80% of his peas were produced by 20% of the peapods.

This led to the formulation of the Pareto Principle, which states that, for many events, roughly 80% of the effects come from 20% of the causes.

In the context of business management, the Pareto Principle is used to help managers identify and determine which set of their inputs are most important. They can use this information to focus on the 20% of resources that are producing 80% of their desired results. This helps to improve efficiency and productivity within an organization.

It is important to note that the numbers 80 and 20 are not fixed; the principle is that a small number of causes is typically responsible for a substantial proportion of the effects. The actual figures could be 70:30, 90:10, etc., depending on the situation. The key point is that the majority of results come from a minority of inputs.

80:20 Rule

80% of results are achieved with only 20% of the effort

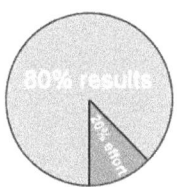

➢ To maximize your output, focus your time on the 20% high impact tasks that produce 80% results.

➢ Such high impact tasks must be high on the priority list at any given time.

Goal Setting

Goal setting is a fundamental component of the planning process in a typical corporate environment. It involves establishing specific, measurable, achievable, relevant, and time-bound (SMART) objectives that align with the company's mission and strategic plan.

Specific: Goals should be clear and well-defined. Vague or generalized goals are unhelpful because they do not provide sufficient direction.

Measurable: Goals should be quantifiable. It is important to have measurable goals so that you can track your progress and stay motivated.

Achievable: Goals should be realistic and attainable. While ambitious goals can push employees towards great achievements, unrealistic goals can result in disappointment and decrease morale.

Relevant: Goals should align with the company's mission and strategic plan. Irrelevant goals can waste valuable resources and divert attention from important objectives.

Time-Bound: Goals should have a clearly defined timeline, including a start and end date. Deadlines help to prevent everyday tasks from taking priority over longer-term goals.

In a corporate setting, goals can be set at various levels including organizational goals, team goals, and individual goals. Organizational goals focus on the broader picture and are linked to the company's mission and strategic plan. Team goals are set for specific teams within the organization and are aligned with the organizational goals. Individual goals are set for each employee, focusing on their personal performance and development, and are aligned with the team and organizational goals.

Goal setting in a corporate environment promotes a focused, aligned, and committed workforce, and is crucial for the company's success. It provides direction, facilitates planning, motivates, and inspires employees, and helps organizations to evaluate and control performance.

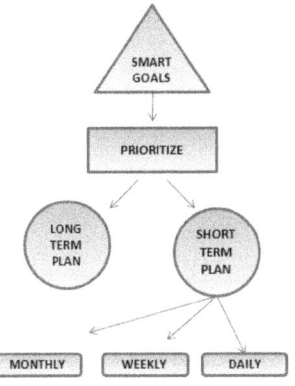

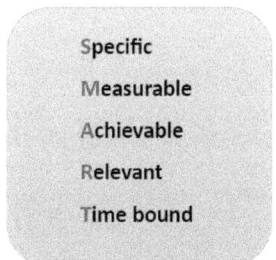

The Value of TIME - Poem

Imagine there is a bank that credits your account each morning with $86,400.

It carries over no balance from day to day.

Every evening deletes whatever part of the balance you failed to use during the day.

What would you do? Draw out every cent, of course!

Each of us has such a bank. It is name is TIME.

Every morning, it credits you with 86,400 seconds.

Every night it writes off, as lost, whatever of this you have failed to invest to good purpose.

It carries over no balance.

It allows no overdraft.

Each day it opens a new account for you.

Each night it burns the remains of the day.

If you fail to use the day's deposits, the loss is yours.

There is no going back. There is no drawing against the "tomorrow".

You must live in the present on today's deposits.

Invest it so as to get from it the utmost in health, happiness and success!

The clock is running. Make the most of today.

To realize the value of ONE YEAR, ask a student who failed a grade.

To realize the value of ONE MONTH, ask a mother who gave birth to a pre-mature baby.

To realize the value of ONE WEEK, ask the editor of a weekly newspaper.

To realize the value of ONE DAY, ask a daily wage laborer with kids to feed.

To realize the value of ONE HOUR, ask the lovers who are waiting to meet.

To realize the value of ONE MINUTE, ask a person who missed the train.

To realize the value of ONE SECOND, ask a person who just avoided an accident.

To realize the value of ONE MILLI-SECOND, ask the person who won a silver medal in the Olympics.

Treasure every moment that you have! And treasure it more because you shared it with someone special, special enough to spend your time.

And remember that time waits for no one.

Yesterday is history.

Tomorrow is a mystery.

Today is a gift.

That's why It is called the present!

(Credits: Marlies Cohen)

CHAPTER 7

DECISION MAKING

Undoubtedly, decision-making stands as one of life's most formidable challenges. The trajectory of success or failure hinges upon our ability to make informed choices.

"I recall an anecdote from *Tirukkural*, a couplet in the Tamil language by the revered saint Thiruvalluvar:

'Enni thuniga karumam thuninthapin. Ennuvam enbathu izhukku.'

The meaning is: 'Think wisely before acting. Once you have acted, refrain from looking back with regret.'"

Daily Decisions

From Wardrobe to Boardroom

From mundane selections like what to wear or eat to weighty business decisions, we engage in decision-making every day. These choices collectively shape our personal and professional paths.

Avoidance Is Not the Answer

While it may be tempting to shy away from decisions, doing so only exacerbates complexities. Inaction rarely leads to favorable outcomes.

The Pitfall of Passing the Buck

Consider those who habitually delegate decisions to others—a common phenomenon. Regrettably, such individuals seldom achieve true success.

The Uncertainty of Right and Wrong

The true nature of a decision—whether right or wrong—only reveals itself after it is made. Regardless of the outcome, we can learn and adapt.

Navigating Options

Ultimately, decisions emerge from the array of options before us. Our ability to weigh these alternatives shapes our journey.

Let us delve more into the process of decision-making.

There are two major types of decisions.

- *Programmed Decision* – a simple, routine matter for which a manager has an established decision rule.
- *Nonprogrammed Decision* – a new, complex decision that requires a creative solution.

Decision-making steps

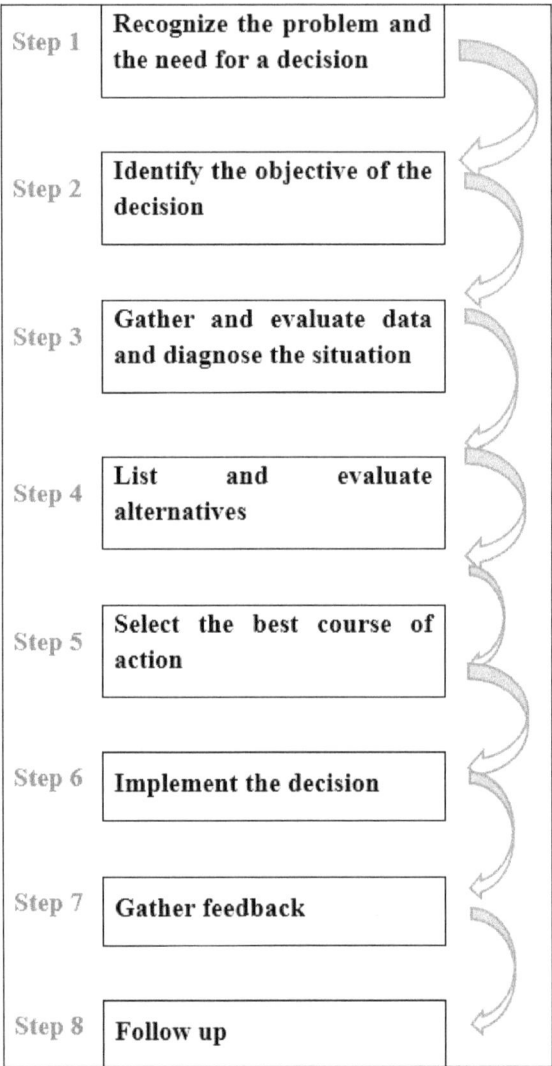

Step 1	Recognize the problem and the need for a decision
Step 2	Identify the objective of the decision
Step 3	Gather and evaluate data and diagnose the situation
Step 4	List and evaluate alternatives
Step 5	Select the best course of action
Step 6	Implement the decision
Step 7	Gather feedback
Step 8	Follow up

Decision-making models

There are three basic decision-making models available.

- Rational model
- Bounded rationality model

- Garbage can model

Let us look at the above briefly:

Rational model

Rationality – a logical, step-by-step approach to decision-making, with a thorough analysis of alternatives and their consequences.

The outcome will be completely rational.

The decision maker uses a consistent system of preferences to choose the best alternative.

The decision-maker is aware of all alternatives.

The decision-maker can calculate the probability of success for each alternative.

Boundary rationality model

Bounded Rationality – a theory that suggests that there are limits to how rational a decision-maker can actually be.

Managers suggest the first satisfactory alternative.

Managers recognize that their conception of the world is simple.

Managers are comfortable making decisions without determining all the alternatives.

Managers make decisions by rules of thumb or heuristics.

Garbage can model

A theory that contends that decisions in organizations are random and unsystematic.

The Quality, Timeliness, Acceptance, and Ethical Appropriateness of a Decision Influence its Effectiveness.

Managers Take Six Steps in Making an Effective Decision Using the Rational Decision-Making Process

ANALYZE THE SITUATION

- What are the key elements of the situation?
- What constraints affect the decision?
- What resources are available?

SET OBJECTIVES

- Is the problem stated clearly?
- Do people understand what they will work on?
- By what criteria will decision-making be judged?

SEARCH FOR ALTERNATIVES

- Do people involved in the problem make the decision?
- Have they sought complete information?
- Do those with information make the decision?
- Do they use diversity to generate ideas?
- Are all ideas encouraged?

EVALUATE THE ALTERNATIVES

- Do participants know that they are evaluating?
- Are the criteria for assessment clear and understood?
- Are differences of opinion included in the evaluation?
- Are some alternative pilots tested?

MAKE THE DECISION

- Do employees know that they are making the decision?
- Are they aware if they are satisficing or optimizing?

- Do action plans fit with the decision?
- Are they committed to the decision?

EVALUATE THE DECISION

- Are responsibilities for data collection, analysis, and reporting clear?
- Is there a comprehensive evaluation plan?
- Is there an evaluation schedule?

Managers Can Ask the following Questions When Evaluating Objectives

Criteria	Questions to ask
Relevance	Do the objectives relate to and support the basic purpose of the organization?
Practicality	Do the objectives recognize obvious constraints?
Challenge	Do the objectives provide a challenge for managers at all levels in the organization?
Measurability	Can managers quantify the objectives?
Schedulable	Can managers monitor the objectives at interim points to ensure progress?
Balance	Do the objectives provide a proper balance on all activities, given organizational goals?
Flexibility	Are the objectives sufficiently flexible of is the organization likely to find itself locked into a particular course of action?
Timeliness	Given the organization's environment, is this the proper time to adopt these objectives?
Technology	Do the objectives fall within the boundaries of current technological development?
Growth	Do the objectives help the organization grow, not just survive?

Cost effectiveness	Do the objectives expected costs clearly outweigh their benefit?
Accountability	Can managers assess the performance of those responsible for attaining the objectives?

Gathering information/ideas

This is a particularly crucial step for decision-making, as these ideas are the inputs based on which the decision will be made.

- Brainstorming
- The Nominal Group Technique
- The Affinity Diagram
- The Delphi Method
- Electronic Meetings

Brainstorming

Generally, a group of people assemble and share ideas during a brainstorming session.

There will be one facilitator who will collate the ideas for further debate.

- Topic
- Take turns sharing ideas
- Record each idea
- No comments/criticisms
- Keep the tempo moving
- One idea per turn
- Members may pass
- Keep going until ideas are exhausted

Nominal group technique

The Nominal Group Technique (NGT) is a structured method for group brainstorming that ensures equal participation from all members. Developed by Andre Delbecq and Andrew Van de Ven in the late 1960s, NGT is particularly useful in corporate environments for problem-solving and decision-making.

Steps involved in NGT:

1. **Silent Idea Generation**: Participants independently write down their ideas.
2. **Round-Robin Sharing**: Each member shares one idea at a time without discussion.
3. **Group Discussion**: Ideas are discussed for clarity and evaluation.
4. **Voting**: Participants rank the ideas anonymously to prioritize them.

Benefits:

- **Equal Participation**: Ensures all voices are heard, minimizing dominance by outspoken individuals.
- **Structured Process**: Keeps discussions focused and productive.
- **Consensus Building**: Facilitates agreement on the most promising solutions.

NGT is effective in diverse settings, helping teams to collaboratively generate and prioritize ideas, leading to more informed and democratic decision-making.

Affinity diagram

Use the ideas which came out of the brainstorming session to develop an affinity diagram.

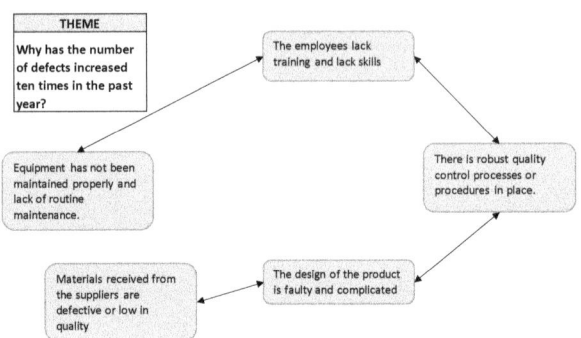

How to conduct the affinity sorting session.

- Clarify the list of ideas. Record them on small cards.
- Randomly lay out cards on a table, flipchart, wall, etc.
- Sort the cards into "similar" groups in silence – based on your gut reaction. If you do not like the placement of a particular card – move it. Continue until consensus is reached.
- Create header cards consisting of a concise 3-5-word phrase description, the unifying concept for the group. Place header card at top of the group.
- Discuss the groupings and try to understand how the groups relate to each other.

next step would be,

- Inquire if ideas are clarified.
- Use 3-5 words in the phrase on the header card to describe the group.
- If possible, have groupings reviewed by non-team personnel.

- To sort, physically get up and gather around the area the cards are placed.
- Team members will ultimately reach an agreement on placement – if for no other reason than exhaustion.
- Sorting begins when all team members are ready.
- If an idea fits in more than one category or group, after discussion, make a second card and place it in both groups.

Delphi technique

- Problem stated
- Questionnaires
- Anonymous & Independent
- Compile results
- Distribute copies of results
- New round begins
- Does not require physical presence
- Time consuming

Electronic meetings: (online)

Most used in recent times, which saves time. Ideas are collected through questionnaires and using algorithms decision-making is done.

Decision-making models

- **Six Thinking Hats**
- **Decision Matrix**

Six Thinking Hats

The **Six Thinking Hats** method, developed by Dr. Edward de Bono, enhances creative conversations by ensuring diverse viewpoints and thinking styles are represented. Here is how it works:

Blue Hat (The Big Picture):

Focuses on managing the process, setting agendas, and summarizing.

Asks questions like: "What is our goal? What process should we follow?"

White Hat (Facts & Information):

Analyzes data objectively.

Asks: "What information do we have? What data supports this?"

Red Hat (Feelings & Emotions):

Explores emotions, intuition, and gut reactions.

Asks: "How do we feel about this? What is our emotional response?"

Black Hat (Negative):

Critically evaluates risks, problems, and drawbacks.

Asks: "What could go wrong? What are the downsides?"

Yellow Hat (Positive):

Focuses on benefits, opportunities, and optimism.

Asks: "What are the advantages? How can this work?"

Green Hat (New Ideas):

Encourages creativity, innovation, and fresh perspectives.

Asks: "What if? How can we think outside the box?"

By wearing these metaphorical "hats," teams explore different angles without debate or criticism, leading to more effective thinking.

Decision Matrix

A **Decision Matrix** is a structured tool for evaluating and prioritizing options based on multiple criteria. Here is how to create one:

Define Criteria:

Brainstorm and refine evaluation criteria relevant to your situation.

Assign relative weights to each criterion based on importance.

Create the Matrix:

Draw an L-shaped matrix.

Label one edge with criteria and weights, and the other edge with options.

Evaluate Options:

Use one of these methods:

Rating Scale: Rate each option against criteria (e.g., 1-3 or 1-5).

Rank-Order: Rank options for each criterion.

Pugh Matrix: Compare alternatives to a baseline option.

Analyze Results:

The highest-scoring option is likely the best choice.

Remember, both methods enhance decision-making by providing structure and clarity. Feel free to explore these tools further or ask if you need more information!

Lateral thinking

The thinking process is very essential for decision-making process. Recent times it is also called 'Critical thinking.'

Lateral thinking, also known as **horizontal thinking** or **divergent thinking**, is an approach to problem-solving that encourages creative solutions beyond straightforward answers. Here is what you need to know:

Definition:

Lateral thinking involves breaking away from traditional linear thinking patterns.

It emphasizes thinking outside the box and exploring unconventional solutions.

Designers and problem solvers use indirect and creative methods to see problems from radically new angles.

Comparison with Vertical Thinking:

Vertical thinking (reason-based) follows step-by-step logic, gathering data and reaching a logical conclusion.

Lateral thinking combines imagination and intuition, generating ideas beyond existing information.

Both approaches can complement each other, enhancing creativity and refining big ideas.

In summary, lateral thinking encourages disruptive reasoning and helps uncover innovative solutions.

Edward de Bono

Psychologist Edward de Bono introduced the term in his 1967 book, "The Use of Lateral Thinking."

He argued that our brains are often trained to seek predictable solutions, even if they are not the best options.

Lateral thinking aims to move past cognitive biases and foster inventiveness.

One of my favorite authors who authored some wonderful books on 'Thinking.'

Edward de Bono, a prolific thinker, and author introduced several influential concepts beyond lateral thinking and the **Six Thinking Hats**. Let us explore a few of them:

Conceptual Thinking:

De Bono emphasized the need for better conceptualization. He believed that clear, precise concepts lead to effective communication and problem-solving.

His book "The Edward de Bono Code Book" proposes new words based on numbers, each representing a useful idea or situation without a single-word representation.

Parallel Thinking:

Similar to Six Thinking Hats, this method encourages considering several aspects of a problem simultaneously.

Instead of debating, participants focus on one perspective at a time, reducing conflict and enhancing creativity.

Po:

De Bono introduced the concept of "Po," which represents a provocative operation. It disrupts habitual thinking patterns and encourages fresh insights.

By applying Po, you deliberately challenge assumptions and explore unconventional ideas.

CoRT Thinking Tools:

De Bono developed the CoRT (Cognitive Research Trust) program for teaching thinking skills to children.

These tools cover various thinking processes, including decision-making, problem-solving, and creativity.

Focus on Language:

De Bono believed that improving language could transform humanity.

He advocated for better communication, precise terminology, and the creation of new words to express complex ideas.

Remember, Edward de Bono's legacy extends far beyond lateral thinking, and his ideas continue to inspire innovative approaches to problem-solving and communication!

Two Brains, Two Cognitive Styles

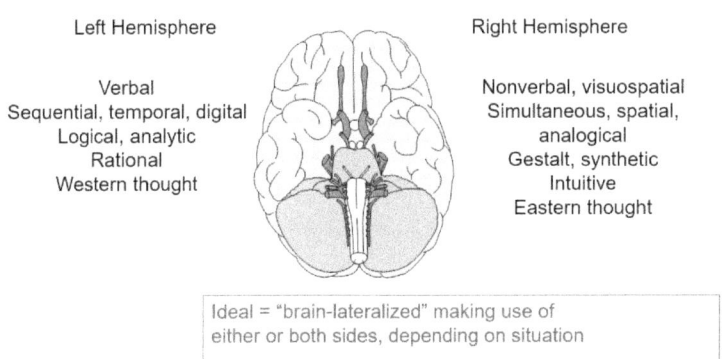

Ethical decision-making

Ethics play a vital role while making decisions, irrespective of the outcome.

Ethical decision-making involves analyzing and evaluating various options to make choices that align with moral principles and values. It is a process used to determine the best course of action in situations that involve moral dilemmas or complex issues.

Here are some key aspects of ethical decision-making:

Identifying the Ethical Issue: Recognize the moral dilemma or the ethical aspects of a situation.

Gathering Information: Collect relevant facts, stakeholders' perspectives, and potential consequences.

Evaluating Alternatives: Consider different courses of action and their ethical implications.

Making a Decision: Choose the option that aligns best with ethical principles and values.

Implementing the Decision: Put the chosen course of action into practice.

Reflecting on the Outcome: Assess the results and learn from the experience to improve future decision-making.

Ethical decision-making is essential in various fields, including business, healthcare, law, and everyday personal decisions. It helps ensure that actions are responsible, fair, and respectful towards others.

Let us look at one example of an ethical decision-making process.

Scenario: You are a manager at a company, and you discover that one of your suppliers is using child labor in their manufacturing process. This supplier offers the best prices and has been a reliable partner for years.

Identifying the Ethical Issue: Recognize that using a supplier who employs child labor is a serious ethical concern.

Gathering Information: Investigate the extent of the child labor issue, understand the legal implications, and consider the impact on your company's reputation and values.

Evaluating Alternatives:

Continue collaborating with the supplier while pressuring them to change their practices.

Terminate the contract with the supplier and find a new one, even if it means higher costs.

Report the supplier to the authorities and industry bodies.

Making a Decision: Choose the option that aligns best with your company's ethical standards and values. For instance, you might decide to terminate the contract and find a new supplier who adheres to ethical labor practices.

Implementing the Decision: Communicate your decision to the supplier and begin the process of finding a new, ethical supplier.

Reflecting on the Outcome: Assess the impact of your decision on your company, the supplier, and the broader community. Learn from the experience to improve future decision-making processes.

This example illustrates how ethical decision-making involves careful consideration of various factors and a commitment to doing what is right, even when it may be challenging or costly.

For your information

Examples of SWOT Analysis

1. Apple Inc:

Strengths: Strong brand, innovative products, loyal customer base.

Weaknesses: High product pricing, Dependence on iPhone

Opportunities: Expanding into new markets

Threats: Competition, changing preference of customers

2. Tesla:

Strength: Electric vehicle technology

Weaknesses: Production challenges, limited global manufacturing facility

Opportunities: Growing demand for EV, globally

Threat: Competition from traditional manufacturers

CHAPTER 8

LEADERSHIP

Leaders are not born; they are made.

"The development of leadership qualities is essential, and this book serves as a guide on that journey. Let us begin by understanding the definition of a leader.

A leader is someone who leads—whether in a company, a country, a business, or a community. They lead from the front, unwaveringly focused on achieving the ultimate objective or goal."

Some of the greatest leaders who inspired me are: (Actually the list is long, but I am restricting considering the size of the book).

"One can gain immense knowledge and inspiration from these leaders."

Mohandas Karamchand Gandhi (Mahatma Gandhi)

Mahatma Gandhi, born on October 2, 1869, in Porbandar, India, left an indelible mark on the world through his unwavering commitment to nonviolent resistance and social justice. Let us delve deeper into his life and contributions:

Nonviolent Struggle (Satyagraha/Ahimsa):

Gandhi's most significant legacy lies in his philosophy of **satyagraha**, which means "truth force" or "soul force." He believed that nonviolent resistance could transform society and achieve justice.

Through civil disobedience, boycotts, and peaceful protests, he led movements against British colonial rule. His campaigns, such as the Salt March and Quit India Movement, galvanized millions of Indians.

Champion of Social Justice:

Gandhi tirelessly fought against discrimination and inequality. He advocated for the rights of the untouchables (Dalits), women, and marginalized communities.

His efforts led to the abolition of untouchability and the promotion of communal harmony. He emphasized the dignity of all human beings.

Simplicity and Self-Sufficiency:

Gandhi's personal life reflected his principles. He wore simple khadi (handspun cotton) clothes and lived in ashrams. His lifestyle emphasized self-reliance and minimalism.

He encouraged Indians to spin their own cloth, boycott British goods, and support local industries.

Peace and Harmony:

Gandhi believed that peace could only be achieved through understanding and dialogue. He worked tirelessly to bridge religious and communal divides.

His efforts during the partition of India in 1947 aimed to prevent violence and promote peaceful coexistence.

Legacy and Global Influence:

Gandhi's impact extended beyond India. Figures like Martin Luther King Jr., Nelson Mandela, and Cesar Chavez drew inspiration from his methods.

His commitment to truth, compassion, and justice continues to resonate worldwide.

In summary, Mahatma Gandhi's life exemplified courage, compassion, and unwavering dedication to humanity. His teachings remain relevant as we strive for a more just and peaceful world.

Nelson Mandela

Nelson Mandela (1918–2013), a South African activist and former president, played a pivotal role in ending apartheid and advocating for human rights globally.

Apartheid Resistance:

Mandela's leadership within the African National Congress (ANC) challenged apartheid. Despite *27 years of imprisonment*, he remained unwavering in his commitment to justice.

His release in 1990 marked a turning point, leading to negotiations that dismantled apartheid and paved the way for democratic elections.

First Black President:

In 1994, Mandela became South Africa's first Black president after universal suffrage elections. His presidency focused on reconciliation, unity, and healing a divided nation.

Social Reforms:

Mandela prioritized education, healthcare, and economic development. His policies aimed to address poverty and inequality, especially for marginalized Black communities.

He exemplified dedication, courage, and sacrifice, refusing to compromise on freedom and justice.

Nelson Mandela's legacy extends beyond borders, inspiring generations to fight for equality and human dignity.

Ratan Tata

Ratan Naval Tata, born on December 28, 1937, in Mumbai, India, was a prominent industrialist and philanthropist. He was the great-grandson of Jamsetji Tata, the founder of the Tata Group, and was raised by his grandmother after his parents separated when he was ten. Tata graduated from Cornell University with a degree in architecture and later completed the Advanced Management Program at Harvard Business School.

Leadership at Tata Group

Ratan Tata joined the Tata Group in 1962, starting his career on the shop floor of Tata Steel. He became the chairman of Tata Sons, the holding company of the Tata Group, in 1991, succeeding J.R.D. Tata. Under his leadership, the Tata Group transformed from a largely India-centric conglomerate into a global powerhouse. Some of the notable acquisitions during his tenure include:

- **Tetley Tea** (2000): This acquisition made Tata Global Beverages the second-largest tea company in the world.
- **Corus Group** (2007): Tata Steel's acquisition of Corus made it one of the top steel producers globally.
- **Jaguar Land Rover** (2008): This acquisition by Tata Motors marked a significant entry into the luxury car market.

Ratan Tata's vision was to make the Tata Group a global entity, and he succeeded in expanding its footprint across various sectors, including steel, automotive, IT, communications, and beverages. His tenure saw the group's revenues grow manifold, and he was instrumental in fostering a culture of innovation and ethical business practices.

Philanthropic Activities

Ratan Tata was as renowned for his philanthropy as for his business acumen. He believed in using wealth for the greater good and was actively involved in various charitable initiatives through the Tata Trusts, which control 66% of Tata Sons' equity. Some of his notable philanthropic contributions include:

- **Education**: Tata Trusts have funded numerous educational institutions and scholarships, including significant donations to Cornell University and Harvard Business School. Tata Hall at Harvard is named in his honor.
- **Healthcare**: The trusts have supported healthcare initiatives, including cancer treatment facilities and rural health programs.
- **Rural Development**: Tata was committed to improving the quality of life in rural India through initiatives in agriculture, water management, and livelihood support.

Ratan Tata's personal investments also reflected his philanthropic spirit. He invested in over 40 startups, focusing on sectors like healthcare, education, and technology, aiming to foster innovation and entrepreneurship in India.

Legacy and Recognition

Ratan Tata's leadership style was characterized by humility, integrity, and a commitment to ethical business practices. He was known for his hands-on approach and his ability to inspire and motivate his team. His contributions to business and society earned him numerous accolades, including:

- **Padma Bhushan** (2000) and **Padma Vibhushan** (2008): India's third and second-highest civilian honors, respectively.
- **Honorary Knight Grand Cross of the Order of the British Empire** (2014): For his services to UK-India relations.
- **Carnegie Medal of Philanthropy** (2007): Recognizing his philanthropic efforts.

Ratan Tata's vision extended beyond profits to encompass social responsibility and sustainable development. He believed that businesses should play a pivotal role in building a better society. His leadership not only transformed the Tata Group but also set a benchmark for corporate governance and social responsibility.

In summary, Ratan Tata's legacy as a business leader is marked by his transformative vision for the Tata Group, his extensive philanthropic contributions, and his unwavering commitment to ethical business practices.

We mourn the loss of this esteemed individual on the 9th of October 2024, whose absence is irreplaceable.

Mustafa Kemal Pasha

Mustafa Kemal Atatürk (1881–1938) was a remarkable leader who played a pivotal role in shaping modern Turkey. Here are some of his major accomplishments:

Military Victory at the Battle of Gallipoli (1915): As a distinguished soldier in the Ottoman Empire, Mustafa Kemal led his forces to victory against invading armies during World War I.

Leader of the Turkish National Movement: After fighting against the puppet Ottoman Sultanate in Istanbul (formerly Constantinople), Kemal's efforts, along with his nationalist associates in Ankara, led to the

Ottoman Emperor's flight. He then became the leader of the Republic of Turkey, founded in 1923.

Introduction of Sweeping Reforms: Atatürk implemented revolutionary social and political reforms to modernize Turkey. These included the emancipation of women, the abolition of Islamic institutions, and the adoption of Western legal codes, dress, calendar, and alphabet (replacing Arabic script with Latin).

Protection of Women's Rights: Atatürk championed women's rights, granting them voting rights and encouraging their participation in public life.

His legacy endures, and his image, busts, and statues can be found throughout Turkey, honoring his immense contributions.

N. Kamaraj

N. Kamaraj, an Indian independence activist and statesman, emerged from humble beginnings to become a legislator in the Madras Presidency. His remarkable leadership qualities and contributions to society are noteworthy:

Selflessness and Simplicity: Kamaraj's low social origins allowed him to connect with low-caste and Dalit voters. He emphasized personal contact, visiting villages across Tamil Nadu multiple times.

Chief Minister of Madras: Serving as chief minister from 1954 to 1963, Kamaraj spearheaded industrial and agricultural progress in Tamil Nadu. His administration made the state one of the best-governed regions in India.

Kingmaker Role: After Nehru's death in 1964, Kamaraj played a pivotal role in reshaping the Congress party. He advocated for senior leaders to relinquish ministerial posts and focus on organizational work, leading to significant resignations. Kamaraj's influence was crucial in shaping the party's direction.

Mid-Day Meals Scheme: Kamaraj's enduring legacy includes the mid-day meals scheme, which combated illiteracy by providing nutritious meals to schoolchildren across India.

In 1976, he received the Bharat Ratna, India's highest civilian award, recognizing his immense contributions to the nation.

Ho Chi Minh

Ho Chi Minh, a legendary leader, played a pivotal role in leading Vietnam to independence. His leadership style was shaped by his nationalist and Marxist-Leninist beliefs. Here are key aspects of his leadership:

Dedication to the Cause: Ho Chi Minh's unwavering commitment to Vietnamese independence was remarkable. He persevered through challenges, inspiring others to join the movement.

Adaptability and Resilience: He adeptly adapted to changing circumstances, demonstrating resilience. Despite setbacks, he remained steadfast in his pursuit of freedom.

Relationship-Building and Communication: Ho Chi Minh excelled in forging connections with diverse groups. His effective communication conveyed his vision for Vietnam, motivating others to join him.

His legacy as the "Father of the Nation" endures, inspiring generations of Vietnamese.

Mao Zedong

Mao Zedong, born in 1893 in Shaoshan, Hunan province, China, was a pivotal figure in shaping modern China. His leadership qualities and contributions left an indelible mark:

Visionary Ideologue: Mao was the principal Chinese Marxist theorist. His revolutionary vision centered on agrarian reform, class struggle, and the empowerment of peasants and workers.

Strategic Military Leader: During the Chinese Civil War and World War II, Mao led guerrilla warfare against Japanese aggression. His military acumen was crucial in securing victory for the Communist forces.

Architect of New China: As the leader of the Chinese Communist Party (CCP), Mao played a vital role in establishing the People's Republic of China in 1949. His policies reshaped the nation, emphasizing collectivization, industrialization, and land reforms.

Cultural Revolution: While controversial, Mao's Cultural Revolution aimed to eliminate remnants of old society and promote ideological purity. It had profound social and political consequences.

Mao was not just a national leader, his impact transcended borders. His legacy continues to shape China's quest for equitable prosperity and sustainable development.

Lee Kuan Yew

Lee Kuan Yew, often referred to as the founding father of modern Singapore, played a pivotal role in transforming the city-state from a small, underdeveloped island into a global economic powerhouse. His leadership, vision, and policies have left an indelible mark on Singapore's development.

Born in 1923, Lee Kuan Yew co-founded the People's Action Party (PAP) in 1954 and became Singapore's first Prime Minister in 1959. Under his leadership, Singapore gained full independence from Malaysia in 1965. Faced with numerous challenges, including a lack of natural resources, a diverse population, and regional instability, Lee implemented a series of bold and innovative policies to ensure Singapore's survival and prosperity.

One of Lee's most significant contributions was his emphasis on economic development. He attracted foreign investment by creating a business-friendly environment, establishing strong legal and financial systems, and investing heavily in education and infrastructure. This strategy transformed Singapore into a major global trading hub and financial center.

Lee also prioritized social cohesion and political stability. He promoted a meritocratic society where individuals were rewarded based on their abilities and contributions, regardless of their background. His policies on housing, healthcare, and education ensured that all citizens had access to essential services, fostering a sense of unity and shared purpose.

Despite his many achievements, Lee's leadership style was often described as authoritarian. He maintained strict control over the media and political opposition, arguing that such measures were necessary to maintain stability and order. While this approach has been criticized, it undeniably contributed to Singapore's rapid development and success.

Lee Kuan Yew's legacy is a testament to his vision, determination, and pragmatic approach to governance. His leadership not only shaped Singapore's past but continues to influence its present and future, making him one of the most influential leaders of the 20th century.

Qualities of a Leader

In the corporate environment, exceptional leaders exhibit the following ten qualities:

Vision and Clarity: Great leaders have a sharp vision for their team or organization. They inspire others by articulating a compelling future state.

Strong Communication Skills: Effective communication is crucial. Leaders listen actively, express ideas clearly, and foster open dialogue.

Emotional Intelligence: Leaders understand and manage their emotions and those of their team. They empathize, build relationships, and navigate conflicts.

Decisiveness: Leaders make informed decisions promptly. They weigh options, consider risks, and take action confidently.

Accountability: Exceptional leaders take responsibility for their actions and outcomes. They hold themselves and their team accountable.

Adaptability and Learning Mindset: Leaders embrace change, learn continuously, and adapt to evolving circumstances.

Empowerment and Delegation: They empower team members, delegate effectively, and trust others to contribute.

Integrity and Authenticity: Leaders act ethically, maintain consistency, and build trust through authenticity.

Resilience and Perseverance: They bounce back from setbacks, stay focused, and lead with resilience.

Inspiration and Motivation: Great leaders inspire others, create a positive environment, and motivate their teams toward shared goals. .

Leadership styles

In the corporate world, leadership styles vary based on context and individual preferences. Here are **three common leadership styles**:

Autocratic Leadership:

Description: Autocratic leaders make decisions unilaterally, without seeking input from their team. They maintain strict control over processes and expect compliance.

Advantages: Quick decision-making, clear direction, and efficient execution.

Disadvantages: Limited creativity, reduced employee morale, and potential resistance.

Example: A CEO dictating company policies without consulting other executives.

Democratic Leadership:

Description: Democratic leaders involve team members in decision-making. They seek input, encourage collaboration, and value diverse perspectives.

Advantages: High engagement, better problem-solving, and increased trust.

Disadvantages: Slower decision-making, potential conflicts, and consensus challenges.

Example: A project manager facilitating team discussions to reach a consensus on project goals.

Laissez-Faire Leadership:

Description: Laissez-faire leaders provide autonomy to their team. They trust employees to manage their tasks independently.

Advantages: Empowerment, creativity, and flexibility.

Disadvantages: Lack of guidance, potential chaos, and accountability issues.

Example: A tech startup founder allowing developers to choose their work methods.

Remember, effective leaders adapt their style based on the situation, organizational needs, and team dynamics.

Difference between Responsibility and Accountability

In a corporate context, **responsibility** and **accountability** have distinct meanings:

Responsibility:

Definition: Responsibility refers to the duties and tasks assigned to an individual. It is about fulfilling specific roles or completing assigned work.

Focus: Task-oriented; it centers around what needs to be done.

Ownership: Can be shared among team members.

Duration: Often temporary until the task is completed.

Transferability: Can be delegated to others.

Measurement: Based on effort and execution.

Feedback: Evaluates how well the task was executed.

Example: Imagine a project manager responsible for creating a project plan. Their duty is to outline tasks, assign deadlines, and coordinate team efforts.

Accountability:

Definition: Accountability emphasizes an individual's obligation to produce specific results or outcomes. It goes beyond completing tasks—It is about accepting consequences.

Focus: Outcome-oriented; it centers around achieving results.

Ownership: Typically rests with a single person.

Duration: Continues even after the task is done until the desired outcome is achieved.

Transferability: Remains with the person even if the task is delegated.

Measurement: Based on whether the desired outcome was achieved.

Feedback: Assesses whether the intended results were met.

Example: Consider a sales manager accountable for meeting quarterly revenue targets. Their responsibility is not only to lead the sales team but also to ensure revenue goals are achieved. If targets are missed, they are answerable for the outcome.

In summary, *responsibility is about tasks*, while accountability involves *delivering results* and accepting the impact of those results on the organization.

Traits of a good leader

Effective leaders exhibit a range of essential qualities that contribute to their success. Here are **twelve key leadership traits**:

Self-Awareness: Understanding oneself, including strengths, weaknesses, and emotions, is crucial. Self-aware leaders adapt better and recognize their impact on others.

Respect: Consistently showing respect fosters trust, eases tensions, and improves effectiveness. Valuing others' perspectives and building belonging are essential.

Compassion: Compassionate leaders not only listen but also act on what they learn. Taking meaningful action builds trust and collaboration.

Vision: Leaders with a sharp vision inspire and guide their teams. Communicating this vision effectively is essential for success.

Communication: Effective communication ensures alignment, clarity, and understanding. Leaders convey ideas, listen actively, and foster open dialogue.

Learning Agility: Adapting to change and continuous learning are critical. Agile leaders stay relevant and navigate complex environments.

Collaboration: Building strong relationships and working well with others lead to successful outcomes. Collaboration fosters creativity and innovation.

Influence: Leaders flex their influence to motivate and guide their teams. Persuasion, negotiation, and inspiring action are key skills.

Integrity: Honesty, ethics, and consistency build trust. Leaders with integrity uphold their values and maintain credibility.

Courage: Courageous leaders take calculated risks, make tough decisions, and stand up for what is right. They inspire confidence in others.

Gratitude: Recognizing and appreciating team members' efforts boosts morale and strengthens relationships. Grateful leaders create a positive environment.

Resilience: Bouncing back from setbacks and maintaining focus on long-term goals are essential. Resilient leaders inspire perseverance.

Remember, these qualities can be learned and improved at all levels of an organization.

Qualities a leader should avoid

While effective leadership traits are essential, there are certain qualities that leaders should *avoid* in a corporate environment:

Unwillingness to Change: Leaders who resist adapting to new ideas or refuse to evolve hinder progress and innovation.

Indecisiveness: Inability to make timely decisions can lead to confusion, missed opportunities, and team frustration.

Lack of Accountability: Leaders must take responsibility for their actions and outcomes. Avoiding accountability erodes trust and undermines team morale.

Apathy: Disinterest or lack of passion negatively impacts motivation and team engagement.

Lack of Integrity: Leaders without integrity damage trust and compromise ethical standards.

Poor Communication: Ineffective communication leads to misunderstandings, conflicts, and inefficiencies.

Remember, self-awareness and continuous learning help leaders avoid these pitfalls and cultivate positive qualities.

CHAPTER 9

ADAPTABILITY AND VISIBILITY

Adaptability and Collaboration in the Workplace

Change is an inevitable part of life. Whether it is adapting to new environments, technologies, or circumstances, our ability to embrace change plays a crucial role in our personal and professional growth. In this context, the book "Who Moved My Cheese?" by Spencer Johnson serves as a valuable reminder of the importance of adaptability.

The Significance of Adaptability

Embracing Change: Change is a constant force, especially in today's dynamic world. Those who resist change often find themselves left behind. To succeed, we must cultivate a positive attitude toward change and be open to learning and adjusting.

Lessons from the Pandemic: The COVID-19 pandemic forced humanity to adapt rapidly. Remote work and online education became the norm. Those who adapted quickly thrived, while others faced challenges. This experience highlighted the need for adaptability in all aspects of life.

Balancing Expectations: Expectations can lead to disappointment if they are unrealistic. While it is essential to aim high, we must also keep our expectations reasonable. Striking this balance ensures that we remain resilient and adaptable.

Developing and practicing the following skills are essential to become more adaptable and visible at work.

Adaptability – Visibility Map

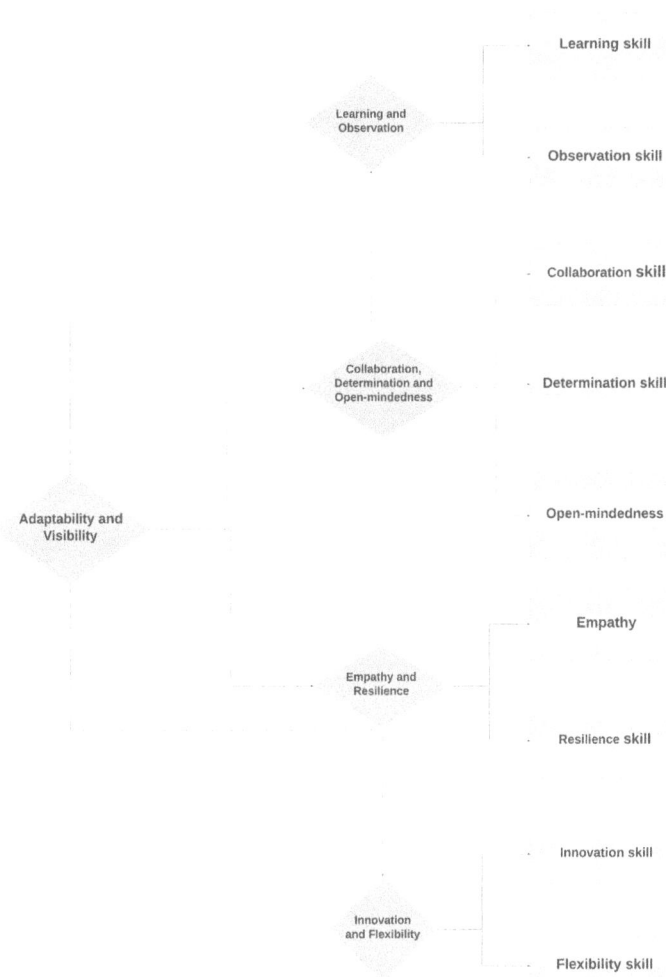

> **Motherhood:**
> The ultimate test of Flexibility and Adaptability

Learning Skills

Learning from Mistakes:

Mistakes are an inevitable part of life. Rather than dwelling on them, focus on extracting valuable lessons. Analyze what went wrong, understand the root cause, and implement corrective actions. The key is to avoid repeating the same mistakes.

Learning from Seniors and Elders:

Leverage the wealth of experience that seniors and elders possess. Engage with them regularly, seek their advice, and learn from their insights. They often have invaluable tricks of the trade that can enhance your own skills.

Helping Others Learn:

Teaching others is a powerful way to reinforce your own learning. Voluntarily assist colleagues or team members. Their questions and challenges provide opportunities for you to deepen your understanding.

Staying Informed:

Cultivate curiosity and stay updated. Keep your eyes and ears open to gather information. Read industry news, attend webinars, and participate in relevant discussions. Remember, learning is not confined to formal education—it is a lifelong journey fueled by curiosity and openness.

Observation skills

Observation Skills: Enhancing Awareness

Observation skills are essential for understanding, recognizing, and analyzing our surroundings. They complement mindfulness and effective communication. Here are some key points:

Application of Active Listening:

Active listening enables us to fully engage with situations.

By practicing active listening, we can detail activities and gain deeper insights.

Avoiding Distractions:

Distractions, such as texting during meetings, impede observation.

Stay focused and avoid multitasking when critical information is at stake.

Feedback and Questions:

Regularly seek feedback and ask questions.

Constructive feedback enhances our observational skills.

Collaboration Skills

Collaboration skills are crucial for achieving success in any role or industry. Let us delve into the concept of workplace synergy:

Workplace Synergy

Definition: Synergy occurs when individuals or organizations collaborate to produce outcomes greater than the sum of their individual efforts. It embodies the principle that "the whole is greater than the sum of its parts."

Origins: The term "synergy" is derived from the Greek word "synergos," meaning "to work together." Effective collaboration involves connecting and communicating with cross-functional partners.

Corporate Synergy: In the business context, synergy gained prominence during mergers and acquisitions. When companies merge, they create additional value by combining their strengths. This synergy not only supports each entity but also leads to cost reductions and increased profitability.

Challenges: Achieving corporate synergy requires integrating various aspects, including finances, employees, products, culture, and practices. Proper change management is essential to avoid negative synergy.

Benefits: Workplace synergy strengthens teams, fosters positive work environments, and enhances overall performance. By leveraging diverse talents and perspectives, organizations can achieve more collectively.

Cultivating Collaboration Skills

Collaboration skills encompass communication, interpersonal abilities, emotional intelligence, and personal traits. Just as riding a bike requires coordination among different body parts, successful collaboration relies on understanding and working effectively with others.

Adaptability and collaboration go hand in hand. By embracing change and fostering collaboration, we position ourselves for success in any work environment.

Enhancing Collaboration Skills in the Workplace

Effective collaboration is essential for achieving success in any professional setting. Here are practical steps to enhance your collaboration skills:

Set SMART Goals:

- **Specific:** Clearly define project goals.
- **Measurable:** Set criteria to track progress.
- **Achievable:** Ensure goals are realistic.
- **Relevant:** Align goals with overall objectives.
- **Time-bound:** Set deadlines.

Communicate these goals transparently to your team.

Clear Communication:

Regularly communicate tasks and expectations.

Utilize toolbox talks, standup meetings, or similar forums to clarify roles and address queries.

Prioritize clarity in communication to avoid misunderstandings.

Learn to Compromise:

Be open-minded and flexible.

Listen actively to others' viewpoints.

Avoid ego-driven decisions; consider alternative solutions.

Avoid Blaming Culture:

Foster a blame-free environment.

Accept mistakes gracefully and focus on solutions.

Encourage a culture of learning and improvement.

Celebrate Success:

Acknowledge achievements, no matter how small.

Celebrate milestones as a team.

Allocate a budget for celebratory events.

Remember, collaboration thrives when individuals work together, respect diverse perspectives, and celebrate collective achievements.

Determination Skills

The Power of Determination: Achieving Goals with Unwavering Commitment

What Is Determination?

Determination is the unwavering commitment to achieve a goal, regardless of obstacles or setbacks. It embodies the "come what may, I will do it" attitude that propels individuals forward.

Visualizing Determination:

Imagine an athlete sprinting one hundred meters, their focus narrowing to the finish line, blocking out distractions. Picture an archer in a major tournament, their gaze fixed on the center point of the target. Similarly, determination drives us toward our objectives, shutting out distractions and doubts.

Benefits of Determination

Positive Influence: Highly determined individuals radiate positivity. Their attitude inspires others, leading to better collaboration and performance.

Enhanced Creativity: Determined people find innovative solutions. They keep the end goal in mind, reducing stress and boosting productivity.

Perseverance: Determination fuels resilience. Giving up is not an option; they persist despite challenges.

Motivation for Others: Determined individuals motivate their peers. Their unwavering commitment encourages team members to excel.

Tips to Improve Your Determination:

Analyze Expectations: Set realistic goals and timelines. Allow room for unexpected delays or challenges.

Know Your Abilities: Understand your strengths and limitations. Avoid situations where your weaknesses hinder progress.

Flexibility Matters: Be adaptable. Evaluate alternative ideas objectively. Rigidity stifles determination. Remember, determination is the driving force behind success. Cultivate it, and you will overcome any obstacle on your path.

Open-Mindedness

Open-mindedness is the ability to be judicious, inquisitive, and receptive. Here is why it matters:

What is Open-Mindedness?

Open-mindedness is basically the willingness to consider new ideas, perspectives, and experiences. It involves being receptive to different viewpoints and being able to adapt one's thinking based on current information.

Why is Open-Mindedness Required?

1. **Innovation and Creativity**: Open-minded employees are more likely to think outside the box and produce innovative solutions. This is an important skill for staying competitive in today's fast-paced business world.
2. **Adaptability**: The corporate landscape is constantly changing. Open-minded individuals can adapt more easily to modern technologies, processes, and market conditions.

3. **Collaboration**: In a diverse workplace, open-mindedness fosters better teamwork and collaboration. It helps in understanding and valuing the contributions of colleagues from diverse backgrounds.
4. **Problem-Solving**: Open-mindedness allows employees to approach problems from various angles, leading to more effective and comprehensive solutions.
5. **Decision making**: Open-mindedness is crucial for making unbiased decisions. It fosters an environment conducive to exploring diverse options.
6. **Multi-Cultural environments**: In diverse workplaces, open-mindedness builds trust and confidence. It promotes collaboration across cultures.

Characteristics of an Open-Minded Person:

Willingness to be challenged.

Remaining calm in negative situations.

Demonstrating empathy and humility.

Practicing active listening.

Developing Open-Mindedness:

Reduce Ego:

Ego can hinder open-mindedness. Stay humble and avoid superiority.

Be neutral and unbiased when handling situations.

Respect Others' Viewpoints:

Acknowledge that different perspectives exist.

Respect diverse opinions.

Ask Positive Questions:

Positively frame questions to understand others' viewpoints.

Seek clarity and deeper understanding.

Interact with Diverse Groups:

Engage with different peer groups and gatherings.

Learn from varied experiences.

Remember, observation skills and open-mindedness contribute to a richer understanding of the world around us. Keep practicing and stay receptive!

Open-mindedness is a crucial skill in the corporate environment. Let us break it down:

Benefits for Employees

1. **Personal Growth**: Being open-minded helps employees learn and grow, both professionally and personally. It encourages continuous learning and self-improvement.
2. **Career Advancement**: Open-minded individuals are often seen as flexible and adaptable, qualities that are highly valued for leadership roles and career advancement.
3. **Enhanced Relationships**: Open-mindedness leads to better communication and stronger relationships with colleagues, creating a more positive and supportive work environment.

Benefits for Employers

1. **Increased Innovation**: Companies with open-minded employees are more likely to innovate and stay ahead of the competition.
2. **Better Decision-Making**: Open-minded teams consider a wider range of perspectives, leading to more informed and balanced decisions.

3. **Improved Employee Engagement**: When employees feel their ideas and perspectives are valued, they are more engaged and motivated.
4. **Positive Work Culture**: Open-mindedness contributes to a culture of respect, inclusivity, and collaboration, which can improve overall employee satisfaction and retention.

How to Foster Open-Mindedness

1. **Encourage Diverse Perspectives**: Create an environment where different viewpoints are welcomed and respected.
2. **Provide Training**: Offer workshops and training sessions on topics like cultural competence, active listening, and critical thinking.
3. **Lead by Example**: Leaders should model open-minded behavior by being receptive to feedback and willing to consider new ideas.
4. **Promote a Growth Mindset**: Encourage employees to view challenges as opportunities for learning and growth.

In summary, open-mindedness is a vital skill that benefits both employees and employers by fostering innovation, adaptability, collaboration, and a positive work culture. It is essential for personal growth, career advancement, and organizational success.

Empathy

Cultivating Empathy in the Workplace

Empathy is the ability to understand and share the feelings of others. It is a crucial skill for building strong relationships and fostering a positive work environment. Here are practical steps to demonstrate empathy:

Different Perspectives: Approach problems from various angles. Put yourself in others' shoes to understand their viewpoints. This broader perspective enhances problem-solving.

Question to Understand: Instead of blaming, ask relevant questions. Use techniques like the "7 Whys" to uncover root causes. Seek to understand rather than assign fault.

Validate Feelings: Repeat what you have understood to clarify. Validate the other person's emotions. Clarity promotes empathy.

Probable Resolutions: Avoid hasty conclusions. Propose potential solutions and seek consensus. Customer service often follows this approach.

Offer Genuine Help: Sincere assistance matters. Lip service without action lacks empathy.

Stay Unbiased: Treat everyone fairly. Bias hinders empathy.

Importance of Empathy

Creating Connections: Empathy builds rapport. It fosters trust and collaboration.

Improving Social Skills: Empathetic individuals communicate effectively. They understand nonverbal cues and emotions.

Enhancing Productivity: Empathy leads to better teamwork. It boosts morale and motivation. Remember, empathy begins with active listening and genuine concern for others. Develop this skill, and you will contribute positively to any team.

Resilience Skills

Resilience is the ability to withstand and bounce back from tricky situations. How we manage adversity matters. Here are key points:

Natural or Developed Skill:

Some people naturally possess resilience, while others develop it over time.

Stress management plays a vital role in building resilience.

Traits of Resilient Individuals:

Self-Confidence: Believing in oneself fosters resilience.

Optimism: A positive outlook helps navigate challenges.

Flexibility: Adapting to change is essential.

Reasonableness: Balancing emotions and logic.

Accountability: Taking ownership of actions.

Self-Awareness: Understanding strengths and weaknesses.

Innovative skill

Innovative Thinking: Beyond Invention

In today's dynamic world, innovation is a buzzword that resonates across industries. It is more than just a trend; It is a mindset that drives progress. Let us break down the key aspects:

ADAPTABILITY AND VISIBILITY

Creativity and Critical Thinking:

Creativity fuels innovation. It is about thinking beyond the obvious, connecting disparate ideas, and imagining new possibilities.

Critical thinking helps evaluate and refine those creative ideas, ensuring they have practical value.

Invention vs. Innovation:

Invention refers to creating something entirely new—a groundbreaking idea or product.

Innovation, on the other hand, involves improving existing solutions, making them more efficient, effective, or user-friendly.

For instance, the first camera was an invention, but the evolution to DSLR cameras represents innovation.

The Sukiyabashi Jiro Story (Japan)

A Culinary Symphony

Sukiyabashi Jiro, located near Tokyo, transcends mere dining. It is a culinary sanctuary where time slows down, and flavors dance on the edge of perfection.

Owned and operated by the venerable sushi master, Jiro Ono, this unassuming restaurant has etched its name in gastronomic history.

Three Michelin Stars and Beyond

Imagine a tiny, unmarked entrance tucked away in the Ginza Subway Station. Follow the discreet yellow C6 sign, descend the stairs, and step into another world.

The restaurant sign, elegantly inscribed in Japanese characters, whispers, "DO NOT TAKE PHOTOS." You have arrived at Sukiyabashi Jiro.

Jiro achieved the unthinkable: three Michelin stars—an accolade reserved for the culinary elite. But there is a twist—the restaurant was removed from the Michelin Guide in 2019.

Why? Because reservations are not open to the public. To secure a seat at Jiro's counter, you must navigate a labyrinth of connections, concierges, and whispered recommendations.

The Omakase Experience

Picture yourself sitting at the wooden counter, inches away from Jiro himself. The air hums with anticipation.

Jiro's hands move like a maestro's—precise, deliberate. Each piece of nigiri is a revelation.

The rice, seasoned to perfection, cradles the freshest fish—maguro, hamachi, uni, and more. The soy sauce brushed on with reverence, enhances without overpowering.

The Price of Perfection

And the bill? Brace yourself. One plate of sushi at Sukiyabashi Jiro costs around 55,000 yen (approximately 300 US dollars).

But this is not about money; It is about mastery. Jiro Ono (Chef and owner), (Died at the age of 98 in the year 2023) embodies dedication.

His mantra: "You must dedicate your life to mastering a skill." For him, it is not just about making better sushi; It is about seeking excellence and touching perfection. That is innovation.

A Lesson Beyond Sushi

Jiro Ono teaches us more than culinary finesse. His relentless pursuit of mastery applies to any craft.

Whether you are a sushi chef, a writer, or a painter, immerse yourself. Seek the sublime. Strive for that elusive three-star moment—the one where time stands still, and your creation becomes a symphony.

So, next time you dream of sushi, remember Sukiyabashi Jiro—a place where rice meets raw fish, and perfection blooms under the subway overpass.

Creativity Beyond Arts:

Creativity is not limited to artistic endeavors. Apply it to all aspects of work.

Consider diverse perspectives and unconventional approaches.

Be Original:

Innovations must be unique. Explore a variety of ideas.

Do not shy away from unconventional solutions.

Problem-Solving Resilience:

Expect challenges during the creative process.

Overcome setbacks with determination and adaptability.

Lateral Thinking:

Think outside the box. Explore different angles.

Try multiple approaches until you find success.

Collaboration and Communication:

Collaborate with others. Share ideas openly.

Effective communication ensures your innovative thoughts are understood.

Continuous Learning:

Stay updated with industry trends and developments.

Embrace lifelong learning.

Learn from Failures:

Failures are stepping stones to innovation.

Analyze mistakes and adapt.

Remember, innovative thinking is not limited to degrees—It is about curiosity, resilience, and a willingness to explore new paths.

Flexibility skill

Being flexible means withstanding stress, challenges, and changes. Here is why it matters:

Nothing Is Permanent:

Life constantly evolves. Flexibility allows us to adapt.

Resilience and flexibility go hand in hand.

Success Stories:

Successful individuals often embrace flexibility.

Rigid attitudes hinder growth.

Example: A colleague's flexibility led to a promotion after resolving an issue.

Technology and Age:

Some resist technology due to rigidity.

Flexible learners thrive, regardless of age.

Adaptability and Decision-Making:

Adaptability and flexibility are vital for facing uncertainty.

Employers value these traits for future growth.

Benefits of Being Flexible

Wider Accessibility:

Flexibility opens doors to diverse opportunities.

You connect with a larger group.

Consultation in Decision-Making:

Flexible individuals are consulted during critical decisions.

Their balanced perspectives contribute significantly.

Developing Flexibility

Improving flexibility skills in a corporate workplace involves a combination of mindset shifts and practical strategies. Here are some key steps:

1. **Embrace Change**: Cultivate a positive attitude towards change. View new challenges as opportunities for growth rather than obstacles.
2. **Continuous Learning**: Stay updated with industry trends and enhance your skill set through courses, workshops, and reading. This makes adapting to new roles and responsibilities easier.
3. **Effective Communication**: Develop strong communication skills to understand and convey ideas clearly. This helps in navigating different perspectives and finding common ground.
4. **Time Management**: Prioritize tasks and manage your time efficiently. Flexibility often requires juggling multiple responsibilities, so being organized is crucial.
5. **Collaboration**: Work well with diverse teams. Be open to different working styles and be willing to compromise when necessary.
6. **Stress Management**: Practice mindfulness, exercise, or other stress-relief techniques. Staying calm under pressure enhances your ability to adapt.
7. **Seek Feedback**: Regularly ask for feedback from colleagues and supervisors. Use it constructively to improve and adapt your approach.

By integrating these practices, individuals can enhance their flexibility, making them more resilient and valuable in a dynamic corporate environment.

Teamwork

Success cannot be achieved without teamwork, especially in a project execution environment.

Teamwork is the collaborative effort of a group of individuals working together towards a common goal. It involves sharing responsibilities, leveraging each member's strengths, and supporting one another to achieve collective success. Effective teamwork requires clear communication, mutual respect, and a willingness to cooperate and compromise. It is characterized by a sense of unity and a shared commitment to the team's objectives.

Teamwork is a cornerstone of success in any corporate environment. It fosters collaboration, enhances productivity, and drives innovation. Here are some key reasons why teamwork is essential:

1. **Enhanced Problem-Solving**: When team members collaborate, they bring diverse perspectives and skills to the table. This diversity leads to more creative solutions and better decision-making.
2. **Increased Efficiency**: Tasks can be divided according to each member's strengths, ensuring that work is completed more efficiently. This division of labor allows for faster completion of projects and higher quality outcomes.
3. **Improved Communication**: Effective teamwork requires clear and open communication. This not only helps in avoiding misunderstandings but also builds trust among team members. Trust is crucial for a positive work environment and for the smooth execution of tasks.
4. **Employee Engagement and Morale**: Working in a team can boost morale and job satisfaction. When employees feel they are part of a supportive team, they are more likely to be engaged and motivated. This leads to higher retention rates and a more positive workplace culture.
5. **Learning and Development**: Teamwork provides opportunities for employees to learn from each other. This continuous learning environment helps in the professional growth of individuals and the overall development of the organization.
6. **Adaptability and Resilience**: Teams can adapt more quickly to changes and challenges. The collective strength of a team makes it easier to navigate uncertainties and produce effective strategies to overcome obstacles.

In summary, teamwork is vital in a corporate setting as it enhances problem-solving, efficiency, communication, employee engagement, learning, and adaptability. By fostering a collaborative environment, companies can achieve greater success and create a more dynamic and resilient workforce.

Coaching and Mentoring

Let us dive into the concepts of coaching and mentoring, their differences, importance, and their effectiveness in a corporate environment.

Coaching:

Focus: Coaching is typically performance-driven, aimed at improving an individual's skills and performance in their current role.

Duration: It is often short-term and specific to particular goals or projects.

Approach: Coaches use structured methods and techniques to help individuals achieve specific outcomes. They ask powerful questions, provide feedback, and hold individuals accountable.

Relationship: The relationship is usually more formal and professional, with the coach often being an external expert.

Mentoring:

Focus: Mentoring is development-driven, focusing on the overall growth and career development of the mentee.

Duration: It is usually long-term, with a broader scope that includes personal and professional growth.

Approach: Mentors share their experiences, provide guidance, and offer advice. They function as role models and provide support based on their own career journeys.

Relationship: The relationship is often more informal and personal, with the mentor usually being a more experienced colleague within the organization.

Importance of Coaching and Mentoring

Both coaching and mentoring are crucial for several reasons:

Skill Development: They help individuals develop new skills and improve existing ones.

Career Growth: They provide guidance and support for career advancement.

Employee Engagement: They increase employee engagement and satisfaction by showing that the organization is invested in their growth.

Knowledge Transfer: They facilitate the transfer of knowledge and expertise within the organization.

Effectiveness in a Corporate Environment

In a corporate setting, coaching, and mentoring can be highly effective:

Enhanced Performance: Coaching helps employees improve their performance, leading to better results for the organization.

Succession Planning: Mentoring prepares employees for future leadership roles, ensuring a smooth transition and continuity.

Cultural Integration: Both practices help integrate new employees into the company culture and align them with organizational values.

Innovation and Problem-Solving: They encourage creative thinking and problem-solving by providing different perspectives and insights.

Helping Employees Climb the Corporate Ladder

Coaching and mentoring play a significant role in helping employees advance in their careers:

Personalized Development: They offer tailored development plans that address individual strengths and weaknesses.

Networking Opportunities: Mentors can introduce mentees to key contacts and networks within the industry.

Confidence Building: Both practices help build confidence by providing constructive feedback and encouragement.

Goal Setting and Achievement: They assist employees in setting realistic career goals and developing strategies to achieve them.

In summary, coaching and mentoring are powerful tools that can significantly impact an individual's career growth and the overall success of an organization. By investing in these practices, companies can foster a culture of continuous learning and development, leading to a more engaged and capable workforce.

Role of a mentor

A mentor plays a crucial role in an employee's career development by providing guidance, support, and valuable insights. Here are some key aspects of a mentor's role:

Knowledge Sharing: Mentors share their expertise and experiences, helping mentees understand industry dynamics and develop necessary skills.

Goal Setting: They assist mentees in setting realistic and achievable career goals, often using frameworks like SMART (Specific, Measurable, Achievable, Relevant, Time-bound) goals.

Feedback and Development: Mentors provide constructive feedback, helping mentees improve their performance and grow professionally.

Emotional Support: They offer encouragement and emotional support, helping mentees navigate challenges and stay motivated.

Accountability: Mentors help mentees stay accountable to their goals and commitments, ensuring they stay on track.

Networking: They often introduce mentees to valuable professional networks, opening doors to new opportunities.

Overall, mentors play a pivotal role in shaping the career paths of their mentees, fostering both professional and personal growth.

Motivation

Motivation Skills in the Corporate Environment

Individual Motivation: Motivation at the individual level is crucial for personal growth and productivity. In a corporate setting, an individual must cultivate self-motivation to achieve personal and professional goals. This involves setting clear, achievable objectives, maintaining a positive mindset, and seeking continuous improvement. Techniques such as time management, self-reflection, and celebrating small victories can enhance motivation. Additionally, staying aligned with the company's vision and values can provide a sense of purpose and drive.

Team Member Motivation: As a team member, motivation extends beyond personal goals to include contributing to the team's success. Effective communication, collaboration, and a supportive attitude are key. Motivated team members actively participate in discussions, share ideas, and provide constructive feedback. They also recognize and appreciate the efforts of their colleagues, fostering a positive and cohesive team environment. Building strong relationships and trust within the team can significantly boost collective motivation and performance.

Leadership Motivation: Leaders play a pivotal role in motivating their teams. A motivated leader inspires and energizes their team through sharp vision, effective communication, and leading by example. They set realistic yet challenging goals, provide necessary resources, and offer regular feedback and recognition. Understanding individual team members' strengths and aspirations allows leaders to tailor their approach, ensuring each member feels valued and motivated. Additionally, fostering an inclusive and positive work culture where employees feel safe to express ideas and take risks is essential for sustained motivation.

Corporate Environment: In the corporate environment, motivation is influenced by organizational culture, policies, and practices. Companies can enhance motivation by creating a supportive and engaging workplace. This includes offering professional development opportunities, recognizing, and rewarding achievements, and promoting work-life balance. Transparent communication and involving employees in decision-making processes can also boost motivation. Furthermore, aligning individual and team goals with the company's mission and values ensures that everyone is working towards a common purpose, enhancing overall motivation and productivity.

Motivation is a multifaceted skill that plays a critical role at all levels within a corporate environment. Whether as an individual, team member, or leader, fostering motivation involves a combination of personal drive, supportive relationships, and a positive organizational culture. By understanding and implementing effective motivational strategies, individuals and organizations can achieve greater success and fulfillment.

How to stay motivated

Maintaining motivation can be challenging, but there are several practical strategies you can use to stay driven and focused:

1. **Set Clear Goals**
   - **Define Specific Objectives:** Break down larger goals into smaller, manageable tasks.
   - **Set Deadlines:** Establish timelines to create a sense of urgency and purpose.
2. **Create a Routine**
   - **Consistent Schedule:** Develop a daily routine that includes time for work, exercise, and relaxation.
   - **Prioritize Tasks:** Focus on high-priority tasks first to ensure important goals are met.
3. **Stay Organized**
   - **Use Tools:** Utilize planners, to-do lists, or digital apps to keep track of tasks and deadlines.
   - **Declutter:** Maintain a clean and organized workspace to reduce distractions.
4. **Seek Inspiration**
   - **Read and Learn:** Engage with motivational books, podcasts, or videos.
   - **Role Models:** Look up to individuals who inspire you and learn from their experiences.
5. **Reward Yourself**
   - **Celebrate Milestones:** Acknowledge and reward yourself for achieving small goals.
   - **Take Breaks:** Allow yourself time to rest and recharge to avoid burnout.

6. **Stay Positive**
   - **Positive Affirmations:** Use affirmations to boost your confidence and outlook.
   - **Surround Yourself with Positivity:** Engage with positive people and environments.
7. **Stay Healthy**
   - **Exercise Regularly:** Physical activity can boost your mood and energy levels.
   - **Eat Well:** Maintain a balanced diet to keep your body and mind in optimal condition.
8. **Seek Support**
   - **Connect with Others:** Share your goals and progress with friends, family, or colleagues.
   - **Join Groups:** Participate in communities or groups with similar interests for mutual support.
9. **Reflect and Adjust**
   - **Self-Reflection:** Regularly assess your progress and make adjustments as needed.
   - **Learn from Setbacks:** View challenges as opportunities to learn and grow.
10. **Stay Flexible**
    - **Adapt to Change:** Be open to changing your plans if necessary and stay resilient in the face of obstacles.

Implementing these tips can help you maintain motivation and achieve your goals more effectively.

> **For your information**
>
> **Ganbatte**
>
> **Ganbatte** is a widely used Japanese phrase that translates to "DO YOUR BEST" or "HANG IN THERE".
>
> It is often used to encourage someone to persevere and give their best, in all situations, whether tackling a difficult task, preparing for an examination, or pursuing a goal.
>
> The essence of 'Ganbatte' lies in its emphasis on determination, resilience, and the unwavering spirit to overcome challenges.
>
> For individuals, adopting the 'Ganbatte' mindset can be incredibly beneficial. It serves as a powerful motivator, fostering a positive attitude and encouraging people to stay focused and committed to their objectives.
>
> By embracing this mindset, individuals can build resilience, enhance their problem-solving skills, and improve the overall performance.
>
> This approach not only aids in achieving personal success but also contributes to personal growth and development.
>
> Moreover, the 'Ganbatte' spirit can create a supportive environment where people encourage each other to strive for their best. This collective encouragement can lead to more positive and productive community, whether in a workplace, school, or any other setup.

Fall seven times, stand up eight - Resilience and perseverance.

The nail that sticks out is struck. Be creative and encourage teamwork

A frog in the well does not know the ocean

CHAPTER 10

NEGOTIATION SKILLS

Like it or not, everybody is a negotiator. Negotiation happens at work as well as every path of your life.

Getting familiar with negotiation techniques will enable you to develop, maintain, and improve important relationships and make you more efficient.

Instead of spending hours arguing and fighting with people and trying to force them to do what you want, you can reach agreements, find solutions to tough problems, and keep work moving ahead more friendly and with less effort if you negotiate effectively.

In addition, being a good negotiator helps you achieve important objectives and achieve what you need for yourself, your department, society, and the organization.

Effective negotiation is a valuable skill. It can help you to achieve what you want in your career and in your personal life too. Negotiation is all about being able to settle differences and reach an agreement through consensus, without arguments or conflict. You could be negotiating a new salary, a deal on a new car, or even which restaurant you and your partner eat at tonight.

Effective negotiation leads to a situation where all parties arrive at a compromise and are satisfied with the outcome. A true *Successful negotiation*, however, is when you get where you want by convincing others to your point of view.

Few Tips on Negotiation

Negotiation is something fluid and unpredictable – you need to be ready to adapt, improvise, react, and think creatively. You cannot always be prepared for what the other parties might say or do, or what their agenda might be.

For this reason, your strategy for negotiation should read more like a map than a linear list. It should have lots of different possible routes and a few different acceptable outcomes.

Before any negotiation, you should have an ultimate goal in mind (your stretch goal), plus a few minimum acceptable outcomes (baselines), pinpointed on your map. This way if you cannot reach your stretch goal, you have got somewhere to fall back to.

As well as comparing a negotiation strategy to a map, Wheeler also uses the analogy of a recipe, saying that you would not make a recipe without preparing the ingredients - so you should not enter a negotiation without preparing.

It is also recommended that you should be flexible enough to be ready to produce a Plan B that you have not prepared. That way if something comes up that you did not expect, you can be ready and willing to take an option you had not considered before.

It is important to not react emotionally during a negotiation - you cannot control a situation completely, but you can control how you react. You should be calm, alert, patient, proactive, practical, and creative. Wheeler recommends identifying the situations beforehand that make you react emotionally, and either avoid them or prepare responses in advance.

Pay attention to what the person you are negotiating with is saying, as well as their body language and tone. It is vital that you understand exactly what the other person wants and can pick up on their anxieties and things they want to avoid.

The Golden Rule of negotiation is 'Never say no unless you really have to' – try to work with whatever is on offer. As soon as you say no, the negotiating comes to an end, even if an agreement has not been reached, which is not the end goal.

First impressions are so important when negotiating – you are weighing each other up and establishing the atmosphere in which the negotiation is going to take place. Instead of going in guns blazing, saying "I want," say "How can we solve this problem together?"

When you are negotiating, emphasize what the person might lose, rather than what they can gain - this motivates people more.

Keep it simple and do not confuse or frustrate the other person with too much choice.

Finally, just like chess, negotiating gets better with experience. As you get better at reading other people and moving tactically, the more skilled you will become at moving across the board.

(Source: The Art of negotiation, Micheal wheeler)

Negotiation Strategies

Negotiation can take a wide variety of forms, from a trained negotiator acting on behalf of a particular organization or position in a formal setting, to an informal negotiation between friends.

Negotiation can be contrasted with mediation, where a neutral third party listens to each side's arguments and attempts to help craft an agreement between the parties. It can also be compared with arbitration, which resembles a legal proceeding.

In arbitration, both sides make an argument as to the merits of their case and the arbitrator decides the outcome. This negotiation is also sometimes called positional or hard-bargaining negotiation.

There are two relatively distinct types of negotiation. They are known as distributive negotiations and integrative negotiations.

Different negotiation theorists may use different labels for the two general types and distinguish them in different ways.

Distributive Negotiation

Distributive negotiation is also sometimes called positional or hard-bargaining negotiation. It tends to approach negotiation on the model of haggling in a market. In a distributive negotiation, each side often adopts an extreme position, knowing that it will not be accepted, and then employs a combination of guile, bluffing, and brinkmanship in order to cede as little as possible before reaching a deal. Distributive bargainers conceive of negotiation as a process of distributing a fixed amount of value.

The term distributive implies that there is a finite amount of the thing being distributed or divided among the people involved. Sometimes this type of negotiation is referred to as the distribution of a "fixed pie." There is only so much to go around, but the proportion to be distributed is variable.

Distributive negotiation is also sometimes called win-lose because of the assumption that one person's gain results in another person's loss. A distributive negotiation often involves people who have never had a previous interactive relationship, nor are they likely to do so again in the near future. Simple everyday examples would be buying a car or a house.

Integrative Negotiation

Integrative negotiation is also sometimes called interest-based or principled negotiation. It is a set of techniques that attempts to improve the quality and likelihood of a negotiated agreement by providing an alternative to traditional distributive negotiation techniques.

While distributive negotiation assumes there is a fixed amount of value (a "fixed pie") to be divided between the parties, integrative negotiation often attempts to create value in the course of the negotiation ("expand the pie"). It focuses on the underlying interests of the parties rather than their arbitrary starting positions, approaches negotiation as a shared problem rather than a personalized battle, and insists upon adherence to objective, principled criteria as the basis for agreement.

Integrative negotiation often involves a higher degree of trust and the forming of a relationship. It can also involve creative problem-solving that aims to achieve mutual gains. It is also sometimes called win-win negotiation.

Positions vs Interests

A position is what you say you want or must have. Positional bargaining is usually distributive - and may be inefficient in the sense that value may be left on the table at the time of settlement because each party did not know what the other really wanted - but it may help one party gain more short-term profit. An interest is both an objective or need and reasons why you want what you want. Interest-based bargaining add integrative potential.

In a negotiation, it is important to be able to distinguish between positions and interests – both yours and the parties with whom you are negotiating. Depending on which one you decide to focus on will affect your negotiation style and influence the outcomes. It is always good to ask yourself why you want what you want. This will help you get a better understanding of what your real goals are and could open, better deals for you.

Strategy Vs Tactics

The distinction between strategy and tactics:

Strategy:

Definition: A strategy is a **long-term plan** that outlines an organization's overarching goals and how it plans to achieve them.

Focus: It provides the **big picture** and guides decision-making at an elevated level.

Purpose: A solid strategy reflects the core values of the organization and sets the direction for all activities.

Example: If a furniture company aims to expand market share, its strategy might include offering competitive prices and maintaining stock availability.

Tactics:

Definition: Tactics are the **specific actions** taken to achieve strategic goals.

Focus: They are more **concrete** and oriented toward shorter time frames.

Purpose: Tactics have a finite timeline and measurable impacts.

Example: Analyzing manufacturing processes to minimize waste and inefficiencies (thus reducing costs) could be a tactic for the furniture company.

In summary, strategy provides the path toward achieving an organization's mission, while tactics are the practical steps taken along that path.

Negotiation Tactics

Tactics play a crucial role in any negotiation process. Various tactics may be encountered or employed during negotiations, ranging from fair to unfair, depending on the participants' styles and the significance of the outcomes. Often, these tactics are subtle and difficult to identify.

Below are some commonly used tactics:

Auction

An auction is a typical example of open negotiation where prices are negotiated between parties. Sellers and buyers gather in one place and bid for each item, with the highest bid winning. Some sellers may manipulate prices unfairly, so buyers must be vigilant to secure the best deal.

Brinkmanship

Brinkmanship is a one-sided negotiation tactic where one party sets the terms, forcing the other party to either accept or walk away. This hard bargaining approach pushes the other party to the brink, often used when the seller knows the buyer has no alternatives.

Bogey

The bogey tactic involves exaggerating a minor issue to make it seem significant, then trading it as a concession to win the negotiation.

Barter

Barter involves exchanging goods or services between a seller and a buyer without any cash transaction. While effective in some cases, it is less common today.

Bundle

Bundling is a successful negotiation tactic where additional items or services are offered along with the main item to attract the other party. For example, a builder might offer free maintenance or furnishings when selling an apartment. This tactic often results in a win-win situation.

Deadlines

Setting deadlines is a pressure tactic that forces the other party to make a decision within a specified timeframe. This is common during limited-period discounts, where the seller pressures the buyer to accept the offer quickly.

Do Not Make the First Offer

In negotiations, it is often advisable not to make the first offer. Let the other party present their proposal first, then begin the negotiation. This approach can prevent overbidding and ensure a more favorable outcome.

Good Cop/Bad Cop, Leaking Information, and Bad Faith Negotiation

These tactics are often used in political negotiations, such as alliances or seat-sharing during elections.

Good Cop/Bad Cop: One negotiator is aggressive (bad cop), while the other is reasonable (good cop).

Leaking Information: The weaker party may leak information about better offers from other parties to secure a better deal.

Bad Faith Negotiation: Negotiations conducted without genuine intent, where neither party trusts the other, often resulting in wasted time.

Use Silence When Necessary

Avoid quickly accepting offers during the initial stages of negotiation. Use silence or suspend the negotiation to gain time and put pressure on the other party.

The Nibble

Towards the end of the negotiation process, a small additional benefit (e.g., a 1% discount) is offered to finalize the deal.

Keep It Light

Maintain a neutral facial expression during negotiations to avoid revealing your inner thoughts. A calm and friendly demeanor can keep the negotiation process positive.

If I Do This, Will You Do That

This tactic involves one party offering something and expecting the other party to reciprocate. It is commonly used in negotiations.

Limiting Your Authority Technique

Stating that you need to consult with a higher authority before making a decision is a common tactic to gain time during negotiations.

Be Willing to Walk Away

Be prepared to walk away if the negotiation is not favorable. Having alternatives is essential, especially when purchasing items like automobiles, mobile phones, and appliances.

Splitting the Difference

This tactic involves both parties agreeing to meet halfway, resulting in a win-win situation.

Negotiation Styles

Complex and strategic negotiations involve many conflicting interests. A simple, but typical, example is the buyer wants to buy at the lowest possible price and the supplier wants to sell at the highest possible price.

How we manage such negotiation conflicts determines the outcome of our negotiation. According to Thomas-Kilmann Conflict Mode Instrument, conflict resolution can be viewed along two dimensions:

1. Assertiveness, i.e., the extent to which we attempt to satisfy our own concerns; and
2. Cooperativeness, i.e., the extent to which we attempt to satisfy the other party's concerns.

The figure below illustrates five commonly referenced conflict resolution, or negotiation styles, within this framework:

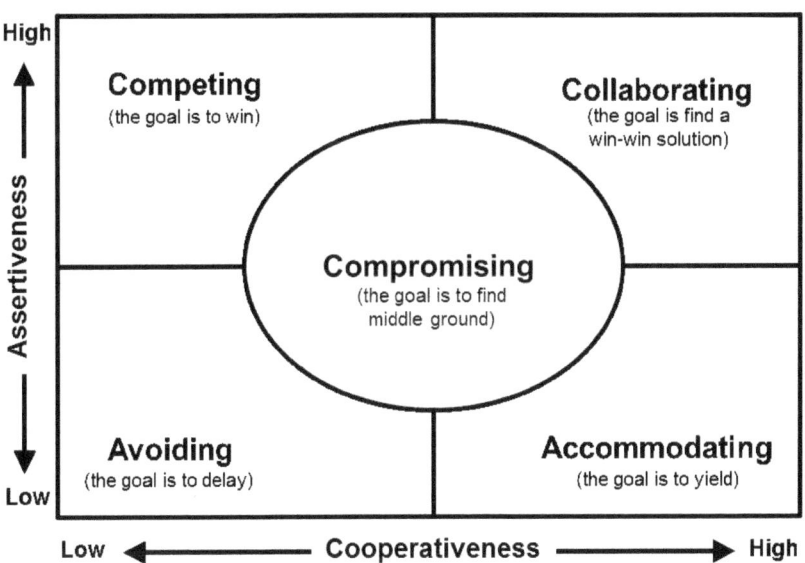

Negotiation styles vary from one individual to another, their background, beliefs, and skills, as well as the general context in which they occur. The following five unique styles are considered from different viewpoints.

Competing (I win – You lose)

Competing is assertive and uncooperative, a power-oriented mode. This style of negotiation is best described as competitive and is one of the most widely used styles in negotiating. Negotiators using this style are looking out for their own needs, asking themselves 'What do I need to get from this discussion / process?'

Competitive negotiators have strong instincts for all aspects of negotiating and are often strategic. They use a variety of tactics to get what they want. Because their style can dominate the bargaining process, competitive negotiators often neglect the importance of relationships.

Competing style is appropriate if your power balance is high, you have a good Plan B and you think he needs you more than you need him. This style is most effective when results are needed quickly, or you are certain there is no room for negotiation. Good examples of this style are buying a new car or a lawyer representing their client or commodity-based selling.

Accommodating (I Lose – You Win)

This style of negotiation is all about the relationship and is the polar opposite of the Competing style. Accommodating negotiators believe that the only way to ultimately get what they want is to satisfy all the demands of the other party, hoping maybe in time the other party will do the same.

Accommodators are sensitive to the emotional states, body language, and verbal signals of the other parties. They can, however, feel taken advantage of in situations when the other party places little emphasis on the relationship. This style, is naturally, well-liked by the opposite party.

Examples of this style are when a person injures another person and willingly offers to pay all medical expenses hoping the injured party does not sue.

Avoiding (I Lose – You Lose)

Individuals who do not like or do not wish to negotiate often resort to this style. They do not negotiate unless warranted. When negotiating, avoiders tend to defer and dodge the confrontational aspects of negotiating; however, they may be perceived as tactful and diplomatic. Avoiding is the strongest position of all—the other side has to make concessions just to get the process started.

An example of this style is two co-workers who cannot agree on the delivery of a project and avoid communicating with each other but happily talk to other co-workers about it!

In some cases, users of this style are unassertive and uncooperative because of their personality. They do not immediately pursue their own concerns or the other parties nor do they ever address the conflict. This style could be a vengeful style and while the adopters of this style will not address the conflict, they will seek ways of retribution. When this occurs, the avoiding style can be difficult to spot as it can go undercover for a time; it escalates to a 'passive-aggressive style.'

This style is usually in response to a highly competitive style. The avoider will shut down communication and contact and will seemingly disappear off the radar. While this is in play, mutual resentment builds and cracks to total breakdown of the relationship may occur, leading to a lose-lose scenario.

Compromising (I Lose / Win Some – You Lose/ Win Some)

The old adage 'pick your battles' applies here. This style values the relationship and acknowledges that there is a loss, but it is better to compromise than completely lose. A compromising style results in both parties getting more or less half of what they originally wanted.

This style is common when the negotiating parties have an elevated level of trust between each other and are time poor.

Compromisers are individuals who are eager to close the deal by doing what is fair and equal for all parties involved in the negotiation. They can be useful when there is limited time to complete the deal; however, compromisers often unnecessarily rush the negotiation process and make concessions too quickly. This style should not be confused with Collaborating (I win – You win).

Collaborating (I Win – You Win)

Collaborative negotiators are innovators! They recognize that both parties have needs that must be met and take the time to find creative solutions to this common conundrum. Collaborators are good at using negotiations to understand the concerns and interests of the other parties. In business, this style of negotiating is often seen as the "Holy Grail."

Collaboration is great when both parties have the power to implement a truly Win-Win business plan. When both sides are strong and both want the deal, then collaboration is possible. Most business-to-business negotiators plan for this type of negotiation. Some organizations are well known for their collaborative style of negotiating. A good example of this style is Toyota Motor Company which is known for being completely focused on a collaborative approach to collaborating with their suppliers resulting in greater commitment and cooperation and well-built cars!

It needs to be recognized that this style of negotiating is somewhat wonderful ideologically and is the most challenging to effect because in reality, it is high on resources and time. It can, in some instances, create problems by transforming simple situations into more complex ones.

The above negotiation styles are also referred to as conflict-handling modes. All five styles are useful in different situations.

Each of us is capable of using all five negotiation styles. None of us can be characterized as having a single style of dealing with conflict. But certain people use some styles better than others and, therefore, tend to rely on those styles more heavily than others—whether because of our temperament (nature) or because of our upbringing (nurture).

So, if you ever wonder "Which is the best negotiation style?" the answer is "It depends." Your negotiation style will be the product of both your personal predispositions and the requirements of the situation in which you find yourself.

Most people choose the style that is likely to reward them with either the quickest conflict resolution or the biggest profit prize.

Types of Negotiators

Three basic kinds of negotiators have been identified by researchers involved in The Harvard Negotiation Project. These types of negotiators are: soft bargainers, hard bargainers, and principled bargainers.

Soft Bargainers

These people see negotiation as too close to competition, so they choose a gentle style of bargaining. The offers they make are not in their best interests, they yield to others' demands, avoid confrontation, and maintain good relations with fellow negotiators. Their perception of others is one of friendship, and their goal is agreement. They do not separate the people from the problem but are soft on both. They avoid contests of wills and will insist on agreement, offering solutions, easily trusting others and changing their opinions.

Hard Bargainers

These people use contentious strategies to influence, utilizing phrases such as "this is my final offer" and "take it or leave it." They make threats, are distrustful of others, insist on their position, and apply pressure to negotiate. They see others as adversaries and their ultimate goal is victory.

Additionally, they will search for one single answer and insist you agree on it. They do not separate the people from the problem (as with soft bargainers), but they are hard on both the people involved and the problem.

Principled Bargainers

Individuals who bargain this way seek integrative solutions and do so by sidestepping commitment to specific positions. They focus on the problem rather than the intentions, motives, and needs of the people involved. They separate the people from the problem, explore interests, avoid bottom lines, and reach results based on standards (which are independent of personal will). They base their choices on objective criteria rather than power, pressure, self-interest, or an arbitrary decisional procedure. These criteria may be drawn from moral standards, principles of fairness, professional standards, tradition, and so on.

Trade-off

Balancing of Factors:

It involves finding a balance between two desirable but incompatible features or goals that cannot both be achieved simultaneously.

Exchange or Compromise:

It is also a situation where achieving something you want requires giving up something else, which is also desirable but less so.

For instance, in a democracy, there is a trade-off between individual liberty and maintaining an orderly society.

Common mistakes during negotiation

Here are **common negotiation mistakes** to avoid:

Insufficient Preparation:

Solution: Thoroughly research and plan before negotiating. Understand your objectives, the other party's interests, and your BATNA (Best Alternative to a Negotiated Agreement).

Focusing on Positions Instead of Interests:

Solution: Dig deeper to understand the underlying motivations behind the other party's demands. Focus on mutual interests for better outcomes.

Letting Emotions Impact Your Judgment:

Solution: Keep emotions in check. Stress and anxiety can hinder effective communication and escalate tensions. Channel negative feelings to your advantage.

Not Having the Right People in the Room:

Solution: Ensure relevant stakeholders are present during negotiations. Missing key decision-makers can lead to suboptimal outcomes.

Assuming Win-Lose Is the Only Option:

Solution: Seek win-win outcomes whenever possible. Collaborate rather than compete, fostering better relationships.

Succumbing to Pressure Tactics:

Solution: Be aware of manipulative tactics. Stay focused on your goals and avoid making hasty decisions under pressure.

Not Understanding or Preparing for Cross-cultural Negotiation:

Solution: Cultural differences impact negotiation styles. Learn about cultural norms and adapt your approach accordingly.

Poor Ethics in Negotiation:

Solution: Maintain ethical behavior. Trust and integrity are crucial for successful negotiations.

Remember, effective negotiation involves both strategy and avoiding these pitfalls!

Negotiation techniques

Here are some effective negotiation techniques to achieve better outcomes:

Begin With Open-Ended Questions:

Start by asking open-ended questions to understand the concerns and commitments of the other party. Actively listen and use their words to demonstrate understanding.

Know What You Want to Achieve:

Define your goals in advance and find ways to achieve them without compromising the other side. Look for mutually acceptable solutions that benefit both parties.

Do not Settle for Less Than Your Primary Goal:

Be clear about your primary goal and key performance indicators. Be willing to walk away if your objectives are not met, but also seek compromise where possible.

Previsualize the Negotiation:

Envision the negotiation, considering priorities for all involved. Avoid assumptions and clarify needs through win-win practices.

Understand Their Real Motivators:

Respect the other party's interests and find ways to meet them. Curiosity and humility are essential. Uncover their real desires and motivators.

Remember, effective negotiation involves a mix of strategy, empathy, and clear communication!

How to manage a difficult negotiator

Dealing with a difficult negotiator can be challenging, but there are effective strategies you can employ:

Stay Calm: Keep your emotions in check. Difficult behavior can be unsettling, but maintaining composure helps you think clearly and respond effectively.

Be Prepared: Thoroughly understand your goals, interests, and potential trade-offs. Anticipate their tactics and have a well-prepared strategy.

Focus on Solutions: Shift the conversation from positions to interests. Seek mutually beneficial solutions rather than getting stuck in a win-lose mindset.

Acknowledge Disagreements: When faced with adversarial behavior, take a deep breath, and acknowledge the disagreement. Avoid escalating tensions.

Transfer the Focus: Redirect the conversation to productive topics. Clarify concerns and steer away from unproductive behavior.

Remember, effective negotiation involves adaptability and maintaining a constructive approach even with challenging counterparts!

How to be a good negotiator

Becoming a skilled negotiator involves developing several essential **skills**. Here are some key ones:

Communication: Clearly express your goals and boundaries. Actively listen to others' ideas and needs to find common ground.

Emotional Intelligence: Understand and manage emotions. Use positive feelings to build trust and channel anxiety into excitement. Read others' emotions effectively.

Preparation: Research, practice, and know what you want to achieve. Be ready for different scenarios.

Problem-Solving: Think creatively to find win-win solutions. Enlarge the pie by creating value for all parties.

Timing: Choose the right moment for negotiations. Timing matters.

Approach: Treat negotiation as a conversation. Engage in civil discussion and seek mutually beneficial outcomes.

Remember, practice and experience play a crucial role in honing these skills!

For your information
25 Golden rules at office

DRESS CODE:

Keep your shirt tucked in unless it is a casual day … then let loose.

Fresh clothes only, no repeats without a wash.

Go easy on the makeup. Less is more.! 👍

Shine those shoes and belts, they deserve it!

Wrinkle-free zone: iron those shirts and trousers.

Light on perfume or cologne

No caps or hats inside the office

Rock those prescription glasses with formal frame

Jewelry: Less is more 👍

Avoid smoking

PROFESSIONAL ETIQUETTE:

Business cards: offer with two hands and accept with two hands.

Keep religious symbols personal… not for display

Often use two wonderful words…Thank you and Sorry

Mind your voice at office

Keep smiling 😊

For your information

25 Golden rules at office

OFFICE CONDUCT:

Silent or vibrate mode for mobile phones.

Personal call… step away from the desk and attend

Avoid discussing personal issues at office.

Rest room chats… avoid

Follow the pantry rules and do not linger too long.

Dry lunch at work desk

Carry a proper office bad 👋

TECHNOLOGY USE:

Office computers are for work. Not for personal or social media.

Keep personal data off, the office computers.

Passwords are private… do not share with anyone. 👍

CHAPTER 11

PUBLIC SPEAKING SKILLS

My first public speaking experience

During my initial speech before a large audience, primarily composed of my colleagues, I was tasked with presenting on a specific topic.

Feeling apprehensive, I sought counsel from my supervisor, Mr. X.

He offered me a single piece of advice: (in a lighter vein)

"Sathya, simply imagine that everyone in the audience is an idiot and speak."

When my turn arrived, I approached the podium with a dry throat and a sense of nervousness. I took a sip of water and glanced at the audience. Mr. X was seated in the front row, smiling.

I began with a slight stumble, but soon my speech flowed seamlessly. Throughout the presentation, I avoided looking at Mr. X.

Upon concluding my speech and returning to my seat, Mr. X called me over and said, "Not bad."

Since that day, I have adhered to his advice diligently, whether in the office, at public meetings, or in academic settings.

Ice Breaker

Icebreakers are important before starting any communication process, particularly during public speaking.

What is an 'ice breaker'?

An icebreaker in the context of communication and public speaking is an activity or prompt used at the beginning of a presentation or meeting to engage the audience, break down barriers, and create a relaxed atmosphere.

Here are a few examples:

Personal Anecdote: Share a short, relatable story about yourself. This helps to humanize you and make the audience feel more connected.

Raise-Your-Hand Questions: Ask the audience simple questions that require a show of hands. This encourages participation and gets people involved right away.

Humor: Start with a light, self-deprecating joke. This can help to ease tension and make the audience more receptive.

Interactive Polls: Use tools like Mentimeter to conduct live polls. This can be a fun way to gather opinions and get everyone engaged.

Fun Facts: Share an interesting or surprising fact related to your topic. This can pique curiosity and set the stage for your presentation.

Icebreakers are effective because they help to create a positive and engaging atmosphere, making the audience more likely to listen and participate.

Few inspiring speakers

Abraham Lincoln

One of the most famous examples of Abraham Lincoln's effective communication is his Gettysburg Address, delivered on November 19, 1863, during the American Civil War. This speech is renowned for its brevity, clarity, and profound impact.

In just 272 words, Lincoln honored the fallen soldiers and redefined the purpose of the war. He began with the now-iconic phrase, "Four score and seven years ago," referencing the founding of the United States and emphasizing the nation's commitment to equality.

He continued by stating that the Civil War was a test of whether a nation "conceived in Liberty, and dedicated to the proposition that all men are created equal" could endure.

Lincoln's speech was powerful because it was concise and focused. He used simple yet profound language to convey his message, ensuring it was accessible to all listeners. He concluded with a call to action, urging the living to dedicate themselves to the unfinished work of those who fought and to ensure that "government of the people, by the people, for the people, shall not perish from the earth".

This address exemplifies Lincoln's ability to communicate complex ideas succinctly and movingly, leaving a lasting impression on his audience and shaping the nation's history.

Mark Antony

One of the most famous examples of effective communication is Mark Antony's speech after Julius Caesar's assassination, as depicted in William Shakespeare's play "Julius Caesar." This speech is a masterclass in rhetoric and persuasion.

Mark Antony begins with the iconic line, "Friends, Romans, countrymen, lend me your ears; I come to bury Caesar, not to praise him". He uses this opening to gain the crowd's attention and establish a connection. Throughout the speech, Antony employs irony and repetition, particularly with the phrase "Brutus is an honorable man," to subtly undermine the conspirators who killed Caesar.

He skillfully appeals to the emotions of the crowd by presenting Caesar's will, which generously bequeaths money and land to the citizens of Rome. Antony also vividly describes Caesar's wounds and the betrayal by Brutus, stirring the crowd's anger and turning them against the conspirators.

This speech demonstrates how effective communication can influence and mobilize an audience, using a combination of emotional appeal, strategic repetition, and rhetorical questions.

Swami Vivekananda

Swami Vivekananda's speech at the Parliament of the World's Religions in Chicago on September 11, 1893, is a remarkable example of effective communication and has left a lasting impact on the world.

When Swami Vivekananda addressed the audience, he began with the words, "Sisters and Brothers of America," which immediately drew a standing ovation from the crowd. This simple yet powerful opening established a sense of unity and brotherhood among the diverse audience.

In his speech, Vivekananda introduced Hinduism to the Western world, emphasizing its principles of tolerance and universal acceptance. He spoke about the ancient and inclusive nature of Hinduism, which respects all paths to God. He highlighted the importance of harmony and the need to end sectarianism and fanaticism.

One of the most memorable parts of his speech was when he quoted a hymn from the Rigveda: "As the different streams having their sources in different places all mingle their water in the sea, so, O Lord, the different paths which men take through different tendencies, various though they appear, crooked or straight, all lead to Thee". This beautifully illustrated the idea that all religions ultimately lead to the same truth.

Swami Vivekananda's eloquence, sincerity, and profound message resonated deeply with the audience, earning him widespread admiration and respect. His speech not only introduced Hinduism to the West but also promoted the values of religious tolerance and universal brotherhood.

Sadhguru Jaggi Vasudev

Sadhguru Jaggi Vasudev is renowned for his captivating oratory skills, which blend profound wisdom with humor and relatable anecdotes.

One notable example is his TED Talk in 2009, where he shared his journey from skepticism to enlightenment.

In this talk, Sadhguru described a pivotal moment in his life when he experienced a deep sense of inclusiveness with the universe while sitting on a rock. His storytelling was vivid and engaging, making the audience feel as if they were part of his journey. He used simple yet powerful language to convey complex spiritual concepts, making them accessible to everyone.

One more example is his response to a question about managing challenging times in life. Sadhguru explained that most people suffer from their own psychological conditions and emphasized the importance of managing one's thoughts and emotions. He illustrated his point with a humorous story, making the audience laugh while also delivering a profound message.

These examples highlight how Sadhguru's oratory skills lie in his ability to connect with his audience, use humor effectively, and simplify complex ideas into relatable stories.

Presentation skills

One of the most important skills one needs to develop is presentation skills.

Communication skills and public speaking skills are two important skills which will enhance the presentation skills.

Those days we used to present using OHP (Overhead projector) and later slide projector. (2K kids may not have seen these)

1980s and 1990s – OHP and Slide projector

Even though there are many software tools now available in the market for delivering a presentation, PowerPoint is still widely used.

(I tried once through the software "Prezi" and struggled. So, the moral of the story is that learn and understand the software tool, well, before presenting.)

Presentation skills are essential for effectively conveying information, engaging your audience, and leaving a lasting impression. Whether you are a business professional, educator, or student, mastering these skills can significantly enhance your presentations. Here are some key aspects to consider:

Understanding Slide Layouts and Themes

Familiarize yourself with different slide layouts and themes in PowerPoint. Choose layouts that suit your content and maintain consistency throughout your presentation.

Advanced PowerPoint Features:

Beyond the basics, explore advanced features like custom animations, slide transitions, and master slides. These allow you to create visually appealing and dynamic presentations.

Using Multimedia:

Incorporate images, videos, and audio to enhance your message. Visuals can reinforce key points and keep your audience engaged.

Data Visualization Techniques:

Learn how to create effective charts, graphs, and infographics. Clear data visualization helps convey complex information concisely.

Slide Timing and Pacing:

Practice delivering your presentation within a specific time frame. Adjust slide timing to maintain a steady pace and avoid rushing.

Collaboration and Sharing:

Utilize collaboration features to work on presentations with others. Share your slides easily for feedback or remote presentations.

Remember, confident body language and connecting with your audience are equally crucial.

Effective PowerPoint presentation

Let us dive into the specifics of creating an effective PowerPoint presentation:

Slide Design and Layout

Consistency: Maintain a consistent design throughout your slides. Use the same font, colors, and alignment.

Minimalism: Avoid clutter. Limit text per slide and use bullet points or visuals.

Font Size: Ensure readability by using a font size of at least 24 points.

Background: Choose a simple background that does not distract from your content.

Number of Slides:

There is no fixed rule, but consider:

Introduction: 1-2 slides

Content: one slide per main point

Conclusion: one slide summarizing key takeaways

Extras: Slides for visuals, data, or examples

Content on Slides:

Headings: Use clear, concise headings.

Bullet Points: Keep them short (3-5 points per slide).

Images: Use relevant images to illustrate concepts.

Charts/Graphs: Visualize data effectively.

Writing Notes:

Speaker Notes: Add notes for each slide. These help you remember key points.

Practice: Rehearse with your notes to ensure smooth delivery.

Delivery Tips:

Eye Contact: Look at your audience, not just the screen.

Voice: Vary your tone and pace.

Body Language: Stand straight, use gestures, and avoid fidgeting.

Remember, *practice makes things, perfect*!

Here is a concise table summarizing the dos and don'ts for corporate PowerPoint presentations:

Do	Do not
Know your audience and tailor your content.	Include excessive details.
Create interest with visuals and anecdotes.	Clutter slides with too much information.
Use high-quality images and charts.	Forget to proofread for errors.

Do	Do not
Infuse personality and humor.	Treat it as a throwaway presentation.
Keep simple colors	Just read what is written in the slide.
Proper body language	Add too many videos in the slide.
Ensure the environment is apt (like the Air conditioning, water availability, etc.)	Fumble during presentation.

Normal meetings at the office

Tips for conducting effective meetings and meeting etiquette:

- Prepare an agenda and circulate it well in advance to all the participants, so that they come prepared.
- Appoint a moderator for the meeting, and the moderator carries the meeting as per the agenda. Allow every participant to express their points during the meeting.
- Ideally, 1 hour should be the time limit for any meeting.
- Avoid serving coffee or tea snacks during the meeting which districts the group.
- Do not use a laptop during meetings, give attention only to the meeting.
- One can relieve the participant, once their portion of work is complete so that they can continue with their routine work.
- It is a good practice to have one day of the week as meeting meeting-free day.
- Avoid planning meetings in the morning session (forenoon), because the employee will be at his peak of energy, in the morning. Plan meetings during the second half.

- Do not deviate from the agenda as it will dilute the purpose of the meeting.
- Ask someone to note down the minutes of the meeting.
- The minutes of the meeting should mention the action date and the person to whom the action is assigned.
- Request all participants to keep the mobile in silent mode.
- It is a good practice to start the meeting with a value moment or a safety moment.
- Do not get into arguments or debates during the meeting and ensure it is constructive.
- Avoid long PPT presentations during the meeting unless otherwise it is required.
- Introduce the participants if they are new to the organization.
- Avoid business lunch during meetings and utilize lunch time, for interacting with the participants and developing rapport.
- Ensure sufficient lighting, air conditioning, and water are available during the meeting.
- For multi-center meetings work out a convenient time zone so that the participants are comfortable.
- The dress code during the meeting is particularly important in particular when clients or vendors are participating in the meeting.
- Finally, avoid planning too many meetings in a day and avoid planning meetings on Friday afternoon. Declare any one day in a week as a meeting-free day.

Voice modulation

To enhance tone modulation, consider practicing exercises such as counting numbers with varying volumes, humming to develop resonance, articulating the "huh" sound to control pitch, and engaging in breathing exercises for better vocal control. Additionally, vocal scales, lip trills, and tongue twisters can improve diction and clarity, which are crucial for articulate voice modulation.

Some exercises for voice modulation

'Voice modulation' is the process of changing the tone and pitch of your voice to convey the desired emotion or emphasis. It is a powerful tool for effective communication, whether you are giving a speech, singing, or engaging in everyday conversations.

Let us dive into some exercises and examples to enhance your voice modulation:

Breath Relaxation:

This technique relieves tension in the breathing process, which can obstruct optimal voice production.

Exhale after taking a typical breath, ensuring that your shoulders and chest are relaxed.

Focus on centered abdominal breathing, avoiding tension in the chest, neck, or shoulders.

Try making a "hiss" sound during exhalation to engage your vocal folds.

Jaw Release:

Relieves stress in the mouth and jaw area.

Place your hands below your cheekbones and massage the facial muscles from cheekbones to the jaw.

Allow your jaw to open naturally as you glide your hands down your face.

Lip Trills:

Release lip tension and connect breathing and speaking.

Make a trill or raspberry sound by loosely placing your lips together and expelling air in a steady stream.

Practice with "h" sounds and then transition to "b" sounds.

Glide up and down scales while repeating the b-trill.

Tongue Trill:

Engages respiration and voice while relaxing the tongue.

Position your tongue behind your upper teeth.

Exhale and make an "r" sound with your tongue.

Keep the sound consistent and connected to your breath.

Pitch Practice:

Experiment with your voice by making it higher or lower while saying a sentence.

Observe how different feelings can be conveyed using pitch variations.

For example, try saying the same sentence with excitement (higher pitch) and sadness (lower pitch).

Tone Range:

Change your singing voice from low to high to find your vocal range.

Explore different tones within your natural range to express various emotions.

Character Voices:

Take a dialogue from your favorite tale or a movie and tell it using different voices for each character.

Play with intonations, pitch, and characteristics (e.g., high-pitched, rough, slow, fast).

Notice how these variations create mental images for the listener.

Remember, consistent practice and self-awareness are key to mastering voice modulation.

Whether you are a speaker, singer, or actor, these exercises can help you develop a more expressive and engaging voice!

"In the melodious world of Indian classical music, 'Shruti' and 'Laya' are like the rhythm and melody dancing together. Just as they harmonize to create beautiful compositions, a skilled orator knows that their tone and voice must walk in sync to captivate the audience.

For your information
How to prepare for an interview (Entry level)

Understand the Job Description: Read the job descriptions thoroughly to understand what the organization is looking for in a candidate. Make a list of skills, knowledge and professional and personal qualities required for the job and identify at least one example of how you can demonstrate each requirement.

Research the Organization: Understand the organization's mission, Vision, Values, culture, and recent developments. These information can be found on the company website or google.

Prepare for common interview questions: Some common interview questions include "Tell me about yourself" "Why do you want to work here" "Explain the challenges you faced in a project" etc. Practice your responses for these questions. Make your answers more concise, specific and to the point.

Prepare your own questions: Interview is a two way process. Prepare some thoughtful questions to understand the organization, whether it is a right fit for you, etc. You could ask about the project, growth opportunities, etc.

Dress professionally: First impression is the best impression. Try to wear formal and fully groomed. (This includes virtual interview too)

Plan your journey: Be on time to the interview. If it is out of your city, arrive one day early.

Follow up: After the interview, send a thank you email to express your appreciation for the opportunity. This can help your standout from other candidates.

CHAPTER 12

PERSONALITY DEVELOPMENT

There is a charming Tamil proverb, "Aaal Paathi… AAdai Paathi," which translates to "half man, half cloth." The gist is that people often judge you based on your attire.

Dressing well is key to making a great first impression. I believe that investing in quality clothing is a smart move.

One needs to develop certain etiquette to be successful in a career.

Basic etiquette

1. Dressing and personal grooming
2. Table manners
3. Body language
4. Email etiquette
5. Command over the language

1. Dressing and personal grooming

I will now elaborate on the importance of dressing, as it creates an immediate first impression.

It is essential to understand that appropriate attire varies based on location, climate, occasion, culture, and local traditions.

For instance, in colder regions such as some European countries, suits are commonly worn, whereas in tropical countries like India, they are less prevalent.

In this section, I will outline corporate attire without focusing on any specific country or region. Each nation has its unique traditional dress (for instance, sarees or salwar kameez in some Asian countries), and it is up to the individual to dress appropriately for the occasion.

In a corporate setting, it is crucial to adhere to the company's dress code policy. The dress code in IT-related industries tends to be casual, whereas traditional industries may have entirely different requirements.

Individuals working in customer relations, front office, and marketing roles need to pay extra attention to their attire compared to those in back-office positions.

We will delve into more details in the following pages.

Dressing can be divided into three main categories:
- Formal
- Business Casual
- Casual

Formal Dressing

Formal office dressing is essential for creating a professional and polished appearance. Here are some detailed guidelines for both men and women:

For Men

Suits: A well-tailored suit is a cornerstone of formal office attire. Opt for classic colors like navy, black, or gray. Ensure the suit fits well, with the jacket sleeves ending just above the wrist and the trousers breaking slightly over the shoes.

Dress Shirts: Choose crisp, clean dress shirts in white or light colors. Make sure the shirt is well-ironed and fits properly around the neck and shoulders.

Ties: Select ties that complement your suit and shirt. Solid colors or subtle patterns are usually best. Ensure the tie reaches the top of your belt buckle.

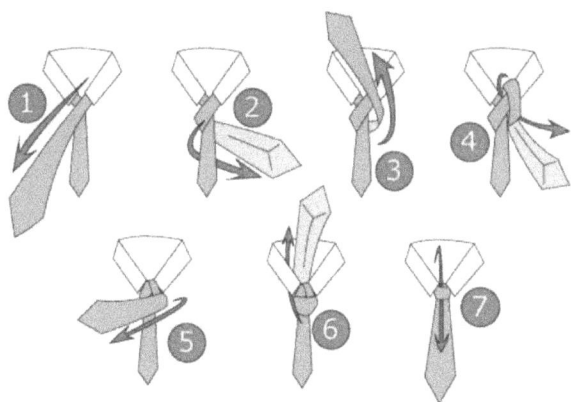

Shoes: Wear polished, closed-toe dress shoes in black or brown. Match your belt with your shoes for a cohesive look.

Accessories: Keep accessories minimal and tasteful. A classic watch and simple cufflinks can add a touch of elegance.

For Women

Suits and Dresses: Women can opt for tailored skirt suits, pantsuits, or conservative dresses. Stick to neutral colors like black, navy, or gray. Ensure the fit is comfortable and professional.

Blouses and Tops: Choose blouses or tops that are modest and well-fitted. Avoid overly bright colors or bold patterns. Light colors like white, cream, or pastels are often preferred.

Shoes: Closed-toe heels or flats are appropriate. Heels should be moderate in height, typically no more than three inches.

Accessories: Keep jewelry and accessories understated. Simple earrings, a watch, and a delicate necklace can enhance your look without being distracting.

Hosiery: Wearing pantyhose or tights is often recommended, especially in more conservative environments.

General Tips

Grooming: Personal grooming is crucial. Ensure your hair is neat and styled appropriately. Men should be clean-shaven or have well-groomed facial hair.

Cleanliness: Always wear clean, ironed clothes. Avoid strong perfumes or colognes, as they can be distracting.

Fit and Comfort: Ensure your clothes fit well and are comfortable. Ill-fitting clothes can be distracting and unprofessional.

Consistency: Adhere to your company's dress code consistently. Observe how colleagues and superiors dress and aim to match that level of formality.

By following these guidelines, you can present yourself professionally and confidently in any formal office setting.

Formal Dressing – Color combination

Here are some classic and professional color combinations for formal office attire:

For Men

Navy Suit with White Shirt and Red Tie

Navy Suit: A versatile and timeless choice.

White Shirt: Crisp and clean, providing a sharp contrast.

Red Tie: Adds a pop of color and conveys confidence.

Charcoal Grey Suit with Light Blue Shirt and Dark Blue Tie

Charcoal Grey Suit: Professional and sophisticated.

Light Blue Shirt: Softens the look and adds a touch of color.

Dark Blue Tie: Complements the shirt and maintains a cohesive look.

Black Suit with White Shirt and Black Tie

Black Suit: Classic and formal.

White Shirt: Timeless and versatile.

Black Tie: Keeps the look sleek and elegant.

Brown Suit with Cream Shirt and Burgundy Tie

Brown Suit: Warm and approachable.

Cream Shirt: Softens the overall look.

Burgundy Tie: Adds a rich, sophisticated touch.

For Women

Black Pantsuit with White Blouse and Black Heels

Black Pantsuit: Classic and powerful.

White Blouse: Clean and professional.

Black Heels: Completes the monochromatic look.

Navy Skirt Suit with Light Pink Blouse and Nude Heels

Navy Skirt Suit: Professional and versatile.

Light Pink Blouse: Adds a feminine touch.

Nude Heels: Neutral and elongates the legs.

Grey Dress with Black Blazer and Black Heels

Grey Dress: Neutral and professional.

Black Blazer: Adds structure and formality.

Black Heels: Keeps the look cohesive.

Dark Green Pantsuit with Cream Blouse and Brown Heels

Dark Green Pantsuit: Unique yet professional.

Cream Blouse: Softens the look.

Brown Heels: Complements the green and adds warmth.

General Tips

Neutral Colors: Stick to neutral colors like black, navy, grey, and brown for suits. These colors are versatile and convey true professionalism.

Accent Colors: Use ties, blouses, or accessories to add subtle pops of color. Stick to muted tones like burgundy, dark green, or light pink to maintain a courteous professional appearance.

Consistency: Ensure your accessories, such as belts and shoes, match your overall outfit. For example, black shoes with a black belt.

By following these color combinations, you can create a polished and professional look suitable for any formal office setting.

Business casual dressing

Business casual attire allows for a bit more flexibility and creativity with color combinations while still maintaining a professional appearance. Here are some great color combinations for both men and women:

For Men

White Shirt with Gray Pants

White Shirt: A classic and versatile choice.

Gray Pants: Neutral and professional, pairing well with almost any color.

Accessories: Consider adding a navy blazer or a patterned tie for a touch of style.

Light Blue Shirt with Khaki Chinos

Light Blue Shirt: Soft and approachable.

Khaki Chinos: Casual yet polished, perfect for a business casual look.

Accessories: Brown belt and shoes to complete the outfit.

Navy Sweater with White Shirt and Dark Jeans

Navy Sweater: Adds warmth and a touch of sophistication.

White Shirt: Keeps the look crisp and clean.

Dark Jeans: Maintain a professional appearance while being comfortable.

Patterned Shirt with Solid Pants

Patterned Shirt: Adds interest and personality.

Solid Pants: Balance the outfit with a neutral base.

Accessories: Simple watch and belt to keep the focus on the shirt.

For Women

Blouse with Pencil Skirt

Blouse: Choose a blouse in a soft color like light pink or blue.

Pencil Skirt: Neutral colors like black, navy, or gray work well.

Accessories: Simple jewelry and a pair of nude or black heels.

Sweater with Dress Pants

Sweater: opt for a fitted sweater in a color like burgundy or forest green.

Dress Pants: Neutral colors like black or gray to keep the look professional.

Accessories: A statement necklace or scarf can add a touch of personality.

Patterned Blouse with Solid Trousers

Patterned Blouse: Adds visual interest and can be paired with neutral trousers.

Solid Trousers: Black, navy, or gray trousers to balance the outfit.

Accessories: Minimal jewelry and a structured handbag.

Cardigan with Blouse and Skirt

Cardigan: A versatile layering piece in a neutral color.

Blouse: Soft colors or subtle patterns work well.

Skirt: A-line or pencil skirts in neutral colors.

Accessories: Simple earrings and a watch to complete the look.

General Tips

Neutral Base: Start with neutral colors like black, navy, gray, or beige for your main pieces. These colors are versatile and easy to mix and match.

Accent Colors: Add pops of color with accessories, such as ties, scarves, or jewelry. Stick to muted tones for a professional look.

Patterns: Incorporate subtle patterns like stripes, checks, or small prints to add interest without being overwhelming.

Consistency: Ensure your accessories, such as belts and shoes, match your overall outfit. For example, brown shoes with a brown belt.

By following these guidelines, you can create stylish and professional business casual outfits.

Casual dressing

Casual dressing is all about comfort and personal style while maintaining a neat and put-together appearance.

Some great combinations for both men and women:

For Men

T-Shirt and Jeans

T-Shirt: opt for a well-fitted t-shirt in a solid color or subtle pattern.

Jeans: Dark wash or classic blue jeans work well. Ensure they are clean and free of rips for a more polished look.

Shoes: Sneakers or loafers can complete this casual yet stylish outfit.

Polo Shirt and Chinos

Polo Shirt: A versatile piece that can be dressed up or down. Choose neutral colors like navy, white, or gray.

Chinos: Khaki or navy chinos are a great alternative to jeans and add a touch of sophistication.

Shoes: Boat shoes or casual loafers work well with this combination.

Button-Down Shirt and Shorts

Button-Down Shirt: A casual button-down in a light fabric like linen or cotton.

Shorts: Tailored shorts in neutral colors like beige or navy.

Shoes: Casual sneakers or sandals for a relaxed look.

Sweater and Jeans

Sweater: A lightweight sweater in a solid color or subtle pattern.

Jeans: Dark wash jeans for a more refined casual look.

Shoes: Casual boots or sneakers.

For Women

T-Shirt and Jeans

T-Shirt: A simple, well-fitted t-shirt in a solid color or with a minimal design.

Jeans: Skinny, straight-leg, or boyfriend jeans in a dark or classic wash.

Shoes: Sneakers, flats, or ankle boots.

Blouse and Skirt

Blouse: A casual blouse in a soft fabric like cotton or silk.

Skirt: A-line or pencil skirts in neutral or pastel colors.

Shoes: Ballet flats or low heels.

Sweater and Leggings

Sweater: A cozy, oversized sweater.

Leggings: Black or dark-colored leggings for comfort and style.

Shoes: Ankle boots or sneakers.

Casual Dress

Dress: A casual dress in a comfortable fabric like cotton or jersey. Patterns like florals or stripes can add interest.

Shoes: Sandals, flats, or casual sneakers.

General Tips

Layering: Layering can add depth and interest to your outfit. Consider adding a denim jacket, cardigan, or light scarf.

Accessories: Use accessories like watches, bracelets, or hats to personalize your look.

Fit and Comfort: Ensure your clothes fit well and are comfortable. Casual dressing is about feeling good while looking good.

By mixing and matching these pieces, you can create a variety of stylish and comfortable casual outfits.

Shoe colors

Choosing the right shoe color for formal dressing is essential to complete your polished look.

THE POWER OF SOFT SKILLS

For Men

Black Shoes

Black Suit: Black shoes are the most formal and versatile option, perfect for black suits.

Navy Suit: Black shoes can also be worn with navy suits for a sleek, professional appearance.

Gray Suit: Black shoes pair well with gray suits, adding a touch of elegance.

Brown Shoes

Navy Suit: Dark brown shoes can complement navy suits, offering a slightly less formal but still professional look.

Gray Suit: Brown shoes can also work with gray suits, especially in lighter shades.

Brown Suit: Match brown shoes with brown suits for a cohesive look.

Burgundy Shoes

Navy Suit: Burgundy shoes add a stylish touch to navy suits, providing a bit of personality while remaining professional.

Gray Suit: Burgundy shoes can also pair well with gray suits for a sophisticated look.

For Women

Black Shoes

Black Suit or Dress: Black shoes are a classic choice that pairs well with black suits or dresses.

Navy Suit or Dress: Black shoes can also be worn with navy outfits for a formal look.

Gray Suit or Dress: Black shoes add a touch of elegance to gray outfits.

Nude or Beige Shoes

Navy Suit or Dress: Nude shoes can elongate the legs and complement navy outfits.

Gray Suit or Dress: Nude shoes also work well with gray outfits, providing a neutral and polished look.

Pastel or Light-Colored Outfits: Nude shoes are versatile and can match various light-colored outfits.

Brown Shoes

Brown Suit or Dress: Brown shoes are a natural match for brown outfits.

Earth Tones: Brown shoes pair well with outfits in earth tones like olive, tan, or beige.

Additional Tips

Consistency: Ensure your belt matches your shoes for a cohesive look.

Material: opt for high-quality leather shoes for a polished and professional appearance.

Maintenance: Keep your shoes clean and well-polished to maintain a sharp look.

By following these guidelines, you can choose the right shoe color to complement your formal attire and create a sophisticated, professional appearance.

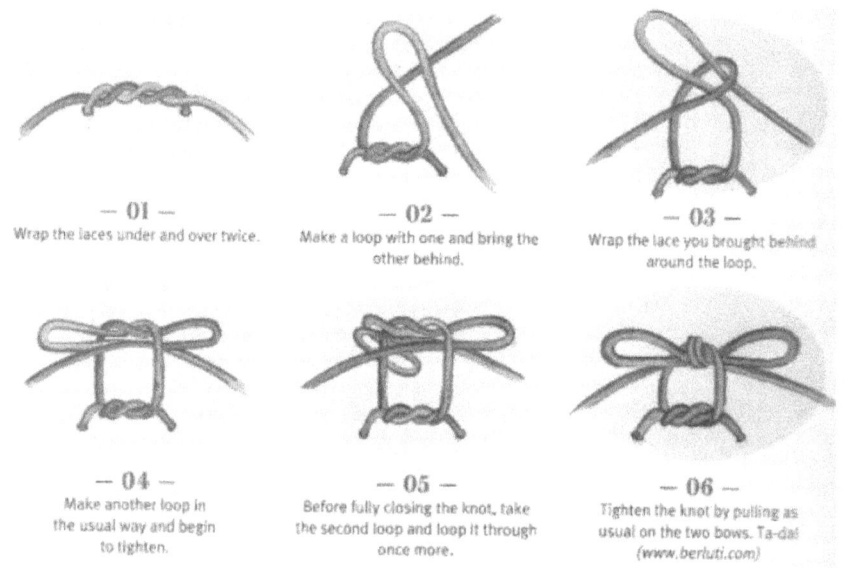

Belts

Choosing the right belt for different dress codes can enhance your overall look.

Here are some guidelines to help you select the appropriate type and color of belts for formal, casual formal, and casual dressing:

Formal Dressing

Type: opt for a classic leather belt with a simple, elegant buckle. Avoid overly large or flashy buckles.

Color: Stick to traditional colors like black or dark brown. Match the belt color with your shoes for a cohesive look.

Casual Formal Dressing

Type: You can choose a leather belt but with a bit more flexibility in design. Braided leather belts or belts with subtle patterns can work well.

Color: Dark brown, tan, or even navy can be good choices. Ensure the belt complements your outfit without overpowering it.

Casual Dressing

Type: Here, you have the most freedom. Fabric belts, woven belts, or even belts with unique buckles can add a fun element to your outfit.

Color: Feel free to experiment with colors. Neutral colors like black, brown, or tan are versatile, but you can also go for brighter colors or patterns to add a pop to your look.

General Tips

Matching: For a polished look, match your belt with your shoes. For example, black shoes with a black belt, brown shoes with a brown belt.

Contrast: If your outfit is neutral, a contrasting belt can add interest. Conversely, if your outfit is colorful, a neutral belt can balance it out.

Socks

When it comes to formal dressing, the color of your socks plays a crucial role in maintaining a polished and professional appearance. Most of us ignore the importance of the socks.

General Rules

Match with Trousers: The safest and most traditional approach is to match your socks with the color of your trousers. This creates a seamless look and gels well your legs. For example, wear black socks with black trousers, navy socks with navy trousers, and so on.

Neutral Colors: Stick to neutral colors like black, navy, gray, or dark brown. These colors are versatile and appropriate for most formal settings.

Specific Combinations

Black Suit: Pair with black or dark gray socks. This maintains the formality and elegance of the outfit.

Navy Suit: Navy or dark blue socks are ideal. You can also opt for dark gray socks for a subtle contrast.

Gray Suit: Dark gray or black socks work well. For a bit of variety, you can also choose navy socks.

Brown Suit: Dark brown or dark green socks complement brown suits nicely. Avoid overly bright colors.

Additional Tips

Avoid Bright Colors: Brightly colored or patterned socks can detract from the overall formality of your outfit. Stick to classic, solid colors for a sophisticated look.

Length: Choose over-the-calf or mid-calf socks to ensure they stay up and cover your legs when you sit down.

Material: Opt for high-quality materials like wool or cotton for comfort and breathability.

By following these guidelines, you can ensure your socks complement your formal attire and contribute to a polished, professional appearance.

Choosing the Right Socks

Material: Look for socks made from moisture-wicking materials like synthetic blends or merino wool. Avoid cotton, as it retains moisture.

Fit: Ensure the socks fit well without bunching up, as this can cause friction and blisters.

Cushioning: Depending on your preference, choose socks with the right amount of cushioning for your comfort.

Handkerchiefs

For Men:

Material: Opt for high-quality cotton or linen. Silk can be used for more formal occasions.

Colors: Stick to classic colors like white, light blue, or grey. Patterns should be minimal and subtle.

Usage: A pocket square can add a touch of sophistication to a suit. It should complement, but not exactly match, your tie.

For Women:

Material: Similar to men, high-quality cotton or linen is ideal. Silk is also an excellent choice for formal events.

Colors and Patterns: Soft, neutral colors work best. Delicate patterns or embroidery can add a feminine touch without being too flashy.

Usage: Handkerchiefs can be carried in a handbag or used as a pocket square in a blazer

Sandals and Chappals

Selecting the right sandals and chappals (flip-flops) involves considering comfort, style, and the occasion. Here is a guide to help you choose and know when to wear them:

How to Select Sandals

Comfort and Fit: Ensure the sandals fit well and provide adequate support. Look for cushioned soles and adjustable straps for a customized fit.

Material: Choose materials that suit your needs. Leather sandals are durable and stylish, while synthetic materials can be more affordable and water-resistant.

Arch Support: If you need extra support, look for sandals with built-in arch support to prevent foot pain.

Style: Consider the occasion. For casual outings, simple designs work well. For more formal settings, opt for sophisticated styles with minimal embellishments.

Purpose: Determine where you will be wearing them. For indoor use, lightweight and soft chappals are ideal. For outdoor use, choose more durable options.

Material: Leather chappals are great for durability and style, while rubber or synthetic ones are perfect for casual, everyday wear.

Design: Choose designs that match your personal style and wardrobe. Classic designs like Kolhapuri chappals are versatile and can be paired with both traditional and modern outfits.

Comfort: Look for features like cushioned insoles and adjustable straps to ensure comfort, especially if you will be wearing them for extended periods.

When to Wear Sandals and Chappals

Casual Outings: Both sandals and chappals are perfect for casual outings like shopping, running errands, or meeting friends.

Beach or Pool: Chappals, especially flip-flops, are ideal for the beach or poolside due to their easy slip-on design and quick-drying materials.

Travel: Sandals are great for travel as they are comfortable for walking and easy to take on and off at security checkpoints.

Semi-Formal Events: Leather sandals can be worn to semi-formal events like casual dinners or outdoor parties. Avoid overly casual designs for these occasions.

Home: Chappals are perfect for indoor use, providing comfort and ease when moving around the house.

By considering these factors, you can select the perfect pair of sandals or chappals for any occasion.

Wristwatches

Choosing the right watch for a corporate office setting involves balancing professionalism, style, and subtlety.

For Men:

Classic Dress Watches:

Material: Stainless steel or leather straps.

Design: Simple, elegant faces with minimal complications (e.g., date function).

Business Casual Watches:

Material: Leather or mesh metal wristbands.

Design: Thin watch faces, neutral color dials, and minimalist appearance.

For Women:

Elegant Dress Watches:

Material: Stainless steel, leather, or ceramic straps.

Design: Small to medium-sized faces, often with subtle embellishments.

Business Casual Watches:

Material: Leather or metal straps.

Design: Simple, elegant designs with neutral colors.

General Tips:

Avoid Digital Watches: Analog watches are preferred for their classic and professional look.

Match with Attire: Ensure the watch complements your outfit. For example, a brown leather strap pairs well with brown shoes and a belt.

Size Matters: The watch should fit your wrist well, not too loose, or too tight.

Smartwatches

Smartwatches can be a fantastic addition to a corporate setting, offering both functionality and style. Here are some considerations for wearing smartwatches in the office:

Benefits:

Productivity Tools:

Notifications: Receive important emails, messages, and calendar reminders without constantly checking your phone.

Health Monitoring: Track your steps, heart rate, and even stress levels, which can help you maintain a healthy work-life balance.

Convenience:

Quick Access: Use features like timers, alarms, and quick replies to streamline your day.

Contactless Payments: Make payments easily without needing to pull out your wallet.

Professional Appearance:

Customizable Faces: Choose watch faces that match your professional attire.

Interchangeable Bands: Swap out bands to suit different outfits and occasions.

Considerations:

Distraction Management:

Ensure that notifications are set to discreet modes during meetings to avoid interruptions.

Use "Do Not Disturb" settings to focus on tasks without constant alerts.

Style and Compatibility:

Match the watch band with your outfit. Leather or metal bands often look more professional than silicone.

Privacy and Security:

Be mindful of the information displayed on your smartwatch, especially in meetings or public spaces.

Smartwatches can enhance your productivity and maintain a professional appearance when used thoughtfully.

With appropriate attire, you are now prepared to make a positive impression on your supervisors, colleagues, and clients.

Next, let us consider table manners, as it is important to remember that you are observed during such occasions.

As one advances in their career, dining with clients, financiers, and influential individuals becomes commonplace. Therefore, mastering this skill is a crucial attribute of a successful corporate manager.

2. Table manners

Table manners are often not emphasized in many settings. I will provide several tips on proper conduct during a corporate lunch or dinner, as well as guidance on the appropriate use of utensils.

Many of us have experienced awkward moments due to a lack of basic table etiquette. However, there is no need for concern; please continue reading…

Handling of multiple utensils

Handling multiple utensils at a formal dinner can seem daunting, but with a few guidelines, you can navigate it with ease.

General Rules

Start from the Outside In: The basic rule is to use the utensils from the outside and work your way inward with each course. For example, the outermost fork is for the first course, and the next fork inward is for the second course.

Utensil Placement: When you are not using your utensils, place them on your plate, not on the table. This helps keep the table clean and organized.

Specific Utensils

Forks: Forks are typically placed on the left side of the plate. The salad fork is usually the outermost fork, followed by the dinner fork.

Knives and Spoons: Knives and spoons are placed on the right side of the plate. The knife closest to the plate is the dinner knife, and the outermost knife is usually for the salad or appetizer. Spoons are placed to the right of the knives.

Dessert Utensils: Dessert utensils are often placed above the plate. The dessert fork and spoon are used for the dessert course and are typically smaller than the other utensils.

Handling Utensils

Holding the Knife and Fork: Hold the knife in your dominant hand and the fork in your non-dominant hand. Use the knife to cut food into bite-sized pieces and the fork to bring the food to your mouth.

Switching Hands: In American style, you can switch the fork to your dominant hand after cutting your food. In European style, you keep the fork in your non-dominant hand.

Resting Position: When taking a break, place your knife and fork in a resting position on your plate. The knife should be placed diagonally across the top right of the plate, with the fork tines down and crossed over the knife.

Additional Tips

Napkin Usage: Place your napkin on your lap as soon as you sit down. Use it to dab your mouth gently if needed.

Pacing: Eat at a moderate pace to keep up with others and avoid finishing too quickly or too slowly.

Avoid Gesturing with Utensils: Do not use your utensils to gesture while speaking. Keep them on your plate when not in use.

By following these guidelines, you can handle multiple utensils with confidence and grace.

How to prepare oneself for a corporate lunch or dinner

Before the Meal

Dress Appropriately: Ensure your attire matches the formality of the event. Business casual is often a safe choice unless otherwise specified.

Arrive on Time: Punctuality shows respect for your host and other guests. Aim to arrive a few minutes early.

Greet Everyone: Shake hands with everyone at the table and introduce yourself if necessary.

During the Meal

Wait for the Host: Do not start eating until the host has begun or given a signal to start.

Use Utensils properly: Start with the outermost utensils and work your way in with each course. Place your utensils on your plate when you are finished.

Mind Your Posture: Sit up straight and keep your elbows off the table.

Engage in Light Conversation: Avoid controversial topics like politics or religion. Instead, discuss light and neutral subjects.

Chew with Your Mouth Closed: Avoid talking with food in your mouth and chew quietly.

Pace Yourself: Eat at a moderate pace to keep up with others and avoid finishing too quickly or too slowly.

Use Napkins Properly: Place your napkin on your lap as soon as you sit down. Use it to dab your mouth gently if needed.

Specific Tips

Bread and Butter: Butter your bread on your plate, not in midair.

Drinks: Look into your glass when drinking, not over it.

Handling Spills: If you spill something, apologize, and ask the server for assistance.

After the Meal

Thank the Host: Express your gratitude to the host before leaving.

Follow-up: Sending a thank-you note or email the next day is a nice gesture.

By following these guidelines, you can navigate corporate meals with confidence and leave a positive impression.

How to cut meat while dining

Cutting meat properly with a knife and fork is an essential skill for formal dining. Here is a step-by-step guide to help you master it:

Holding the Utensils

Knife: Hold the knife in your dominant hand. Your index finger should rest on the top of the blade, and your thumb should be on the side. The other fingers wrap around the handle.

Fork: Hold the fork in your non-dominant hand with the tines facing down. Your index finger should rest on the back of the fork, and your thumb should be on the side.

PERSONALITY DEVELOPMENT

Cutting the Meat

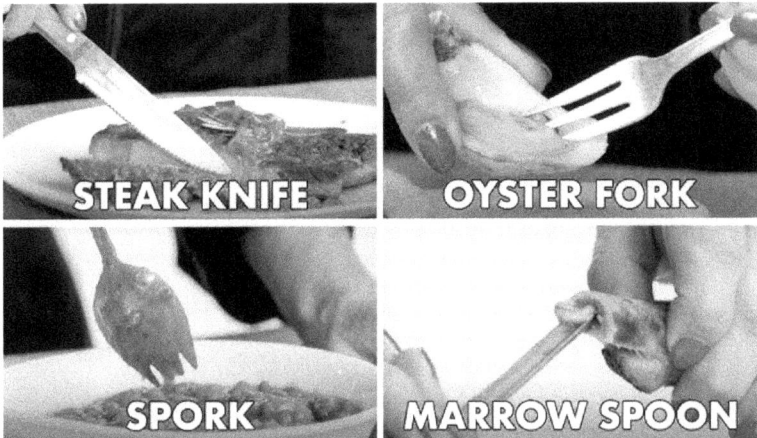

Stabilize the Meat: Use the fork to hold the meat steady. Apply gentle pressure with your index finger on the back of the fork.

Cutting Motion: Place the knife close to the base of the fork and use a gentle sawing motion to cut the meat. Make sure to cut against the grain for maximum tenderness.

Bite-Sized Pieces: Cut the meat into small, manageable pieces. This makes it easier to eat and looks more refined.

Eating the Meat

Switching Hands: After cutting a piece, you can place the knife on the edge of your plate with the blade facing inward. Then, switch the fork to your dominant hand to eat.

Continental Style: Keep the fork in your non-dominant hand and use it to bring the meat to your mouth. This style is often seen as more efficient and elegant.

Resting Position (of cutlery)

Taking a Break: If you need to pause, place your knife and fork in a resting position on your plate. The knife should be placed diagonally across the top right of the plate, with the fork tines down and crossed over the knife.

End process

Once completed place the cutlery upside down on the middle of the plate vertically. This indirectly indicates that you have completed the session.

Additional Tips

Avoid Excessive Noise: Cut gently to avoid making noise with your utensils.

Maintain Good Posture: Sit up straight and keep your elbows off the table.

Use a Sharp Knife: A sharp knife makes cutting easier and more precise.

By following these steps, you can cut meat properly and confidently during any formal dining occasion.

What if the meat is tough?

If you find yourself dealing with tough meat during a formal dinner, here are some strategies to handle it gracefully:

Cut Smaller Pieces

Cut Smaller Bites: Instead of trying to chew through large pieces, cut the meat into smaller, more manageable bites. This can make it easier to chew and less noticeable if the meat is tough.

Chew Slowly

Take Your Time: Chew slowly and thoroughly. This not only helps with digestion but also makes it easier to handle tougher meat. In fact, make the solid into a juicy stuff, and swallow. This helps in good digestion too.

Use Sauces and Side

Combine with Sides: Pair each bite of meat with a bit of sauce or a side dish. This can help mask the toughness and make it more palatable.

Stay Composed

Maintain Composure: If the meat is particularly tough, try to remain composed and avoid showing any frustration. Keep a pleasant expression and continue engaging in conversation.

Discreetly Leave Tough Pieces

Leave Unmanageable Pieces: If some pieces are too tough to eat, it is acceptable to discreetly leave them on your plate. Place them to the side and focus on the more tender parts.

Use of a Napkin

Use Your Napkin: If you need to discreetly remove a piece of meat from your mouth, use your napkin to cover your mouth and remove the piece quietly.

By following these tips, you can handle tough meat without drawing attention to the issue.

Caution: If *alcoholic beverages* are served during dinner or any office event, it is advisable to limit your consumption. Avoid intoxication, as it can create a negative impression. While these gatherings may offer expensive drinks, it is important to resist the temptation to overindulge. Please exercise moderation.

The dessert

Desserts are served normally at the end and depending on the likes of an individual the selection could be made.

Remember to keep some portion of your stomach empty for the dessert.

Here are some popular types of desserts you might like:

1. **Cakes and Pastries**
    Tiramisu: An Italian dessert made with layers of coffee-soaked ladyfingers, mascarpone cheese, and cocoa.

Black Forest Cake: A German chocolate cake with layers of chocolate sponge, whipped cream, and cherries.

Éclair: A French pastry filled with cream and topped with chocolate icing.

2. **Puddings and Custards**

   Crème Brûlée: A French custard topped with a layer of caramelized sugar.

   Panna Cotta: An Italian creamy dessert made with sweetened cream and gelatin, often served with berries or caramel.

   Bread and Butter Pudding: A British dessert made with layers of buttered bread, raisins, and custard.

3. **Tarts and Pies**

   Apple Pie: A classic dessert with a flaky crust and a spiced apple filling.

   Lemon Tart: A French tart with a tangy lemon custard filling.

   Bakewell Tart: A British tart with a layer of jam and almond-flavored sponge.

4. **Ice Creams and Sorbets**

   Gelato: An Italian-style ice cream that is denser and creamier than regular ice cream.

   Sorbet: A refreshing, dairy-free frozen dessert made with fruit puree and sugar.

   Ice Cream Sundae: A classic dessert with scoops of ice cream topped with sauces, nuts, and whipped cream.

5. **Chocolates and Truffles**

   Chocolate Mousse: A light and airy dessert made with whipped cream and chocolate.

   Truffles: Rich, bite-sized chocolates often filled with ganache or flavored creams.

   Chocolate Fondant: A molten chocolate cake with a gooey center.

6. **Fruit-Based Desserts**

   Fruit Salad: A simple and refreshing mix of various fresh fruits.

Poached Pears: Pears poached in a spiced wine syrup, often served with cream or ice cream.

Strawberries and Cream: Fresh strawberries served with whipped cream, a classic British dessert.

7. **Specialty Desserts**

Baklava: A Middle Eastern dessert made with layers of filo pastry, nuts, and honey syrup.

Cannoli: An Italian pastry filled with sweetened ricotta cheese and often garnished with chocolate chips or candied fruit.

Profiteroles: French choux pastry balls filled with cream and topped with chocolate sauce.

These desserts not only satisfy your sweet tooth but also offer a taste of the rich culinary heritage.

3. Posture and Body language

Improving your posture and body language can significantly enhance your confidence and presence.

Let us look at some practical tips.

Stand Tall

Poor Posture	Good Posture	Poor Posture
Forward Head		Forward Head
		Rounded Shoulders
Flat Back	Balanced upright posture	Sway Back / Weak abdominal Muscles

Posture: Keep your shoulders back and relaxed, and your chest slightly forward, but try to be normal.

Head Position: Keep your chin up and your gaze forward. This not only makes you look more confident but also helps with eye contact.

Confident Movements

Avoid Fidgeting: Try to minimize nervous movements like tapping your feet or playing with your hands. Instead, use deliberate and controlled gestures.

Take Up Space: Stand with your feet shoulder-width apart and use open gestures. This shows your confidence.

Eye Contact

Engagement: Maintain eye contact about 60% of the time during conversations. This shows interest and confidence.

Practice: If direct eye contact feels intimidating, start by looking at a spot close to the person's eyes.

Hand Gestures

Open Gestures: Use open hand gestures to appear more approachable and engaged. Avoid crossing your arms or inserting your hands in your pockets.

Purposeful Movements: Use your hands to emphasize points but keep movements natural and not overly exaggerated.

Sitting Posture

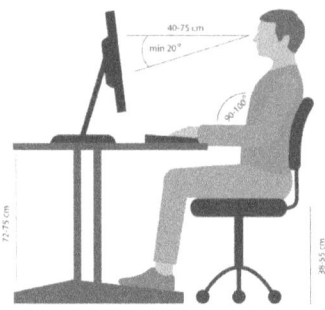

Sit Up Straight: When sitting, keep your back straight and avoid slouching. Your feet should be flat touching on the floor, and your shoulders open and relaxed. Ensure that you are aware of the ergonomics.

Lean Forward: Leaning slightly forward when speaking to someone shows that you are interested and engaged.

Sitting posture in a conference room: Follow the above and also do not look or work on your laptop when someone is talking or presenting.

Practice and Awareness

Mirror Practice: Practice your posture and gestures in front of a mirror to become more aware of your body language.

Feedback: Ask friends or colleagues for feedback on your body language and make adjustments as needed. (Do not ask too many people.)

By incorporating these tips into your daily routine, you will start to see improvements in how you carry yourself and how others perceive you.

Remember, confident body language can make a significant difference in both personal and professional interactions.

4. Email etiquettes

Use a Clear and Professional Email Address:

Ensure that your email address reflects professionalism, preferably using your name. Avoid using casual or unprofessional email addresses that may create a negative perception.

Write a Clear and Concise Subject Line:

Create subject lines that accurately represent the content of the email. A clear subject line helps recipients understand the purpose of your email and facilitates smooth communication.

Use Proper Greetings and Salutations:

Begin your email with a courteous greeting, such as "Dear Mr./Ms." or "Hello [First Name]. Use appropriate salutations, such as "Sincerely" or "Best Regards," to end your email in a professional manner.

When writing an email, the salutation sets the tone for the message. Here are some common types of salutations you can use:

Formal Salutations

1. Dear [Name],
2. To Whom It May Concern,
3. Dear Sir/Madam,
4. Dear [Title] [Last Name],

Semi-Formal Salutations

1. Hello [Name],
2. Hi [Name],

Informal Salutations

1. Hi [First Name],
2. Hey [Name],
3. Greetings,

Professional Salutations

1. Dear Team,
2. Dear [Department Name],
3. Dear [Job Title],

Friendly Salutations

1. Hi there,
2. Hey everyone,

Creative Salutations

1. Good [Morning/Afternoon/Evening],
2. Greetings [Name],

The choice of salutation depends on the context of your email and your relationship with the recipient.

Be Mindful of Tone:

Emails can sometimes be misinterpreted, so choose your words carefully. Use a polite and professional tone and avoid using sarcasm or ambiguous statements that may cause confusion or offense.

Keep It Professional and Formal:

Maintain a professional tone throughout the email. Use complete sentences and proper grammar. Avoid the use of slang, abbreviations, or excessive emojis, as they are not suitable for professional communication. Also, do not write stories.

Keep Your Email Brief and to the Point:

Respect the recipient's time by keeping your email concise and focused. Clearly state the purpose of the email and provide essential information efficiently. Use bullet points or paragraphs to break up lengthy text, ensuring readability.

Use Correct Grammar and Proofread:

Always proofread your email for grammar and spelling errors before hitting the send button. A well-written and error-free email demonstrates attention to detail and professionalism.

Respond Promptly:

Strive to respond to emails in a timely manner. Even if you cannot provide a complete response immediately, acknowledge the receipt of the email and let the sender know when they can expect a detailed response.

Use Proper CC and BCC:

When addressing multiple recipients, use the CC (carbon copy) field for those who need to be informed and the BCC (blind carbon copy) field when recipients do not need to be visible to each other. Be mindful of sharing sensitive information.

Similarly, when you respond to a mail, dot press "Reply All", unless it is warranted to do so.

Use Professional Signature:

Create an email signature that includes your full name, position, and contact details. This allows recipients to easily identify and contact you.

Remember, emails are a reflection of your professionalism and attention to detail. Following these email etiquette guidelines will help you effectively communicate and build positive relationships within your organization.

5. Command over the language

Having a good command over the language you use at work is crucial for effective communication.

In today's world, short messaging services dominate our communication, filled with slangs and acronyms like ROFL, LOL, and GN. While convenient, this trend has led to a decline in the use of proper language.

Handwriting is becoming a lost art, and relying on typing software like MS Word can actually diminish our writing skills due to autocorrect features.

To truly master the language, I highly recommend writing a few sentences by hand every day. It is a simple yet effective way to enhance your command over the language.

Command over the language enhances your ability to articulate ideas clearly, participate in discussions, and write reports or emails proficiently. Strong language skills can open up more job opportunities, facilitate better client interactions, and contribute to career advancement.

Here are some strategies to help you enhance your skills:

Read Regularly: Engage with a variety of materials such as books, articles, and journals. This will expose you to different writing styles and vocabularies.

Write Daily: Practice writing essays, journal entries, or even short stories. Focus on clarity, grammar, and expanding your vocabulary.

Expand Your Vocabulary: Learn new words daily and try to use them in your conversations and writing. Tools like flashcards or vocabulary apps can be extremely helpful.

Engage in Conversations: Speak with native speakers or join language exchange groups. This will improve your fluency and help you understand colloquial usage.

Take a Course: Enroll in a language course or workshop. Structured learning can provide you with a solid foundation and clear progression.

Use Language Apps: Apps like Duolingo, Babbel, or Rosetta Stone can provide interactive and engaging ways to practice. (Duolingo is my favorite.)

Watch and Listen: Consume media in the language you are learning. Watch movies, listen to podcasts, and follow news channels to improve your listening skills and pronunciation.

Seek Feedback: Share your writing with others and ask for constructive feedback. This can help you identify areas for improvement.

Practice Public Speaking: Join a group like Toastmasters to practice speaking in front of an audience. This can boost your confidence and improve your spoken language skills.

Be Patient and Persistent: Language mastery takes time and consistent effort. Celebrate your progress and stay motivated.

Improving the Vocabulary

Expanding the knowledge on vocabulary is essential to develop a command over any language.

Here are some additional tips to help you expand your vocabulary:

Read Widely and Actively: Choose a diverse range of reading materials, including novels, newspapers, academic journals, and blogs. When you encounter unfamiliar words, look them up and note their meanings.

Use a Thesaurus: When writing, use a thesaurus to find synonyms for frequently used words. This can help you discover new words and understand their nuances.

Create a Vocabulary Journal: Maintain a journal where you write down new words, their definitions, and example sentences. Review this journal regularly to reinforce your learning.

Play Word Games: Engage in word games like Scrabble, Boggle, or crossword puzzles. These games can make learning new words fun and challenging. In recent times there are many applications like "wordly" are popular.

Set a Word of the Day: Choose a new word each day and make an effort to use it in your conversations and writing. This practice can gradually build your vocabulary.

Use Flashcards: Create flashcards with new words and their meanings. Review them frequently to help with memorization.

Engage in Conversations: Practice using new words in your daily conversations. This will help you become more comfortable with their usage and context.

Watch Educational Videos: Platforms like TED Talks, YouTube, and educational websites offer videos that can introduce you to new vocabulary in various contexts.

Join a Book Club: Participating in a book club can expose you to different genres and authors, and discussing the books can help reinforce new vocabulary.

Write Regularly: Incorporate new words into your writing. Whether it is a diary entry, a blog post, or an essay, using new vocabulary in context will help solidify your understanding.

Use Language Learning Apps: Apps like Anki, Quizlet, and Memrise offer vocabulary-building exercises and flashcards that can aid in learning new words.

Practice Contextual Learning: Learn new words in context rather than in isolation. Understanding how a word is used in a sentence can help you remember it better.

Engage with Literature: Reading classic literature can expose you to a rich and varied vocabulary. Authors like Shakespeare, Dickens, and Austen use a wide range of words that can enhance your language skills. I would also suggest novels to start with.

Listen to Audiobooks and Podcasts: Listening to audiobooks and podcasts can help you learn new words and understand their pronunciation and usage.

Participate in Writing Workshops: Join writing workshops or online forums where you can receive feedback on your writing and learn new vocabulary from others.

By incorporating these strategies into your daily routine, you can steadily expand your vocabulary and improve your language skills.

Pronunciation

Never ever try to copy the native speaker's pronunciation. Speak in your style, but clearly. (I have noticed, many non-English speakers try to imitate the native English accent and fumble.)

Improving pronunciation is a key aspect of mastering a language. Here are some effective strategies to help you enhance your pronunciation skills:

Listen Carefully: Pay close attention to how native speakers pronounce words. Listen to podcasts, watch movies, and engage with other audio-visual materials in the language.

Use Pronunciation Tools: Utilize online dictionaries and language learning apps that provide audio examples of words. Websites like Forvo and apps like FluentU can be immensely helpful.

Practice Phonemes: Focus on the individual sounds of the language, known as phonemes. Understanding and practicing these sounds can help you pronounce words more accurately.

Record Yourself: Record your speech and compare it to native speakers. This can help you identify areas for improvement and track your progress over time.

Mouth and Tongue Positioning: Pay attention to how your mouth and tongue move when producing different sounds. There are many online resources and videos that demonstrate the correct positioning.

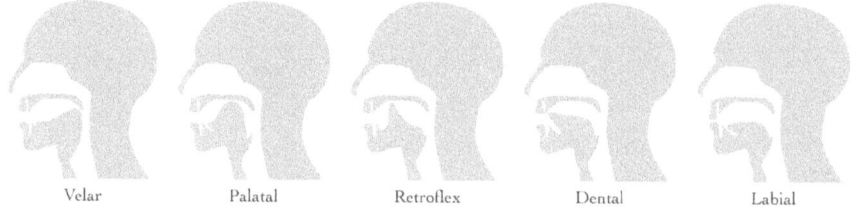

Velar   Palatal   Retroflex   Dental   Labial

- **Velar**: The back of the tongue touches the soft palate. Example: /k/ in "cat."
- **Palatal**: The middle of the tongue touches the hard palate. Example: /j/ in "yes."
- **Retroflex**: The tip of the tongue curls back towards the hard palate. Example: /ɖ/ in "red" (though not common in English, it is found in some dialects).
- **Dental**: The tongue touches the teeth. Example: /θ/ in "think."
- **Labial**: Both lips touch. Example: /p/ in "pat."

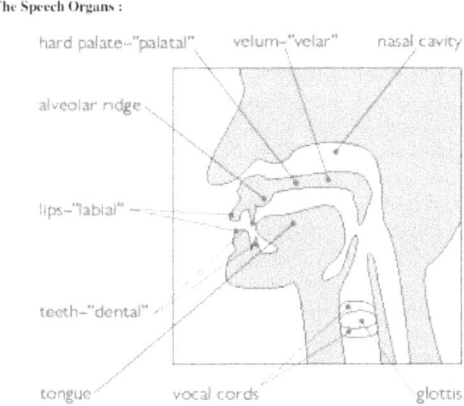

The Speech Organs:

1. The Vocal Cords:

The air that is released by the lungs moves up through the windpipe and reaches first

the Larynx. The Larynx contains two small bands of elastic tissue called vocal cords. These

cords can move towards each other or away from each other. When we speak, it is these

cords that make sound with the help of the air stream and this basic sound is articulated into

different phonemes (our choice from the list of 44 phonemes) by the different speech organs in our mouth. Without vocal cords, speaking can never happen. Immediately above the Larynx is a space behind the tongue which reaches up towards the nasal cavity. This space is called the Pharynx.

The Palate:

The palate forms the roof of the mouth and separates the mouth cavity from the nasal cavity. The front part of the palate is hard and the back part is soft, and both the parts can be felt by the tip of our tongue. The soft palate can be raised or lowered.

The hard palate which is fixed is divided again into two sections; the teeth (alveolar) ridge and the hard palate. The alveolar ridge is the part of tooth gums immediately behind the upper front teeth and the hard palate is between the alveolar ridge and soft palate.

All the three parts of the upper roof – alveolar ridge, hard palate and soft palate are important for the production of vowels and consonants, particularly consonants.

The palate not only starts at the back and ends above the upper teeth, but curves down wards either side (left and right) towards the teeth.

The Teeth:

The upper front teeth have a role to play in the production of consonants represented by 'th' in words like 'this' and 'that'. The lower front teeth are not important in speaking but, if they are absent consonants like / s / and / z / as in 'sign' and 'zeal' will be difficult to be produced.

The Tongue:

The tongue is the most important speech organ because it plays a major role in speech production. Its movements are many which are essential for the production of vowels, consonants, words, and sentences.

To produce the consonants / t / and / d / as in 'ten' and 'deal' the tip of the tongue touches the upper teeth (alveolar) ridge.

To produce the sounds /k / and / g / as in 'kite' and 'game', the back of the tongue presses against the soft palate. To produce the sounds / s / and / z / as in 'seat' and 'zeal', the tip and blade of the tongue go close to the alveolar ridge. Similarly, the movements of the tongue are important in the production of vowels and diphthongs.

The Lips:

The lips take up different positions to produce vowels and consonants. To produce the

consonants / p / and / b / as in 'pen' and 'bell' we bring the lips firmly together, block the air column and then blow it by separating the lips. To produce / f / and / v / as in 'fan' and 'vent' the lower lip is drawn inward and then slightly upwards to touch the upper front teeth.

All the speech organs are important for the right kind of speaking (correct production of sounds, words and sentences) and one should be conscious about the movements of speech organs till the right speaking skills are acquired.

Use Tongue Twisters: Practicing tongue twisters can improve your articulation and help you become more comfortable with difficult sounds.

Slow Down: Speak slowly and clearly. This allows you to focus on pronunciation and reduces the likelihood of making mistakes.

Seek Feedback: Ask native speakers or instructors for feedback on your pronunciation. They can provide valuable insights and corrections.

Practice Regularly: Consistency is key. Dedicate time each day to practice pronunciation, and I would recommend at least 15 minutes a day.

Remember the old proverb…*practice makes a man perfect.*

Engage in Conversations: Regularly speaking with native speakers will help you improve your pronunciation in a natural context.

By incorporating these strategies into your daily routine, you can steadily improve your pronunciation and become more confident in your speaking abilities.

Remember Life is a Marathon… not a Sprint.

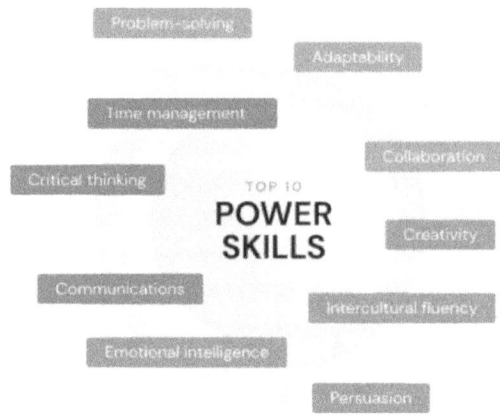

Additional topics

I. 'Work From Home' (WFH), 'Remote work' or 'Telework.'

Post Covid the 'new norm has evolved,' "Work from home." (Remote working)

To be frank, I was never comfortable working from home for a prolonged time period. I would rather prefer the 'Hybrid' model. That is, a few days at the office and a few days at home, in a given month.

There are advantages as well as disadvantages of working from home. Also, we shall look at how to make work from home effective and comfortable.

Advantages of working from home

Working from home offers several advantages for both employees and employers in a corporate environment. Let us explore some of these benefits:

Lower Costs: Employers can reduce overhead expenses associated with maintaining physical office spaces, such as rent, utilities, and office supplies.

Bigger Applicant Pool: Remote work allows companies to tap into a wider talent pool by hiring candidates from different geographic locations. This can lead to better recruitment outcomes.

Improved Employee Retention: Offering work-from-home options can enhance employee satisfaction and reduce turnover rates. Employees appreciate the flexibility and work-life balance it provides.

More Autonomous Employees: Remote work encourages self-management and autonomy. Employees learn to be accountable for their tasks and deadlines, which can positively impact productivity.

Increased Productivity: Fewer social distractions and personalized work environments can lead to higher productivity among remote employees.

Improved Employee Morale: A better work-life balance contributes to happier employees, which in turn boosts morale and job satisfaction.

Environmental Impact: Reduced commuting leads to less traffic congestion and lower carbon emissions, contributing to a more sustainable planet.

Overall, embracing remote work can create a win-win situation for both employees and employers, fostering a more efficient and content workforce.

Disadvantages of working from home

The following are some disadvantages of working from home for both employees and employers in a corporate environment:

Increased Isolation: Remote work can lead to feelings of loneliness and isolation, as employees miss out on social interactions with colleagues.

Home Office Costs: Employees may need to invest in home office equipment (e.g., ergonomic chairs, desks, high-speed internet) at their own expense.

Risk of Overworking: Without clear boundaries, employees might find it challenging to disconnect from work, leading to burnout and excessive working hours.

Impact on Productivity: Some employees struggle to maintain the same level of productivity at home due to distractions, lack of supervision, or inadequate workspaces.

Distractions at Home: Household chores, family members, and pets can disrupt work focus and productivity.

Workplace Disconnect: The absence of face-to-face interactions can hinder team collaboration, creativity, and a sense of belonging.

Disproportionate Work-Life Balance: The blurring of boundaries between work and personal life can make it challenging to switch off after work hours.

Employers also face challenges related to managing remote teams, maintaining company culture, and ensuring consistent performance. It is essential to address these drawbacks proactively to create a successful remote work environment.

Advantages and disadvantages of the Hybrid model

Let us explore the advantages and disadvantages of the hybrid work model in a corporate environment:

Advantages of Hybrid Work:

Flexibility: The hybrid model offers a balance between traditional office work and remote work. Employees can choose where they work, promoting flexibility and accommodating individual preferences.

Increased Productivity: Some employees thrive in a remote environment, while others prefer the structure of an office. Hybrid work allows companies to harness the benefits of both settings, potentially boosting overall productivity.

Environmental Friendliness: Reduced commuting due to remote workdays contributes to a smaller carbon footprint and environmental impact.

Talent Attraction and Retention: Offering a hybrid work option makes a company more attractive to potential hires and helps retain existing talent. Employees appreciate the work-life balance it provides.

Disadvantages of Hybrid Work:

Communication Barriers: Hybrid teams may face challenges in communication. Ensuring effective collaboration across remote and in-office employees requires intentional efforts.

Collaboration Hurdles: Spontaneous interactions, brainstorming sessions, and team-building activities are harder to replicate in a hybrid setting. Maintaining a cohesive team becomes crucial.

Security Concerns: Balancing security protocols for both office and remote work can be complex. Companies need robust cybersecurity measures to protect sensitive data.

In summary, the hybrid work model offers flexibility and productivity gains but requires thoughtful planning to address communication gaps and maintain team cohesion.

How to make oneself comfortable while working from home

The following are some tips to make yourself comfortable while working from home:

Create a Good Workspace:

Remove distractions like pets, children, or spouse.

Set up essentials like a desk lamp, extension cord, and comfortable seating.

Pay Attention to Ergonomics:

Sit or stand at a desk or table.

Keep your forearms level with the table and elbows at 90 degrees.

Use cushions or a footrest if you do not have an adjustable chair.

Take Breaks:

Blink frequently to prevent dry eyes from screen time.

Walk away from your computer to avoid eyestrain and blood clots due to prolonged sitting.

Stay Hydrated:

Keep a water bottle nearby to stay refreshed throughout the day.

Develop a Transition Routine:

Create a ritual to signal the end of work, such as a short walk or a specific activity.

Remember, small adjustments can significantly improve your comfort and well-being while working from home!

II. Work-Life Balance

Maintaining a healthy work-life balance is crucial, especially in today's fast-paced corporate environment. Let us refine and rephrase the advice to emphasize its importance:

Strategies for Achieving Work-Life Balance in a Multinational Corporate Setting

Prioritize Thoughtfully:

Recognize that achieving balance is a personal responsibility. While organizations play a role, individuals must actively manage their priorities.

Understand that everyone's needs and preferences differ, just as organizations have varying demands.

Choosing the Right Workplace:

When evaluating job opportunities, consider not only salary negotiations but also the overall working environment.

Remember that we spend a sizable portion of our waking hours at work, so a positive workplace culture matters.

Family and Personal Commitments:

Acknowledge the people waiting for you at home—parents, spouse, or children. Allocate quality time for them with kindness.

Address home-front issues promptly to prevent strain on relationships.

Effective Time Management:

Prioritize tasks at the office. Avoid procrastination and manage your time efficiently.

At home, resist the urge to open your laptop or mobile unless it is an emergency. Steer clear of office WhatsApp groups during personal time.

Leisure and Travel:

Plan regular weekend outings and at least two extended holidays each year. Consider exploring destinations beyond your home country.

Allocate time for socializing with friends and relatives—they contribute to your overall well-being.

Financial Discipline:

Create a budget and monitor expenses. Avoid unnecessary purchases and strike a balance between frugality and indulgence.

Financial stress can impact work-life balance, so manage your resources wisely.

Engage in Social Activities:

Participate in community service or social initiatives. Giving back can be a stress reliever and provide a sense of purpose.

Connect with others beyond work-related interactions.

Mental Boundaries:

While at the office, focus on work tasks. Avoid dwelling on personal matters.

Similarly, when at home, disconnect from work-related thoughts and immerse yourself in your personal life.

Hobbies and Stress Relief:

Develop a hobby or pursue an artistic interest—music, dance, or a game. Creative outlets are excellent stress busters.

Engage in activities that recharge your mind and spirit. (Refer to the 'time management 'chapter for some more information on designating personal time, daily)

Avoid Negative Influences:

Stay away from negative elements and unhealthy habits.

While some vices are acceptable in moderation, maintain a healthy balance.

By adhering to these principles, you can achieve a harmonious work-life balance, contributing to your overall well-being and productivity.

III. Continuing Education

Continuing education plays a crucial role for corporate employees, benefiting both individuals and organizations. Here is why:

Career Advancement

Skill Enhancement: Continuing education allows employees to acquire new skills and stay updated in their field.

Promotions: Demonstrating ongoing learning can lead to promotions and career growth.

Resume Boost: Certifications and workshops enhance resumes and make employees stand out.

Employee Satisfaction and Retention:

Job Satisfaction: Learning opportunities increase engagement and job satisfaction.

Retention: Companies that invest in employee development retain skilled talent longer.

Internal Talent Pipeline: Upskilling creates a pool of qualified candidates for future roles.

Productivity and Agility: Learning increases productivity and agility.

Agile Workforce: Rapid technological changes require upskilling and reskilling.

Addressing Skills Gaps: Ongoing education helps bridge gaps and adapt to industry shifts.

Attracting Top Talent:

Lifelong Learning Culture: Companies offering education support attract skilled candidates.

Increased Productivity: Skilled employees contribute more effectively to organizational goals.

In summary, continuing education benefits employees by enhancing skills, boosting confidence, and opening career opportunities. For employers, it leads to a stronger workforce, higher retention rates, and a competitive edge in attracting talent.

IV. Rational use of social media

I am not against the use of gadgets and spending time on social media, but against spending too much time on these activities.

Technology has created a *lot of connections* in our life but left many in *loneliness*. Humans are social animals, whereas one-to-one interaction is coming down drastically, off late with the advent of social media. The sad part is even those who live in the same home, interact through WhatsApp.

Responsible use of social media is essential for adults to maintain their well-being and make the most of these platforms. Here are some key points:

Balance and Moderation:

Limit Screen Time: Spending excessive hours on social media can harm psychological well-being, leading to stress, anxiety, and depression.

Set Boundaries: Allocate specific times for social media use and avoid constant scrolling.

Prioritize Real-Life Interactions: Balance online interactions with face-to-face connections.

Mindful Engagement:

Quality Over Quantity: Focus on meaningful interactions rather than accumulating followers or likes.

Avoid Comparisons: Remember that social media often portrays curated versions of people's lives.

Unfollow Negativity: Unfollow accounts that consistently make you feel anxious or inadequate.

Privacy and Security:

Review Privacy Settings: Regularly check and adjust privacy settings to protect your personal information.

Be Skeptical: Verify information before sharing it. Misinformation spreads easily on social media.

Avoid Oversharing: Be cautious about sharing sensitive details publicly.

Positive Use Cases:

Connect with Purpose: Use social media to connect with friends, family, and like-minded individuals.

Learn and Share: Follow educational content, hobbies, and interests.

Support Mental Health: Some studies suggest that social media can compensate for diminishing face-to-face interactions, especially for busy adults.

Remember that responsible social media use can enhance connections, increase self-esteem, and improve a sense of belonging.

V. Corporate ethics and business code of conduct

Workplace ethics and a **code of business conduct** are critical for multinational corporations (MNCs) to maintain integrity, foster trust, and ensure compliance. Let us explore these aspects:

Workplace Ethics in MNCs:

Diverse Cultures: MNCs operate across borders, dealing with diverse cultures, norms, and values. Understanding and respecting these differences is essential.

Leadership Role: Ethical behavior starts at the top. Leaders must model integrity, transparency, and fairness.

Training and Communication: Regular training programs on ethics and cultural sensitivity help employees navigate cross-cultural challenges.

Risk Assessment: MNCs face unique risks (e.g., bribery, human rights violations). Conduct thorough risk assessments to address these challenges.

Code of Business Conduct

A well-defined code outlines expected behavior for employees, contractors, and partners.

Key Elements:

Anti-Corruption: Prohibits bribery, kickbacks, and unethical payments.

Conflicts of Interest: Addresses situations, where personal interests conflict with company duties.

Data Privacy: Ensures protection of sensitive information.

Fair Competition: Promotes fair market practices.

Human Rights: Upholds labor rights, diversity, and inclusion.

Environmental Responsibility: Encourages sustainable practices.

Enforcement and Reporting: Clear procedures for reporting violations and consequences for non-compliance.

Localization: Translate the code into local languages to ensure understanding across regions.

Remember, a strong ethical foundation contributes to MNCs' long-term success and reputation!

Anti-Corruption

Let us explore some key anti-corruption laws from different countries:

Foreign Corrupt Practices Act (FCPA) - United States:

The FCPA, enacted in 1977, was the world's first anti-bribery law. It prohibits companies from using bribes to influence foreign business operations.

The U.S. Securities and Exchange Commission (SEC) and the Department of Justice (DOJ) enforce the FCPA.

The FCPA focuses on preventing bribery of foreign officials and promoting transparency.

United Nations Convention against Corruption (UNCAC):

UNCAC is a global treaty aimed at combating corruption in both public and private sectors.

It covers various aspects, including criminalization, prevention, and asset recovery.

Ratified by over 180 countries, it provides a framework for international cooperation.

OECD Convention on Combating Bribery of Foreign Public Officials:

Adopted in 1997, this convention encourages member countries to criminalize bribery of foreign public officials.

It promotes transparency, accountability, and cooperation in anti-corruption efforts.

UK Bribery Act (2010):

The UK Bribery Act covers bribery in the UK and abroad.

It criminalizes offering, promising, or giving bribes, as well as failing to prevent bribery within organizations.

Corruption of Foreign Public Officials Act (CFPOA) - Canada:

CFPOA prohibits bribery of foreign public officials by Canadian individuals and companies.

It aligns with international standards and emphasizes corporate liability.

Remember that these laws play a crucial role in promoting ethical business practices and combating corruption globally.

Conflict of interest

A **conflict of interest** occurs when an individual's personal interests clash with their professional duties or responsibilities within a company. Here are some common examples:

Outside Employment: An employee working for a company while also having a side job that competes with the employer's interests.

Workplace Relationships: When personal relationships (e.g., family, friends) affect decision-making or create bias.

Selling to the Company: An employee using their position to benefit themselves by selling goods or services to their own company.

Political Commitments: Advocating for personal political beliefs that conflict with the company's values.

Personal Financial Interest: Making decisions that benefit the employee financially but harm the organization.

In business, conflicts of interest often have legal implications, and individuals may be required to remove themselves from such situations.

Insider trading

Insider trading occurs when a director or employee trades their company's public stock or other securities based on important or "material" information about that business. Here are the key points:

Definition:

Insider trading involves buying or selling company stock using nonpublic information.

It is legal if the person reports the trade to the Securities and Exchange Commission (SEC) and the information is already public.

Legal vs. Illegal:

Legal: When insiders (employees, directors) trade with proper disclosure.

Illegal: When insiders use nonpublic information to gain an unfair advantage.

Prevention Measures:

Disclosure: Insiders must report their trades to the SEC.

Monitoring: Regulators watch trading activity around significant events (earnings, acquisitions).

Complaints: Traders' complaints trigger investigations.

Blackout Periods: Some companies restrict trading during critical times (e.g., earnings announcements).

Remember, transparency and ethical behavior are crucial to maintaining market integrity!

Information security

Information security compliance refers to adhering to standards, laws, and regulations that ensure an organization's data and IT assets are adequately protected. Here are key aspects related to IT compliance:

Comprehensive Information Security Policy:

Develop a policy outlining appropriate usage of hardware, software, data protection, access control, and incident response.

Train all personnel on proper security measures when managing sensitive data or systems.

Secured Network:

Implement robust network security measures to prevent unauthorized access.

Regularly test and review network security policies.

Protected User Data:

Safeguard user data through encryption, access controls, and secure storage.

Ensure data integrity and confidentiality.

Regular Reviews:

Continuously review and update information security policies.

Monitor compliance with industry standards and regulations.

Remember, IT compliance is crucial for protecting your organization from cyber threats!

VI. Diversity Equality and Inclusion – DEI

Diversity, equity, and inclusion (DEI) initiatives are gaining prominence in the corporate world. Let us delve into the details:

What Is DEI?

Diversity: Encompasses employing people with a range of social identities (e.g., race, gender, ethnicity, age, disability).

Equity: Focuses on creating systems that ensure equal access and opportunities for all.

Inclusion: Aims to ensure that all voices are heard and valued within the organization.

Why DEI Matters:

Positive Work Culture: DEI initiatives foster a positive work environment by embracing diverse perspectives.

Morale Boost: Exposure to different viewpoints improves employee morale.

Ethical Business: Promotes fairness and ethical practices.

Innovation: Diverse teams drive creative problem-solving and innovation.

Examples of DEI Initiatives:

Gender Parity: Companies implement policies to promote gender equality, such as tailored financial products for women entrepreneurs.

Representation: Ensuring diverse representation at all levels of the organization.

Training and Education: Regular DEI training for employees.

Inclusive Policies: Creating policies that accommodate diverse needs.

Community Engagement: Engaging with diverse communities and supporting social causes.

Remember, DEI is not just about compliance; it is about building a stronger, more inclusive workplace!

VII. Performance Appraisal

Performance appraisal, also known as performance review or performance evaluation, is a systematic process in a corporate environment where the job performance of an employee is evaluated and documented. It is an integral part of career development and consists of regular reviews of employee performance within organizations.

Here is how the process is typically executed:

1. **Setting Clear Expectations:** At the beginning of an appraisal cycle, managers and employees set clear, measurable objectives for the upcoming period. These objectives should align with the company's overall goals.
2. **Ongoing Feedback:** Throughout the appraisal period, managers provide ongoing feedback to employees on their performance. This can be done through regular one-on-one meetings, coaching sessions, and informal check-ins.
3. **Self-Evaluation:** At the end of the appraisal period, employees are often asked to conduct a self-evaluation. This involves assessing their

own performance against the objectives set at the beginning of the period.
4. **Manager Evaluation:** Managers also evaluate the employee's performance based on the set objectives and the feedback collected throughout the period. They consider the quality of work, accomplishment of objectives, and the employee's skills and competencies.
5. **Review Meeting:** The manager and the employee then meet to discuss the evaluation. This is an opportunity for dialogue where the manager provides feedback, recognition, and constructive criticism. The employee can also share their thoughts, discuss challenges faced, and express their aspirations and training needs.
6. **Documentation:** The outcomes of the appraisal are documented and kept in the employee's record. This can be used for making decisions about promotions, compensation, training needs, etc.
7. **Action Plan:** Based on the appraisal, an action plan is developed for the next period. This includes setting new objectives, addressing performance gaps, and planning for career development.

Remember, the goal of performance appraisal is not just to evaluate past performance, but also to develop employees and improve future performance.

During the appraisal process, it is important to identify the training and development plan, which is essential for the growth of the appraisee.

It is a continuous process that promotes understanding, improves communication, and motivates employees.

How to manage a negative performance appraisal

Receiving a negative performance appraisal can be challenging, but it is important to handle it professionally and use it as an opportunity for growth. Here are some steps to handle a negative performance appraisal:

1. **Stay Calm:** It is natural to feel defensive or upset when receiving negative feedback but try to stay calm and composed. Take some time to process the information before responding.
2. **Listen Actively:** Listen carefully to the feedback you are receiving. Try to understand the perspective of your manager and the reasons behind the negative appraisal.
3. **Ask for Clarification:** If you do not understand a point or if you need more information, ask for clarification. It is important to fully understand the feedback in order to address it effectively.
4. **Reflect on the Feedback:** Take some time to reflect on the feedback. Consider the validity of the points raised and how they align with your own perception of your performance.
5. **Develop a Plan:** Based on the feedback, develop a plan to address the areas of improvement. This could involve setting new goals, acquiring new skills, or changing certain behaviors.
6. **Seek Support:** Do not hesitate to seek support. This could be from your manager, HR, a mentor, or even a coach. They can provide guidance and resources to help you improve.
7. **Follow-Up:** After you have developed and started implementing your plan, follow up with your manager. Discuss your progress, any challenges you are facing, and ask for ongoing feedback.

Remember, a negative performance appraisal is not a reflection of your worth as a person. It is an assessment of your performance in specific areas at work. Use it as a learning opportunity and a stepping stone for growth and improvement.

What do you do in case of a biased performance appraisal?

If you feel that the feedback you have received is unfair or biased, it is important to handle the situation professionally and constructively. Here are some steps you can take:

1. **Reflect on the Feedback:** Before reacting, take some time to reflect on the feedback. Try to separate your emotional response from the actual content of the feedback.
2. **Seek Clarification:** If you are unsure why certain feedback was given, ask for more details. It is possible that there may be a misunderstanding that can be cleared up with more information.
3. **Provide Your Perspective:** If you disagree with the feedback, express your perspective calmly and professionally. Use specific examples to support your viewpoint.
4. **Request a Second Opinion:** If you believe the feedback is biased, you might consider asking for a second opinion from another manager or HR.
5. **Document Everything:** Keep a record of all your accomplishments, feedback received, and communication with your manager. This can be useful if you need to provide evidence of your performance.
6. **Speak to Human Resources:** If you feel comfortable doing so, speak to someone in your HR department about your concerns. They can provide guidance on how to handle the situation and can intervene if necessary.

Remember, it is important to communicate openly and honestly with your manager about your concerns. Everyone has biases, and it is possible that your manager may not even be aware of theirs. By addressing the issue professionally and constructively, you can help to improve the feedback process for everyone involved.

VIII. Upskilling

In the current competitive market, continuous upskilling is essential for survival and growth within one's domain.

As you progress through your career, you may find opportunities to build upon your existing skill set. Over time, these new or advanced skills may be why you move into a management position or take on more interesting projects at work.

Although skills development can happen naturally over time, some people choose to actively pursue their professional development goals by upskilling. Likewise, some companies encourage their employees to upskill in order to generate growth opportunities internally.

Upskilling means learning new and enhanced skills that relate to your current role. Think about it as "leveling up" your skills.

Often, you will deepen your knowledge about your role and industry as you gain more experience. Upskilling is typically a more intentional learning process where you will gain exposure to that deeper knowledge sooner through skills development courses, certifications, or mentorship programs.

Depending on your role, you may find it beneficial to elevate your workplace skills, technical skills, or both.

Upskilling and reskilling

Upskilling and reskilling are two terms that tend to go hand in hand. Whereas **upskilling** involves elevating your current skill set, **reskilling** involves learning new cross-functional skills. With reskilling, you may be able to move into a new role or widen the scope of your current role.

Differences between reskilling and upskilling

Upskilling refers to providing current employees with additional skills. These new skills are learned to improve or expand upon a current role or to become qualified for the next step in a person's career path. An example of upskilling could be a software development company training its developers in a new language they will use to develop new products.

Reskilling, on the other hand, refers to learning new skills for an unrelated role or to make a career change. Reskilling often requires an employee to go back to college or a trade school to earn a degree or certification in a different field. An example of reskilling could be a construction worker who goes back to school to become a software developer.

Upskilling develops employees for a linear path in their career, while reskilling is typically used as a lateral movement for a person's career.

Source: Coursera.org

Top upskilling platforms and websites

Here is a list of ten platforms and websites that will provide you with the best content that ranges from being cheaply priced to almost free!

EDX

https://www.edx.org/

edX is a non-profit organization launched by MIT and Harvard University. Its online courses range from Computer Sciences to a small number of art-related courses, such as Inspiring and Motivating Arts and Culture Team.

FutureLearn

https://www.futurelearn.com/

FutureLearn's catalog ranges across all domains from business and media to literature and history. It offers condensed versions of courses similar to a university course. It is a UK-based digital education platform that is jointly owned by The Open University and SEEK LTD. They have over 140 international partners. Although learning in the medium is free, if you want to earn certificates you will need to pay.

Udemy

https://www.udemy.com/

This medium is not exactly free, the courses price starts from $10 and goes up to $300. It has created a medium for instructors to create their own courses across the globe and learners can take advantage of the diverse platform. Luckily, a lot of courses keep popping up for free on Mashable or multiple other platforms.

Coursera

https://www.coursera.org/

One of the biggest online platforms was started by Standford professors Andrew Ng and Daphne Koller. The biggest asset of the platform is that it partners with universities and companies as well. The free courses on this platform are of immense value and can help you upskill at your own pace.

I have completed many courses through coursera.org, on soft skills, and found them more professional and interesting.

JetBrains Academy

https://www.jetbrains.com/academy/

Everyone's beloved Python coding Interface PyCharm's parent company is giving free project-based courses to everyone for a limited period of time. Grab a seat as soon as possible and make use of this invaluable resource.

Code Academy

https://www.codecademy.com/

Coding is something that you might not have considered before, but it is a highly sought-after skill. Based on your reasons for wanting to learn how to code — whether it is for web development, programming, or data science — Code Academy has tailored courses to set you on the right path. The majority of their free courses take less than ½ day to complete, and there is also an option to take on more advanced courses if you are looking to build on your existing coding experience.

Khan Academy

https://www.khanacademy.org/

It has been The Resource for students of all ages. It gives instructional subjects from programming, science to art, and literature. There is no doubt about the quality as it has partnered with multiple organizations such as NASA, MIT, California Academy of Sciences, and even Pixar Studios.

Alison

https://alison.com/

It is another leading online platform that has world-class teachers. From soft skills such as time management and productivity to industry-based skills such as digital photography and web design, they have a broad variety of courses most of which have an average completion time of 2–3 hours. On completion, you will receive a professional certification, or in some cases, you can even go on to secure a diploma in your chosen area.

FreeCodeCamp

https://www.freecodecamp.org/

This delivers bang on what it promises. This is a not-for-profit online organization and the courses range from HTML, CSS, and JavaScript and then move onto project-based courses.

Google Digital Garage

https://learndigital.withgoogle.com/digitalgarage

Google is providing the leading online courses which are approved by industry professionals to everyone. Most of the courses are free and are available for Data and Technology, and Digital Marketing.

(Source: Internet)

(This list is only for information purpose.)

How to develop an upskilling strategy

1. **Identify skills gaps**

   When developing an upskilling strategy, companies must first identify the skill gaps currently within their organization. This step helps businesses ensure their upskilling efforts align with their workforce needs.

2. **Consider the impacts of upskilling efforts**

   Next, companies must consider both the short- and long-term impacts of the upskilling efforts. For example, it can be easy to focus on the newest tool on the market. However, this development might not help the business in the long term. Therefore, an organization should focus on how it can improve its core skills to increase long-term value. However, it is still necessary to stay current with industry trends and to use modern technology so the company can maintain a competitive edge.

3. **Build and select training programs**

   Once the skill gaps have been identified, a business can begin to build and select the training programs that make the most sense for them. In this step, an organization determines factors such as the following:

- Whether a volume training session is needed or if one-on-one lessons would be more beneficial.

- Whether the training can be done internally or if an external educational institution needs to be hired.
- Which types of learning make the most sense – considering mentoring, online courses, training sessions, or post-secondary courses.

4. **Tailor upskilling plans**

   In addition to understanding which upskilling methods are best for all employees, organizations must also consider each worker's career goals and tailor an upskilling plan to them. Since each person possesses different skill sets and goals, a different upskilling strategy is needed for each employee, depending on their current knowledge, role within the organization, how that role is evolving and the modern technology requirements necessary to continue to efficiently perform the job. It is important to communicate with managers throughout this stage of the upskilling strategy to ensure they are having frequent, open conversations with each employee to understand their needs and desires.

5. **Employee encouragement**

   Finally, when providing external learning opportunities, companies might consider offering financial incentives to encourage their employees to participate. Workers who are offered the resources to learn new skills are often more motivated. Financial incentives – such as increased training and development budgets, educational rebates, and employee grants to attend training and conferences – increase the likelihood that employees will take advantage of upskilling opportunities.

Some upskilling strategies include the following:

- **Job-specific upskilling and credential programs.** This strategy offers employees training specific to their jobs that can enhance their current skill sets, e.g., with lessons on specialty software used by only a small portion of the organization. Credential programs – which result in a professional certificate – are also great opportunities for employees to improve their current skill sets.

- **Personal development plans.** Encouraging employees to create a personal development plan that addresses the abilities they want to improve and the new skills they would like to learn empowers them to create their own upskilling program. Employees can choose what they would like to do instead of being told what the company thinks they should do.
- **Devote time during the workday.** Employees with personal development plans should be given time during the workday to dedicate to their upskilling efforts.
- **Use third-party services.** Some companies might be able to custom design their upskilling programs; however, not every organization has the time or resources to do so. These organizations can instead use third-party; learning platforms that feature courses and certifications for different topics, skills, and tools.

Specific upskilling opportunities include the following:

- **Virtual and online courses.** This uses training software and an online training platform to let employees train from home at a time that works for them, rather than forcing workers to attend inconvenient, onsite development sessions at specific times.
- **Mentoring and shadowing.** Most companies have experts on specific subject matter already included in their workforce. Use these experts to train other employees with real-world experience and advice that cannot be taught in a classroom setting. In addition, this enables experts to improve their leadership skills.
- **Lunch-and-learn sessions.** These are beneficial for employees who feel they do not have enough time in their workday to devote to training sessions. Lunch-and-learn sessions let workers use their lunch break for training. These sessions often involve an expert from outside the

company who can teach employees by sharing their knowledge on a specific subject.
- **Microlearning.** This upskilling opportunity focuses on training in quick bursts – such as short videos followed by fast exercises and quizzes that demonstrate understanding. Microlearning sessions typically last between five and 10 minutes, letting employees use them at almost any time, such as during short breaks throughout the day or during a lunch break.

Benefits of upskilling from an organization perspective

Upskilling helps current employees learn new job skills, makes the company more attractive to job applicants, and improves the employee experience. Furthermore, while upskilling programs are expensive, they generate a strong bottom line and return on investment. Creating ongoing training opportunities for workers is often less expensive than addressing workplace problems. Providing free training also increases employee retention rates, thus decreasing turnover and lowering hiring and onboarding costs.

Other upskilling benefits include the following:

- **Improves employee engagement.** Potential and current employees want professional development and training opportunities in their jobs, and they will look for roles that provide these options. Upskilling satisfies these employee demands.
- **Optimizes employee productivity.** Improving employee engagement ultimately increases productivity. Also, if employees do not understand the technology they work with, they will not excel in their jobs. Therefore, upskilling employees in modern technologies is necessary for improving their productivity.
- **Improves employee retention.** Upskilling decreases employee turnover. When workers feel their employer is invested in their professional growth, they are more likely to remain committed to the

company. Upskill training can also make employees happier and more motivated to complete their work.
- **Increases customer satisfaction.** Happy employees often directly affect and improve the customer experience. Furthermore, employees can use their new skills to solve customer issues with more efficiency, creativity, and innovation.
- **Creates an image of a caring employer.** Having an upskilling program shows that an organization is willing to invest in its employees. This can make it easier to attract fresh staff.
- **Keeps up with the industry.** Learning new skills is often necessary to remain competitive. Upskilling is an effective way to ensure organizations maintain and increase their competitive market standing.
- **Creates a flexible team.** Training employees on their current and future goals also creates a flexible team that has a wealth of different skills to call upon when needed.

Benefits of upskilling - Employee/individual perspective

Often, the benefits of upskilling are listed from a company perspective. Namely, companies that invest in upskilling their employees tend to see better employee engagement and a greater retention rate. In the long run, this can save money by reducing recruitment costs.

However, upskilling is beneficial for individuals as well. Through upskilling, you could:

- Progress toward goals
- Remain competitive in the job market
- Qualify for a promotion
- Secure a new job
- Earn a higher salary
- Continue self-improvement

Effective ways to upskill

Here are some effective ways to upskill:

1. **Online Courses and Certificates**: Platforms like Coursera, Udemy, or LinkedIn Learning offer flexible courses that allow you to learn at your own pace.
2. **Stretch Opportunities at Work**: Taking on projects outside your usual remit can help you develop new competencies. Collaborating with people from other teams also hones important collaboration and problem-solving skills.
3. **In-Office Training and Online Resources**: Traditionally, companies have led the way in helping workers upskill through in-office training. Nowadays, you can also hone your skills online by watching YouTube videos or signing up for LinkedIn Learning programs.

Source: Coursera.org

Remember, continuous learning is key to staying competitive in today's dynamic job market!

IX. Personal branding

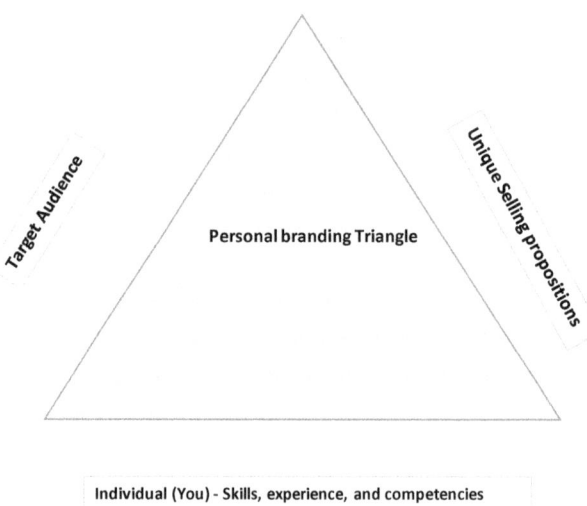

The personal branding conceptual triangle is based on three pillars. First, the branded individual and his skills, competencies, experiences, and what they bring to the table. Second, the perceptions of the branded person and relevant associations of the target audience. Third, a distinction from their peers, by leveraging their points of difference and defining individual Unique Selling Proposition (USP).

The human brand can have a strong focus on career and employment as well as the commercialization of a story, a way of doing business, an intellectual perspective, or knowledge. Thanks to social media, nowadays it is possible to showcase yourself in the digital world, think how you want to be perceived, and what is going to draw people's attention towards you.

The concept of "Personal Branding" was coined in 1997 by Tom Peters in the Fast Company Magazine. Several years later, the term has evolved in different ways as in "human branding," "self-marketing" or "self-branding." One of the main goals of personal branding is to gain relevance in professional paths, in order to do so, some key aspects are required during the effort of becoming a human brand such as visibility, differentiation, and a unique personality to strengthen brand equity.

Scheidt, Gelhard, and Henseler, in their article "Old Practice, but Young Research Field: A Systematic Bibliographic Review of Personal Branding" consider the term, from a process perspective "establishing, maintaining and developing an individual's human brand…an intangible asset linked to a person, which generates economic and social value through its visibility as a result of a personal branding process".

There are a variety of human brands, examples from sports, academics, visual and performing artists, business managers or self-employed, content creators, and professional services.

There are three C's – Clarity, Consistency, and Constancy – that are fundamental to building a strong personal brand.

Clarity means knowing who you are, what you stand for, and what makes you unique.

Consistency involves presenting your clear brand message across all platforms and interactions.

Constancy is about staying active and visible.

Personal branding

Personal branding is the conscious and intentional effort to create and influence public perception of an individual. It involves positioning oneself as an authority in a specific industry, elevating credibility, and differentiating from competitors. The goal is to advance one's career, expand influence, and make a larger impact. Essentially, it is about marketing and promoting oneself as a brand, both personally and professionally. To break it down further:

1. **Define**: Understand who you are, what you enjoy, and your unique skills. Seek feedback from stakeholders (managers, mentors, colleagues) to adjust based on how others perceive you.
2. **Develop**: Showcase your brand through daily actions at work. Consider how your brand can improve the organization. Also, become a stakeholder for others by sharing knowledge and helping them develop.
3. **Communicate**: Use social media (especially LinkedIn) to gain visibility. Network strategically by sharing updates and celebrating others' achievements. Remember, you are always building your personal brand!

How can you start your personal branding?

Building a **personal brand** is essential for career growth and professional success. Here are some steps to get started:

1. **Get to Know Yourself**: Reflect on your mission, passion, and strengths. Understand what makes you unique and what you want to achieve.
2. **Define Your Target Audience**: Identify who you want to reach with your brand. Consider their needs, interests, and pain points.
3. **Write an Elevator Pitch**: Craft a concise statement that summarizes your value proposition. Imagine you have 30 seconds in an elevator to explain who you are and what you do.
4. **Tell a Story**: Share memorable, resonant stories that convey your brand. Stories create emotional connections and make your brand relatable.
5. **Draw Lines in the Sand**: Define your boundaries and values. What do you stand for? What won't you compromise on?
6. **Build and Find Community**: Connect with like-minded individuals, both online and offline. Attend events, join professional groups, and engage with your audience.

7. **Leverage social media (and Be Consistent)**: Choose platforms relevant to your brand and maintain a consistent presence. Share valuable content, engage with followers, and showcase your expertise.

Remember, personal branding is intentional and strategic. It is about expressing your unique abilities and making a positive impact.

Examples of personal branding

Let us now look at, some **personal brand statement examples** from successful individuals:

1. **Chris Do**: A multi-hyphenate—designer, creative strategist, public speaker, founder, and CEO of The Futur (an online education platform). His brand statement: "Bilingual creative who lives at the intersection of business & design.".
2. **Gary Vaynerchuk**: A digital marketing expert, entrepreneur, and author. His brand is built around hustle, authenticity, and social media savvy.
3. **Marie Forleo**: An entrepreneur, author, and host of "MarieTV." Her brand focuses on empowerment, business advice, and personal development.
4. **Seth Godin**: A marketing guru, author, and speaker. His brand emphasizes innovative thinking and challenging the status quo.
5. **Simon Sinek**: Known for his "Start with Why" concept, he is a motivational speaker and author. His brand centers on purpose-driven leadership.

Remember, a personal brand statement should highlight your unique skills, experience, and personality, making a memorable impression on your audience!

(Source: Internet)

LinkedIn serves as a robust platform for employers, employees, and professionals alike. My personal experience attests to its effectiveness.

However, many users fail to leverage its full potential due to inactivity.

Simply opening the application infrequently and then closing it is insufficient. LinkedIn's algorithm is highly sophisticated and capable of generating insightful analytics, but it requires consistent engagement to be truly effective.

LinkedIn profile

Enhancing your **personal brand on LinkedIn** is crucial for career growth and networking. Here are some strategies to optimize your LinkedIn profile:

1. **Optimize Your Profile for LinkedIn SEO**: (Search Engine Optimization)
   - Use relevant keywords in your 'Headline,' 'About' section, and job experiences.
   - Customize your profile URL to make it search-friendly.

2. **Professionalize Your Profile Photo**:
   - Choose a high-resolution, professional-looking photo with good lighting.
   - Keep the background clutter-free.

3. **Craft a Unique and Compelling Headline**:
   - Avoid clichés and focus on a concise description of your expertise and value.
   - Highlight what sets you apart.

4. **Enhance Your LinkedIn Profile Summary**:
   - Treat it as your personal elevator pitch.
   - Showcase your skills, achievements, and personality authentically.

5. **Utilize the LinkedIn Banner**:
   - Use this prime real estate to visually communicate your professional journey.

6. **Share Valuable and Unique Content**:
   - Post engaging, original content that resonates with your audience.
   - Avoid generic posts and focus on quality.

Remember, your LinkedIn profile is your digital business card—make it count!

Building and maintaining the Brand

Twelve Easy Steps to Build Your Personal Brand on social media

If you think about it, you already have a personal brand. Everyone has one. If a potential employer or client were to Google your name, they would probably find your LinkedIn and social media profiles, perhaps followed by any news articles featuring your name or any other websites that mention you. What impression would someone get of you based on the search results? This, essentially, is your personal brand. It is your online reputation.

Personal branding means taking control of your online reputation and shaping it, so people see you in the way you want to be seen.

So, if you search for my name online, you will see my LinkedIn profile, my YouTube channel, and then my other social media profiles. Even just a quick glance at these results is enough to tell you I am an expert in Quality, EPC project execution, and an author.

Of course, social media is not the only way to establish your brand, but it does play a huge role. Here are twelve ways you can use social media to your advantage and sharpen your personal brand.

1. First things first, get your profiles in order. Add a professional, up-to-date photo to your social media profiles, using the same photo across different platforms to ensure consistency. Then clean up your profiles by deleting any content that you would not want potential employers or clients to see. (You can always maintain a private profile for sharing personal things that you do not want employers or clients to see.)
2. Be yourself. While you want to cultivate a professional brand, it is important to let your personality shine through in your social media posts. Write in the way you would normally speak. Be authentic. Be honest. Talk about things that really matter to you (rather than trying to hop on the latest trends). And do not pretend to be someone you are not. This is all part of ensuring your brand stays consistent.
3. Share what you are learning. Something that I have found impactful – and easy – is sharing interesting and relevant news stories from my industry on social media. This really helped me build my profile and stay knowledgeable on what is happening in my field. To keep up to date with interesting and relevant news stories, you can subscribe to industry newsletters or, even easier, set up Google alerts for certain keyword topics. Do be sure to add your own message when you share something on social media – even if it is just "I came across this today and thought I'd share it. What do you guys think?"
4. Join industry groups on social media platforms. Then make yourself known by engaging with posts, answering questions, and liking, commenting, and sharing other people's content in the group.
5. Be generous with your time and knowledge. Be helpful to others online by responding to questions and comments and generally engaging with them. And do take the time to like or amplify other content that you found engaging, inspiring, or useful. Basically, be reciprocal.

6. Make new contacts as often as you can, especially on LinkedIn. You can do this by identifying people you want to connect with in your field and sending a certain number of invites each week, with a short private message. Make a habit of this, and your network will soon grow.
7. Create quick polls to pose interesting questions and boost engagement. You can always mix it up by posting a mixture of professional and more broad questions.
8. Post quality photos and videos from your work life. People love visual content, so if you are at a work conference, attending an industry event, on the way to visit a client, or whatever, share it. You can mix it up with occasional "everyday" photos and videos while still keeping it fairly professional (think your morning cup of coffee when you are working from home, that sort of thing).
9. Really, you can post any sort of content that will help to cement your reputation – it could be advice, thought-provoking questions, excerpts from presentations you have given, pro tips, how-to content, or whatever.
10. If you really want to establish your expertise, consider authoring longer-form articles and sharing them on LinkedIn. I did a lot of this – still do, in fact – and it has played a huge role in growing my personal brand.
11. Use cross-platform tools to make your life easier. For example, you can use a tool like Hootsuite to schedule your posts in advance and share posts across multiple platforms, such as Instagram and YouTube, all from one place. This means you can get maximum value from each piece of content without having to physically post it in multiple places.
12. Try penciling in a specific time each day or week for social media. You may actively want to limit the amount of time you spend on social media (it can be a huge time suck). So, I find it helps to

schedule posts in advance and block out specific times to check in with social media, reply to comments, and see other people's posts.

Everyone understands the importance of social media for business promotion and growth. However, many people do not realize social media is also essential for building your personal brand.

I admire Anand Mahindra (CEO of Mahindra group, India) and his presence on social media.

Personal branding is crucial across all industries, helping to increase sales, build trust and strengthen your company's reputation. Social media plays a significant role in personal branding efforts, so most executives, CEOs, and founders post on two to five social media networks regularly.

Social media platforms

I will highlight eleven social media platforms that can help you build your brand and share tips and best practices for brand building.

Before launching a personal branding campaign on social media, examine where your target audience spends time online. Ensure you are on networks they will see to maximize your visibility.

1. **Facebook**

   Facebook is a popular social networking platform where users post comments and share various content types, including photos and news.

   If you are exploring Facebook for personal branding, keep the following tips in mind:

   Post regularly: Keep your audience interested by sharing regular updates. Posting once daily is ideal, but at least three times a week may be more manageable.

   Conduct Facebook Live Q&A sessions: Once in a while, host a Facebook Live Q&A. These livestream presentations can help

build your personal brand, increase your follower count, and boost engagement with customers and prospects.

Invite people to like your Facebook page: Inviting people to like your Facebook page is an uncomplicated way to add followers.

Run ads on Facebook: Take advantage of Facebook's advertising offerings. With Facebook ads, you can target your demographic by gender, age, location, and more.

Comment and engage on the platform: To build your following, it is essential to engage with your Facebook community by liking and regularly commenting on quality content.

Did You Know?

Other Facebook marketing strategies and tools can help you build your personal brand, including Audience Insights, the Facebook Ad Library, and Facebook Experiments.

2. **'X' (Formerly Twitter)**

    X (formerly Twitter) is a powerful personal branding tool for startup founders. Consider the following tips to build your personal brand on X:

    Stay active: A good rule of thumb is to be active on X daily. One to five posts a day will dramatically increase your audience engagement.

    Follow others: One of the best ways to gain followers is to follow other X accounts. When starting on the network, it is a clever idea to follow at least two people in your industry a day.

    Participate in chats: Another way to increase your following is to participate in ongoing chats or pertinent threads.

3. **LinkedIn**

    LinkedIn is an absolute must for any professional building their personal brand. Some tips include the following:

    Create a profile: Create an individual profile to let others know who you are. Connect with influential people in your industry to network successfully on LinkedIn.

Create a company profile: You should also create a LinkedIn business profile for your company and add it to your personal profile.

Join LinkedIn groups: Join relevant LinkedIn groups to connect with others in your industry and expand your network.

Post articles: You can also post original articles on LinkedIn to establish your credibility and expertise.

Post consistently and often: LinkedIn advises unaccustomed users to post quality content twice a week. As you gain traction, build up to three to five posts weekly. However, it is always better to post fewer high-quality posts than frequent low-quality posts.

Tip

As with any business-related social media presence, be transparent and authentic in your posts. Humility and gratitude are excellent character traits to demonstrate offline and online.

4. **Instagram**

    Instagram is a visual platform, so photos, videos, and descriptive text captions are essential to your personal branding strategy. Some tips include the following:

    Show your personal and business sides: Create an Instagram account that blends your personal and business life. Using Instagram for business expands your company's reach and engagement, but you also want to include posts that showcase you personally.

    Post frequently: Business owners should try to post on Instagram once or twice daily.

    Use hashtags: Harness the power of hashtags to help others discover your content and become new followers. However, be careful not to overuse hashtags; you do not want to be perceived as spam. Try to stay within five to twelve hashtags.

    Interact on Instagram: Be sure to like and comment on others' content to increase your following.

    Did You Know?

Instagram posting best practices include posting consistently, not over-posting, posting only quality content, and telling stories via the Instagram stories feature.

5. **Snapchat**

    Founders of businesses catering to millennials and Gen Zers can use Snapchat as a powerful storytelling tool when building their personal brand. Some tips include the following:

    Create a Snapchat story: Post pictures, videos, and captions to craft a narrative that lasts 24 hours on your Snapchat story. Posting content daily will keep your brand fresh in your followers' minds. Update your Snapchat story about three times daily, every four or five hours. Try an account takeover: Increase your followers by having an influencer take over your account for the day or you can take over another account. Promote the takeover to their followers and yours. Promote your Snapchat: Promote your Snapchat account on other marketing channels so your existing audience knows where to find you.

6. **Quora**

    Executives can use Quora to demonstrate their industry expertise, build credibility, and elevate their personal brand. Some tips include the following:

    Post consistently: There is no set rule for how often you should post on Quora, but It is vital to be consistently active. Try to answer questions, leave comments, and upvote others' answers at least three days a week.

    Focus on a niche: Focus on positioning yourself in one niche so people will know what to expect and want to follow you.

    Ask good questions: Gain exposure by asking insightful questions that resonate with people.

7. **Crunchbase**

    Crunchbase is an excellent platform if your business is growing, particularly if you have a tech company and want to be visible to potential investors. Some tips include the following:

    Establish a social media presence first: Before you can set up a Crunchbase account, you will need an account on Twitter, LinkedIn, or Facebook.

    Fill out your profile: Fill out your profile completely, including a detailed bio, events you have contributed to, and press references. While Crunchbase is not a platform where users post, you can edit your profile anytime to keep it fresh.

8. **Medium**

    Medium is an online publishing platform where users read and author articles. The website allows anyone to create content and establish themselves as an industry expert without dealing with the details involved in setting up a blog. Some tips include the following:

    Focus on a theme: Use Medium to publish content focused on a theme related to your brand or business.

    Be consistent: Plan a consistent content schedule — whether once a week or once a month — to stay relevant and grow your audience.

9. **Pinterest**

    Like Instagram, Pinterest is a visual platform ideal for influencers and product creators. You will use Pinterest to drive traffic to your site, store original pins, and craft a credible and knowledgeable presence. Some tips include the following:

    Set up a business account: Start growing your personal brand on Pinterest by setting up a business account, which is necessary to track data analytics.

    Confirm your website: Confirm your website so your Pinterest picture will appear on all pins from your site automatically.

Be consistent: Pin consistently to build your personal brand and increase website traffic. Pinning a handful of times daily or every other day will be more effective than mass pinning once a week.

10. **YouTube**

    YouTube can help you build brand trust with video — a vital element of creating a personal brand. Making a YouTube channel for your brand is an excellent way to increase brand awareness online and grow your audience. Some tips include the following:

    Post videos based on your brand: First, define your personal brand and publish videos based on your interests and profession. For example, if you are a marketing expert, consider sharing videos that focus on specific marketing niches, such as the benefits of email marketing.

    Be consistent: As with other social media channels, posting consistently on YouTube will provide the best results. If possible, post once a week. If this is not realistic, you can post every two weeks.

11. **TikTok**

    TikTok generally caters to a younger audience, so if your personality and brand fit with the platform, consider it a tool for personal branding. Some tips include the following:

    Focus on your unique brand: With TikTok, you do not have to pay for targeting or go out of your way to reach your audience. TikTok's algorithm places content in front of likely audiences, so it is an excellent tool if you are just getting started.

Be authentic: TikTok is a varied, unique platform, so being your authentic self will serve you well. No need to dance — unless you want to.

Ten Key Elements of a Strong Personal Brand

Personal branding is an essential component of modern entrepreneurship, and establishing a strong personal brand can significantly impact your success. To help you on your personal branding journey, we will explore the ten key elements that make up a robust personal brand, while providing tips and practical advice along the way.

Authenticity

Authenticity is the foundation of a compelling personal brand. Go beyond the surface and present the genuine, unfiltered version of yourself. Share personal anecdotes and values to forge a deep connection with your audience.

TIP: Embed your individual experiences into your content to establish an authentic connection with your audience.

Consistency

Consistency is the linchpin of a resilient personal brand. Maintain uniformity in your message, tone, and visual identity across all platforms to reinforce your brand's recognizability.

TIP: Develop a style guide to ensure the coherence of your branding elements, including logos, fonts, and colors, across all mediums.

Clarity

Ensure that your personal brand message is clear and easily comprehensible. Your audience should swiftly understand your values and offerings.

TIP: Construct a succinct elevator pitch that encapsulates your personal brand in a sentence or two.

Uniqueness

Stand out by emphasizing your unique qualities within your field. Celebrate your quirks and narrate your personal story—no one else has your exact journey.

TIP: Embrace your distinctiveness and use it as a compelling asset to set yourself apart.

VALUE

Infuse your personal brand with value for your audience. Provide knowledge, insights, and solutions relevant to your niche.

TIP: Regularly create content that educates, informs, or entertains your audience to establish yourself as a valuable resource.

Engagement

Actively connect with your audience through various channels. Foster a community around your brand through genuine interaction.

TIP: Respond promptly to comments and messages to nurture meaningful connections with your audience.

Professionalism

Sustain a professional image, irrespective of the casual or informal nature of your personal brand. Consistent professionalism can distinguish you in the market.

TIP: Employ professional language and maintain a polished online presence to enhance your credibility.

Visual Identity

Craft a visual identity that aligns seamlessly with your personal brand. This encompasses your logo, color scheme, and typography.

TIP: Invest in professional graphic design or leverage online tools to ensure a cohesive visual representation of your brand.

Emotional Connection

Forge an emotional connection by weaving compelling stories and demonstrating empathy. Share personal narratives that resonate with your audience's emotions.

TIP: Infuse emotion into your brand by sharing stories and experiences that evoke a strong response from your audience.

Adaptability

Allow your personal brand to evolve with your growth and changing goals. Embrace adjustments while staying rooted in your core values.

TIP: Regularly evaluate and refine your personal brand to ensure it remains relevant and effective as you navigate your entrepreneurial journey.

By focusing on these ten key elements and following the practical advice and tips provided, you can develop a strong and influential personal brand that helps you stand out as an entrepreneur or brand owner in the market.

Avoid Politics, Religion, and Sensitive issues in your posts, as far as possible. Always be positive and spread good news.

Use of keywords – The most important

Personal Keywords:

Your personal keywords include your name, target location, languages you speak, and education. Your name needs to match on all your social platforms (especially LinkedIn) and resume. Use your full name online unless you use an abbreviated name on your resume and all other printed materials you use such as business cards. Also, include your full name as your signature on email.

Professional Goals Keywords:

Choose keywords for the position you want. Include industry keywords as well. Here is where a few hours exploring job postings will pay off. What words are recurring for the positions you want? Research industry keywords to include.

Work History Keywords:

Most of your keywords will be used here. Again, make sure you have done your research and know what keywords employers are using. You need to be truthful when using keywords. The trick is using the words employers use to describe the work you do.

If the company you work for uses puns for job titles like Marketing Guru, change that to read Marketing Manager – if the title matches what you actually do. Where you have a lot of liberty is hard and soft skills.

There are a lot of ways to say you have rock-solid communication skills including problem-solving, confident speaking ability, active listening, and collaboration to name a few.

Use enough keywords when describing your experience, skills, certifications, and job-specific tools and techniques without overstuffing. Your LinkedIn profile, resume, and cover letter need to be readable.

Think like a recruiter. If you submit a cover letter and resume, the recruiter is definitely going to search your LinkedIn profile. But recruiters also search LinkedIn for viable clients even when they have not received a resume. In fact, 95% of recruiters say they search LinkedIn to find candidates for open positions. LinkedIn reports that 70% of the global workforce is made up of passive talent not actively job hunting.

Your keywords need to be an exact match. Job Hunt uses the example of a job description requiring "Microsoft Word" experience. If your resume states "highly skilled with Microsoft Office products" it will not meet the search criteria. You may be well versed in Microsoft Office but if the majority of job postings are only asking for Microsoft Word, you need to include Microsoft Word.

How do you apply keywords to your other social channels? Use your full name or the variation of your name that appears on LinkedIn and your resume. On Facebook, you can add keywords to the "about" section of your profile. Instagram allows a brief description below your name and title. The same is true for Twitter.

Consistency matters. Your resume and social profiles should paint a picture of who you are, what you do, and where you want to go.

Hashtags (#)

Hashtags are words and numbers following the # symbol that categorize and track content on social media platforms. You can add hashtags to social posts, bios, and comments on most major platforms, including Instagram, Facebook, TikTok, Twitter, LinkedIn, YouTube, and Pinterest. They allow users to easily search for and discover posts related to specific topics or themes. Here are some basics about hashtags:

1. **What is a Hashtag?**
   - A hashtag is a way to group social conversations around a certain topic, making it easy for people to find content that interests them.
   - The pound or hashtag symbol (#) was initially used to mark numbers but was first used for hashtags in 2007 by Chris Messina on Twitter. Since then, hashtag use, reach, and effectiveness have grown significantly.
   - Hashtags are now used on nearly all social platforms to connect content to specific topics, events, themes, or conversations.

2. **How to Use Hashtags Effectively:**
   - Always start with #, but avoid using spaces, punctuation, or symbols within the hashtag.
   - Make sure your accounts are public so that non-followers can see your hash-tagged content.
   - Keep hashtags relatively short and easy to remember.
   - Use relevant and specific hashtags; avoid obscure ones.
   - Limit the number of hashtags you use to avoid looking spammy.

3. **Mix of Hashtags:**
   - A good social media strategy includes a mix of popular, relevant, and branded hashtags.
   - Do not rely solely on popular hashtags; find ones that align with your brand and content.

Remember, effective hashtag use can boost your brand's social media reach and engagement!

How to measure the effectiveness of personal branding

Measuring the effectiveness of your **personal brand** involves assessing various metrics. Here are some ways to gauge your impact:

1. **Online Presence**: Monitor your website traffic, social media engagement, and networking opportunities.
2. **Engagement**: Evaluate how actively your audience interacts with your content, such as comments, likes, and shares.
3. **Conversions**: Track specific goals tied to your brand, like job applications, speaking engagements, or business inquiries.
4. **Reach and Impressions**: Measure the number of people exposed to your brand across different channels.

Remember, consistent evaluation helps you refine your brand and make data-driven decisions!

Some common mistakes to avoid in personal branding

When building your **personal brand**, it is essential to avoid common pitfalls. Here are some mistakes to avoid:

1. **Not Knowing "YOU" Before Building Your Brand**: Understand your authentic self and what you represent. Authenticity builds trust.
2. **Not Setting Specific Goals**: Define clear objectives for your brand—whether it is landing a new job, increasing your salary, or becoming a paid speaker.
3. **Building Your Brand Around Someone Else's Idea of You**: Be true to yourself, quirks, and all. Do not conform to others' expectations.
4. **Ignoring the Need for a Personal Brand**: Whether you realize it or not, you already have a brand. Manage it intentionally.
5. **Lacking a Plan to Manage Your Personal Brand**: Develop a strategy for consistent messaging and engagement.
6. **Spreading Yourself Too Thin Across Multiple Channels**: Focus on platforms relevant to your audience.
7. **Being Inconsistent**: Maintain a cohesive brand voice and image across all interactions.
8. **Neglecting Your Profile on Personal Brand Platforms**: Complete your profiles thoroughly.
9. **Expecting Instant Success**: Building a brand takes time and effort. Patience is key!

Remember, your personal brand reflects who you are and for what you stand. Avoid these missteps, and you will be on the right track!

Maintaining your personal branding

Maintaining a consistent **personal brand online** is crucial for professional growth. Here are some practical tips:

1. **Audit Your Current Online Presence**: Review your social media profiles and posts. Remove anything divisive or unprofessional.

2. **Leverage Storytelling**: Share your unique journey, challenges, and victories. Authentic storytelling humanizes your brand and makes it relatable.
3. **Bolster Storytelling with Data and Insights**: Ground your stories in data and real-world experiences. Blend authenticity with evidence to engage your network.
4. **Get On Camera**: Do not overthink it—point the camera at yourself and talk. Authenticity attracts like-minded connections.
5. **Regularly Create and Share Content**: Consistency matters. Share thought leadership content to build authority and trust.
6. **Create an Updated Portfolio**: Showcase your work, projects, and achievements. Keep it current and relevant.
7. **Discuss Your Skills and Experiences**: Engage in conversations about your expertise. Participate in industry discussions.
8. **Increase Visibility in Your Industry**: Attend events, contribute to forums, and collaborate with peers. Be present where your audience is.

Remember, your online persona should align with your authentic self!

Impact of videos photos and pdf/ppt on your content

Let us explore how several types of media—videos, photos, and presentations (PPTs)—can enhance social media posts:

1. **Videos:**
   - **Engagement:** Videos capture attention and encourage users to spend more time on your post. They can convey emotions, tell stories, or showcase products.
   - **Information:** Videos allow you to explain complex topics, or share behind-the-scenes glimpses.
   - **Live Streams:** Live videos create real-time interaction with your audience, fostering engagement and authenticity.

2. **Photos:**
   - **Visual Appeal:** High-quality images catch the eye and evoke emotions. Use them to showcase products, landscapes, events, or personal moments.
   - **Storytelling:** A single photo can tell a powerful story. Use captions to add context and connect with your audience.
   - **Branding:** Consistent visual style reinforces your brand identity.
3. **Presentations (PPTs):**
   - **Educational Content:** Share informative slides on topics relevant to your audience. PPTs can break down complex concepts.
   - **Professionalism:** PPTs lend credibility and professionalism. Use them for business updates, reports, or industry insights.
   - **Visual Variety:** Mix text, images, and graphics for engaging content.

Remember, the choice of media depends on your goals, target audience, and platform. Experiment and analyze what resonates best with your followers!

Exercise caution when you post on social media

Inappropriate Content and Offensive Remarks

One of the most common ways social media can negatively impact your job is through the posting of inappropriate content, such as offensive remarks, hate speech, or discriminatory comments. While freedom of expression is a fundamental right in many countries, it is not absolute. Employers have the right to maintain a positive and inclusive work environment, and inappropriate online behavior can violate company policies or ethical standards.

Various laws have been implemented to prevent offensive and inappropriate content from floating on social media platforms and also protect netizens' freedom of speech. Here are some laws practiced in the US, EU, and India around social media behavior.

- **United States**: The First Amendment protects freedom of speech, but it does not shield employees from the consequences of their social media posts. Private employers are not bound by this protection and can dismiss employees for online behavior that reflects poorly on the company.
- *European Union:* Under the European Convention on Human Rights, individuals have the right to free expression, but this right is subject to restrictions when it conflicts with others› rights or company interests. Courts have upheld employers' rights to terminate employees who engage in hate speech or discriminatory behavior online.
- *India:* In India, there is no specific law regulating social media activity in the workplace. However, employers may terminate employees if their posts violate company policies, the Information Technology Act of 2000, or the Indian Penal Code (IPC), which prohibits hate speech and defamation.

Breaching Confidentiality and Company Policies

Sharing confidential company information on social media can be a serious breach of trust, often leading to immediate termination. Many employees, knowingly or unknowingly, disclose sensitive information about the company's operations, client details, or business strategies. This is not only unprofessional but can also result in legal action, particularly if a non-disclosure agreement (NDA) has been signed.

"Please be aware that it is insufficient to merely possess knowledge of your own skills; it is equally important that others are made aware of them as well."

X. Personality Check card

Self-assessment is crucial for personal development. I have compiled the following checklist to facilitate your self-evaluation. The traits listed are fundamental for achieving success in life.

For any traits where your score is average or below, please focus on improving those areas.

(This is for your personal use only and need not be shared with others.)

Sathya's (Personality) self-check card							
Personal trait/ quality	Description	Excellent	Very good	Good	Average	Poor	Very poor
Perseverance	The ability to keep going despite challenges and setbacks. This trait helps you stay committed to your goals and see tasks through to completion.						
Determination	A strong resolve to achieve your objectives. Determination drives you to overcome obstacles and maintain focus on your goals.						
Resilience	The capacity to recover quickly from difficulties. Resilience helps you bounce back from failures and adapt to change.						

Patience	The ability to wait calmly and handle delays or frustrations without getting upset. Patience is crucial in managing stress and maintaining positive interactions.						
Confidence	Believing in your abilities and expressing yourself assertively. Confidence helps you communicate more effectively and take on new challenges.						
Curiosity	A desire to learn and understand more. Curiosity drives you to seek out new knowledge and experiences, enhancing your adaptability and problem-solving skills.						
Integrity	Being honest and having strong moral principles. Integrity builds trust and respect in your relationships.						

Humility	Recognizing your own limitations and being open to feedback. Humility allows you to grow and improve continuously.						
Self-Discipline	The ability to control your impulses and stay focused on your goals. Self-discipline helps you manage your time and responsibilities effectively.						
Optimism	Maintaining a positive outlook even in challenging situations. Optimism can improve your resilience and make you more approachable.						
Empathy	The ability to understand and share the feelings of others. Empathy helps you connect with people on a deeper level and improve your interpersonal relationships.						

Creativity	Thinking outside the box and producing innovative solutions. Creativity can enhance problem-solving and adaptability.						
Accountability	Taking responsibility for your actions and their outcomes. Accountability builds trust and reliability.						
Flexibility	Being open to new ideas and willing to adjust your approach. Flexibility helps you adapt to changing circumstances.						
Mindfulness	Being present and fully engaged in the moment. Mindfulness can improve your focus and reduce stress.						
Gratitude	Appreciating what you have and expressing thanks. Gratitude can enhance your overall well-being and relationships.						

Assertiveness	Communicating your needs and opinions confidently and respectfully. Assertiveness helps you stand up for yourself while maintaining positive interactions.						
Empowerment	Encouraging and supporting others to achieve their potential. Empowerment fosters a collaborative and motivating environment.						
Emotional Intelligence	Recognizing and managing your own emotions and those of others. Emotional intelligence is key to effective communication and relationship-building.						
Open mindedness	Being receptive to different perspectives and ideas. Open-mindedness can lead to more inclusive and innovative solutions.						

Reliability	Being dependable and consistent in your actions. Reliability builds trust and ensures that others can count on you.					
Generosity	Willingness to give your time, resources, or support to others. Generosity fosters positive relationships and a supportive environment.					
Honesty	Being truthful and transparent in your interactions. Honesty is fundamental to building trust and integrity.					
Compassion	Showing kindness and concern for others. Compassion helps you connect with people and provide meaningful support.					
Enthusiasm	Displaying a positive and energetic attitude. Enthusiasm can motivate others and create a dynamic atmosphere.					

Respectfulness	Treating others with consideration and valuing their perspectives. Respectfulness enhances collaboration and mutual understanding.						
Loyalty	Being faithful and supportive to people and commitments. Loyalty strengthens relationships and fosters a sense of security.						
Tactfulness	Handling sensitive situations with care and diplomacy. Tactfulness helps you navigate difficult conversations and maintain harmony.						
Initiative	Taking proactive steps to address issues and improve situations. Initiative demonstrates leadership and a willingness to go above and beyond.						

Graciousness	Being courteous and showing gratitude. Graciousness can enhance your interactions and leave a positive impression.						
Tenacity	The determination to keep going despite difficulties. Tenacity helps you stay focused and achieve long-term goals.						
Diligence	Careful and persistent effort in your work. Diligence ensures high-quality results and reliability.						
Courage	The ability to face fear and take risks. Courage allows you to step out of your comfort zone and embrace new challenges.						
Self - motivation	The drive to achieve your goals without needing external encouragement. Self-motivation keeps you proactive and focused.						

Resourcefulness	The ability to find quick and clever ways to overcome difficulties. Resourcefulness helps you adapt and solve problems efficiently.						
Prudence	Exercising good judgment and caution in decision-making. Prudence helps you avoid unnecessary risks and make wise choices.						
Altruism	Selflessly caring for the well-being of others. Altruism fosters a supportive and compassionate environment.						
Decisiveness	The ability to make decisions quickly and effectively. Decisiveness helps you take action and move forward confidently.						
Self-reflection	Regularly assessing your own behavior and performance. Self-reflection promotes continuous personal growth and improvement.						

| Listening | Actively paying attention to and understanding what others are saying, without interrupting or judging. | | | | | |

Once you are done with it, start working on improvising the traits which you have identified.

XI. MBTI – Personality development assessment tool

The **Myers-Briggs Type Indicator (MBTI)** is a popular personality assessment tool developed by Katharine Cook Briggs and her daughter Isabel Briggs Myers, based on Carl Jung's theories. It categorizes individuals into 16 personality types based on preferences in four dichotomies: Extraversion vs. Introversion, Sensing vs. Intuition, Thinking vs. Feeling, and Judging vs. Perceiving.

Advantages of the MBTI

1. **Self-Awareness and Personal Growth**: The MBTI helps individuals gain insights into their own personalities, strengths, and weaknesses. This self-awareness can lead to personal growth and improved decision-making.
2. **Improved Communication**: Understanding different personality types can enhance communication and reduce conflicts in personal and professional relationships. It helps people appreciate diverse perspectives and adapt their communication styles accordingly.
3. **Team Building**: In organizational settings, the MBTI is often used for team building. It helps managers understand team dynamics and leverage the strengths of different personality types to improve collaboration and productivity.

4. **Career Development**: The MBTI can guide individuals in choosing careers that align with their personality types, leading to greater job satisfaction and performance.

Disadvantages of the MBTI

1. **Lack of Scientific Validity**: Critics argue that the MBTI lacks empirical support and reliability. Studies have shown that the test-retest reliability is low, meaning individuals might get different results if they retake the test after some time.
2. **Over-Simplification**: The MBTI's binary choices (e.g., Extraversion vs. Introversion) are seen as overly simplistic. Human personalities are complex and cannot be fully captured by a dichotomous framework.
3. **Predictive Limitations**: The MBTI does not predict behavior or success in specific roles. It provides a snapshot of preferences rather than a comprehensive analysis of abilities or potential.
4. **Commercialization and Misuse**: The widespread use of the MBTI in corporate settings has led to its commercialization. Some organizations may misuse the test for hiring or promotion decisions, which is not its intended purpose.

Conclusion

While the MBTI offers valuable insights into personality and can be a useful tool for personal and professional development, it is important to be aware of its limitations. It should be used as a starting point for self-reflection and growth rather than a definitive measure of one's abilities or potential.

The 16 MBTI personality types are categorized based on preferences in four dichotomies: Extraversion (E) vs. Introversion (I), Sensing (S) vs. Intuition (N), Thinking (T) vs. Feeling (F), and Judging (J) vs. Perceiving (P). Here are the types:

Analysts

1. **INTJ (Architect)**: Imaginative and strategic thinkers with a plan for everything.
2. **INTP (Logician)**: Innovative inventors with an unquenchable thirst for knowledge.
3. **ENTJ (Commander)**: Bold, imaginative, and strong-willed leaders.
4. **ENTP (Debater)**: Smart and curious thinkers who cannot resist an intellectual challenge.

Diplomats

5. **INFJ (Advocate)**: Quiet and mystical, yet very inspiring and tireless idealists.
6. **INFP (Mediator)**: Poetic, kind, and altruistic people, always eager to help a good cause.
7. **ENFJ (Protagonist)**: Charismatic and inspiring leaders, able to mesmerize their listeners.
8. **ENFP (Campaigner)**: Enthusiastic, creative, and sociable free spirits.

Sentinels

9. **ISTJ (Logistician)**: Practical and fact-minded individuals, whose reliability cannot be doubted.
10. **ISFJ (Defender)**: Very dedicated and warm protectors, always ready to defend their loved ones.
11. **ESTJ (Executive)**: Excellent administrators, unsurpassed at managing things or people.
12. **ESFJ (Consul)**: Extraordinarily caring, social, and popular people.

Explorers

13. **ISTP (Virtuoso)**: Bold and practical experimenters, masters of all kinds of tools.

14. **ISFP (Adventurer)**: Flexible and charming artists, always ready to explore and experience something new.
15. **ESTP (Entrepreneur)**: Smart, energetic, and very perceptive people.
16. **ESFP (Entertainer)**: Spontaneous, energetic, and enthusiastic people.

Each type offers a unique perspective on how individuals perceive the world, make decisions, and interact with others.

> *"Success lies in a masterful consistency around the fundamentals."*
> **– Robin Sharma**

'Robin Sharma' recommends the following TEN MANTRAs for SUCCESS

"Speak good words"

Speaking good about others helps make friends and reduce enemies while saying good about situations cultivates a positive outlook towards life. It is also about focusing and being grateful for what you have instead of cribbing about all the things you lack in life.

"Take long walks"

Walking is a great exercise – not just for the body, but also for the soul. It helps one destress and think clearly – thus making better decisions in life.

"Read wise books"

Reading has many benefits – it broadens your worldview, gives you more ideas, improves your vocabulary and writing, and many more. Most successful people in the world have one common habit – they read a lot to stay ahead of others.

"Be polite and punctual"

Being polite and kind to others and punctual (especially at the workplace) makes you more trustworthy and credible. This can help you get more important tasks at work, thus helping you grow and be successful.

"Keep each promise"

Sticking to your words will make you more trustworthy as a person – both in your personal and professional life. This will also make people respect you as a person.

"Get up early"

Most successful people in the world have this one common habit – they all prefer waking up between 4 to 5.30 am. They utilize this time for yoga, meditation, exercising, reading, or journaling which helps them grow as a person and stay ahead of others.

"Rest properly"

While it is important to work hard to be successful in life, resting and having quality sleep are equally crucial. This will keep you going in the long run.

"Put in the work"

It's not just hard work but also smart work, which helps successful people stay ahead of the rat race.

"Be patient"

It is often said 'Good things come to those who wait' (and persist), and rightly so. Smart work and persistence do pay off in the long run.

"All will turn out great"

Lastly, believe in yourself and trust the Universe for everything to fall into place.

> *"If four things are followed. - having a great aim, acquiring knowledge, hard work, and perseverance – then anything can be achieved."*
>
> **– APJ Abdul Kalam**

www.ingramcontent.com/pod-product-compliance
Ingram Content Group UK Ltd.
Pitfield, Milton Keynes, MK11 3LW, UK
UKHW020245240426
12048UKWH00026B/1614